ANNE UBERSFELD

Reading Theatre

Translated by Frank Collins
Edited and with a foreword by
Paul Perron and Patrick Debbèche

UNIVERSITY OF TORONTO PRESS
Toronto Buffalo London

© University of Toronto Press Incorporated 1999
Toronto Buffalo London
Printed in Canada

ISBN 0-8020-4455-7 (cloth)
ISBN 0-8020-8240-8 (paper)

Toronto Studies in Semiotics
Editors: Marcel Danesi, Umberto Eco, Paul Perron, and Thomas A. Sebeok

Reading Theatre is a translation of *Lire le théâtre 1* (© Editions Belin 1996)

Printed on acid-free paper

Canadian Cataloguing in Publication Data

Ubersfeld, Anne
   Reading theatre

   (Toronto studies in semiotics)
   Translation of: Lire le theatre.
   Includes bibliographical references and index.
   ISBN 0-8020-4455-7 (bound) ISBN 0-8020-8240-8 (pbk.)

   1. Theater – Semiotics. I. Collins, Frank. II. Perron, Paul. III. Debbeche, Patrick. IV. Title. V. Series.

   PN2039.U2313 1999   792'.01   C98-933021-4

University of Toronto Press acknowledges the financial assistance to its publishing program of the Canada Council for the Arts and the Ontario Arts Council.

Contents

Acknowledgments

We would like to thank the staff of the University of Toronto Press who worked on *Reading Theatre:* Ron Schoeffel, who encouraged the project from the very beginning; Barbara Porter, who managed the project from beginning to end; Denise Wake, who supervised the production; Will Rueter, who designed the cover. We would also like to thank Ruth Pincoe for her diligent work in copy editing the manuscript. The unflagging care and professionalism of all these individuals contributes greatly to the scholarly reputation of the University of Toronto Press. They were always a joy to work with.

Toronto, 1999

Foreword

Students and practitioners of the theatre are generally aware of Anne Ubersfeld's important theoretical contributions to the study of dramatic texts and performance. The originality of her work undoubtedly stems from the fact that she has practised a number of professions linked to the theatre, and the experience gained in each one supplements the others. She was director of the *Institut d'études théâtrales*, at the University of Paris-Sorbonne; for several years she directed amateur theatre companies; she was a theatre critic for *l'Humanité, France Nouvelle*, and *Révolution*. As a literary historian she has written numerous learned articles and major studies,[1] and she also established a number of critical editions of classical texts (including *Andromaque, Hernani, Lorenzaccio, le Mariage de Figaro*, and *Ruy Blaz*) that, as Guy Rosa notes, 'renewed their interpretation to such a degree that their influence on recent production has been noticeable and recognized' (Rosa 1991, 849).[2] The combination of these diverse professions has had an impact on her decisive contribution to the semiology of the theatre. In addition, Rosa points out that many of her articles contributed to opening the way for the semiotic analysis of theatre. '[O]ne has to recognize that when *Lire le théâtre* and *l'École du spectateur* appeared no comparable works existed. Methodically covering all aspects of text and performance in her concern for bringing together the different forms of structural analysis without ignoring the specificity of each, these pioneering works have remained and have now become classics' (ibid., 849).

Yet, until now none of Ubersfeld's works have been available in translation in their entirety; North American audiences had to rely on commentaries by leading semiotic theoretists (for example: M. Carlson [1993]; K. Elam [1980]; M. De Marinis [1993]; A. Helbo [1987]; S. Melrose [1994];

P. Pavis [1982]; F. de Toro [1996]). This translation makes one of her major theoretical works that had a fundamental impact on the semiological investigation of drama directly accessible to English speakers for the first time. *Lire le théâtre* [*Reading Theatre*] was widely acclaimed[3] and cited for its innovativeness and originality when it was first published in 1977, and it was considered to be such an important breakthrough that it was re-edited four times in five years.

The originality of Anne Ubersfeld's contribution is that she has adapted a semio-pragmatic perspective to the study of drama and performance. It should be noted, though, that this perspective is related both to the application of semiotic theory and to its philosophical and aesthetic underpinnings. She questions at one extreme the philosophical and semantic postulates of the theory, and at the other, the relationship between the object language and its instruments through numerous applications and analysis. What characterizes Ubersfeld's descriptive practice is the recourse to methodology in which operational concepts and discovery procedures are made explicit. In her work methodology constitutes a meeting ground of the theory of signs and the social sciences. Although she adopts certain semiotic tools from the Paris School of Semiotics,[4] it should be stressed that she redefines and reframes them from the point of view of theatrical practice.

Reading Theatre can be situated within the context of science-theoretical developments in theatre research that occurred in Europe during the 1970s. Indeed, much of this research, whether it focuses on a meta level of analysis – that is, on the fundamentals and theory of theatre research in general – or concentrates on the object level, from either a more theoretical or a descriptive perspective, can be grouped under the umbrella of semiotics. However, one of the major stumbling blocks encountered in early semiological theatre research can be directly attributed to the lack of a unanimous definition of the sign *per se*, and more specifically of the theatrical sign.

Initially theatre semiotics was dependent on a theory of signs inherited from Saussurian linguistics. Certain theoreticians from the Prague School, for example, Jan Mukařovský, attempted to break away from the binary definition of sign by introducing a ternary model in which a work of art was considered

as an autonomous sign composed of: (1) an artifact functioning as a perceivable signifier; (2) an 'aesthetic object' which is registered in the collective consciousness and which functions as 'signification'; (3) a relationship to a thing signified (this relationship refers not to any distinct existence – since we are talking about an autonomous sign – but to the total context of social phenomena, science, philosophy, religion, politics, economics, and so on, of any given milieu) (Mukařovský 1934, 9).

Nonetheless they remained very much part of the Prague tradition. Mukařovský and other members of the Prague School contributed to the semiotics of theatre by emphasizing the interdefinition of the various components of dramatic art.[5]

Although the principles governing the theory of the sign (arbitrariness, value, and system) are at the origin of most semiological analyses of Saussurian inspiration, the orthodox linguistic usage of these operational concepts does raise serious methodological and theoretical problems. In general linguistic theory, one can define and delimit the constituent units of a system, but this is not always the case in all other semiological systems. André Martinet (1969), for example, differentiated natural language from other 'means of communication' by postulating in the former the principle of the *double articulation*: the first articulation is situated at the level of 'morpheme' signs, the second at that of 'phonemes.' This distinction, seemingly adequate for verbal sign systems, is not pertinent when one attempts to analyse units as large as sentences or other semiotic systems such as gestures. The usefulness of the double articulation approach seems to be less and less significant as one moves from highly codified and structural systems such as American Sign Language to poly-sign-systems such as theatre performance. For example, can gestures having a communicative intent be broken down into minimal units and analysed in terms of 'gestemes'? (For an overview see Nespoulous, Perron, and Lecours 1986.)

The influence of linguistic analysis based on segmentation and the identification of minimal units led to an impasse in theatrical research which made it difficult, if not impossible, to account for the poly-system that distinguishes the dramatic text from other verbal arts, that is, from literature in general. In this type of analysis, the segmentation of a sequence was dependent on the dual principles of hierarchization and interdefinition. Such principles could be respected in the analysis of a literary text. However, when faced with a dramatic text, it is necessary to take into account the specificity of theatre which, as Roland Barthes writes, is made up of 'a density of signs and sensations built up on stage, starting from the written argument; it is that oecumenical perception of sensuous artifice – gestures, tone, distance, substance, light – which submerges the text beneath the profusion of its external language' (Barthes 1972, 75). In this vein Ubersfeld herself points out that there exists a quasi-necessary conflict between the various modes of segmentation of dialogue, gesture, time, and didascalia insofar as they cannot be hierarchized or interdefined.

A number of critics[6] have commented on the subtlety with which Anne Ubersfeld tackles the problem of the duality of text-performance which is fundamental to the semiological analysis of dramatic text. She does not restrict herself to the written text that she considers incomplete, filled with blanks (*troué*); in fact, her analysis takes into account the tension between text and performance. However, it should be clear that the text remains the primary object of study and performance its horizon of analysis. Ubersfeld recognizes the importance of this distinction, but she also warns us against the temptation of reifying the text by means of a sociohistorical coded reading that would result in a fixed and determined performance. Each performance constitutes a unique realization or production that transcends and even rejects the assumption of fidelity to a specific text.[7] Yet, at the same time the text is a fundamental component of the art of theatre from two points of view – methodological and discursive. From the methodological point of view, for the analyst and, generally speaking, the practitioners of theatre, the text is a primary corpus that cannot be set aside. From the discursive point of view the text is present in performance, insofar as it is verbalized on stage. Ubersfeld remarks that the text has a dual existence: it precedes and accompanies performance, and it embodies matrices of 'performativity' that constitute its theatrical specificity, defined by Roland Barthes as that which 'must be present in the first written germ of a work, it is a datum of creation not of production ... [it] is from the first carried along by the externality of bodies, of objects, of situations; the utterance immediately explodes into substances' (Barthes 1982, 75).

Anne Ubersfeld's contribution to the study of the theatrical sign is to emphasize its paradoxical nature with respect to the referent. Here she takes into account its specificity by modifying and adapting the traditional definition of sign inherited from Saussurian linguistics that refuses to consider the objects of the 'real' world which the signs of the natural language designate.[8] For her the sign manifested in performance can be considered as having three domains of referentialization: the dramatic text, itself (reflexive), and the natural world. This is contrary to the sign of the literary text that constructs its own internal referent and a semiotics of the natural world.

We did note that in her analysis of dramatic action Anne Ubersfeld adapted A.J. Greimas' actantial model, which was influenced by two of the major twentieth-century scholars of folklore and anthropology: Vladimir Propp, who provided the syntagmatic or syntactic aspect of the theory, and Claude Lévi-Strauss, who provided the paradigmatic one. In working out his own model Greimas took the thirty-one functions that were initially developed by Propp and reformulated them in terms of: (a) actants (subject/object; helper/opponent; sender/receiver), defined as things or beings that accomplish or undergo an act independently of all other determinations; (b) actantial structures[9] (subject → object; helper → opponent; sender → receiver) and a canonical narrative schema. Greimas (1987, 48–83) developed an elementary syntax that could organize any type of narrative discourse. Propp's model was broken down into three successive sequences that correspond to the syntagmatic unfolding of the actantial model in which two sequences of communication – a mandate sequence and an evaluation sequence – frame an action sequence and transform the states. From this he worked out a semiotics of manipulation (how the sender manipulates the subject), then a semiotics of action (how the subject acquires competence in order to carry out performance), and finally a semiotics of evaluation or sanction (the passing of judgments on self, on others, and on things).[10]

For Ubersfeld, the standard actantial model that theoretically can account for transformations in all types of narratives is not specific to theatre. She modifies the above canonical model by bracketing off the sender/receiver/helper relations and concentrates on what is more characteristic of theatre, the subject → object ← opponent, or conflictual relation. She notes that it is possible then to identify a number of triangles that materialize the relatively autonomous relations between actants that occur in most classical scenes with two or three characters: the subject and opponent are vying for an absent object; or, the subject and object unite against the opponent; or, the sender designates the object of his/her quest to the subject. What characterizes the dramatic text compared with the novel is that in theatre there exists not one but at least two actantial models whereby, for example, objects or opponents can indeed assume the role of subjects in their own right. Finally, Ubersfeld notes that in most cases related to theatre the models proposed are unstable; they vary throughout the work and there are often shifts or even substitutions from one model to another along the way.

Ubersfeld addresses the key question of the representation of space with respect to the stage and to the written text. She frames her discussion of theatrical space from the perspective of the stage construction of spatial signs and from the point of view of the relationship between space and dramatic text. Patrice Pavis has written 'It is perhaps regrettable that Anne Ubersfeld, too preoccupied by signs in the text, only examines space, time, and scenic details on the textual level, neglecting the presentational one' (1977, 226). However, contrary to this statement, Ubersfeld in fact analyses the space of performance, since she defines textual space as flat and demonstrates in a very subtle way that theatrical space is an unspoken element (*un non-dit*) of the text, a zone filled with gaps – specifically the lack of the theatrical text – that the articulation of the performance-text unfolds. Some theorists have restricted the model proposed by Ubersfeld to only the written text. However, a closer reading of her work shows that she is mainly preoccupied by the space of performance (cf. chapter IV, section 2.2).

Ubersfeld's systematic exploration of the referential, iconic, poetic, and socio-historical networks of theatrical space provide valuable tools for directors and actors whose primary work is, first of all, to construct a concrete space in which the physical activities (gesture, movement, etc.) unfold. This space is then transformed into complex spatial signs where symbolic, poetic, praxic, and socio-historical relations are established. The importance of her account of spatial configurations and the choices and selections of different spatial networks directors have to make is illustrated in the example she gives of *Phèdre*:

[directors] can spatialize *Phèdre* in terms of conflict between several spaces, in terms of the problematics of the body divided, or again in terms of various other matrices of spatialization. The choice depends on the relation, at the time of performance, between the staging of the play and the play's contemporary referent, and with the code currently in force. It becomes uniquely interesting to make note of the choice made by the director, among the various matrices of spatialization the text offers (chapter IV, section 3.5. 'Space and Poetics: Consequences').

In chapter V, 'Theatre and Time,' Anne Ubersfeld shows once again, and rightly so, that the written text cannot in and by itself account for theatrical time. As a matter of fact, she argues that temporal signifiers in performance, for example with respect to rhythm and pauses, are far more difficult to apprehend and describe than spatial signifiers. However, in theatre, there exists a fundamental relationship between space and time

insofar as time can be perceived only through space and space is the signifier of time. Ubersfeld's approach to the question of time in theatre is
derived from the structuralist narratological framework. She introduces
distinctions such as the 'here and now' of enunciation, reported time (of
represented action), and duration. What concerns her in the treatment
of theatrical time, above and beyond stage time, are the numerous modu-
lations and ramifications that account for the relations of individuals to
their socio-historical, ideological, or personal histories.

Another important point she makes concerns the spectators' mode of
reception of spatial and temporal signs. It should be noted that the time
of performance is the time experienced by and for the spectator, who
participates fully in the process of signification when confronted with spatial and temporal signifiers or the discourse of characters. That the spectator plays an active role in performance is a secret to no one today;
however, Ubersfeld underscores the fact that the spectator's role is part
and parcel determined by the cultural constraints of the era. The manner
in which she envisages reception can be linked to recent work done on
the semiotics of passions (see Greimas and Fontanille 1993, 95–102),
which accentuates the role of sensitivization or the different ways in
which various cultures, places, and epochs treat the same sign systems.
She warns against performances that have become stereotypical and fos-
silized. Moreover, she states that 'sender-scriptors' have a fundamental
responsibility in this respect and that they should not lose sight of the fact
that they are always addressing a new public with its own aesthetic and
socio-cultural values. For her, the theoretical implications are that there
exists a dialogue between the two sender-scriptors (the author and the
director) that cannot be deciphered at the textual level and only becomes
meaningful within the context of the production of signification at the
time of performance. In other words, a semiotics of theatre must come to
grips with a multitude of dimensions including the dialogue between
author and director; director and actor; director and audience of her or
his era; actor and audience; and why not even current director and directors from other eras. These complex issues are explored in detail in *Lire le
théâtre II: L'école du spectateur,* 1981.

Reading Theatre is indeed a pioneering work that opens up new avenues
of investigation in the analysis of the dramatic text and performance. It is
a timely book, situated at the crossroads of current debate on the theory
of dramatic art since, on the one hand, it takes into account the findings
of semiotics derived from narratology, but on the other, it proposes a

model more particularly articulated in terms of the object-semiotics or the ensemble performance-text. In short, this is a useful and seminal work for students, directors, actors, and anyone interested in theatre in general.

PAUL PERRON AND PATRICK DEBBÈCHE
UNIVERSITY OF TORONTO

Introduction

Everyone knows – or accepts as truth – that you cannot read theatre. Professors are not unaware of this. Almost inevitably they know the anguish of explaining or trying to explain a textual document to which the key lies outside itself. Actors and directors embrace this truth more than anyone else and they view all academic explanations, which they see as unwieldy and useless, with scorn. Ordinary readers accept this wisdom as well. Whenever they take a stab at it, they realize the difficulty of reading a text that most decidedly does not appear to be intended for reading the way one reads a book. Not everyone is technically versed in mounting a play, nor does everyone have the unique imagination needed to conceive a work of fictive performance. This, however, is what each of us does, and this private act cannot be justified either theoretically or practically, for reasons which will soon be evident.

Are we thus obliged either to give up on reading theatre or to accept reading theatre as if it were some other kind of literary object? Are we to read Racine's theatre as if it were a vast poem, *Bérénice* as an elegy, and *Phèdre* in the way we read Dido's passionate episode in Virgil's *Aeneid*; must we read Musset in the way we read the work of a novelist, and Perdican as we do Fabricius? Should we read *La Tour de Nesle* the way we do *Les Trois Mousquetaires*, and *Polyeucte* as we do Pascal's *Pensées*?

We can admit that we cannot 'read' theatre, but we must do so nonetheless. First of all, this is true for everyone involved in theatre, in whatever capacity; amateurs, professionals, and dedicated spectators all turn to or return to the text as origin or reference. Amateur and professional readers of literature also read theatre, especially in France – professors, pupils, students – because the classic works of French literature from the Middle Ages to the twentieth century are, in large measure, works of theatre. Of course, one would rather study them staged, put them on, or see them put on. But performance is an instantaneous thing, a perishable thing. The text alone lasts. This book's only ambition is to provide some very simple keys to reading theatre and to indicate certain procedures for that reading. This is not a matter of discovering secrets hidden in a theatrical text and bringing them to light. Our task, less ambitious but more demanding, is to try to determine ways of reading which will allow us not only to cast light on a particular and unique textual practice, but also to show, if possible, the links that exist between this textual practice and a different one – that of performance.

Of course we will refer to other existing analyses of performance and of the text-performance relationship. The hope is eventually to study, elsewhere, the ways in which we read performance.[1] The specificity of the theatrical text is the first and essential question we must tackle. Perhaps by freeing ourselves from both the terrorism of the text and the terrorism of the stage, we can seek the elements of a response to the conflict between those who attach special status to the literary text and those who, caught up solely in the practical matters of production, have no time for its status as the product of an act of writing. In this battle between academics and theatre people, between theoreticians and theatrical practitioners, the semiologist cannot be the arbiter but can instead offer a principle of organization. The combatants on both sides use sign-systems. These sign-systems need to be both studied and constituted, so as to establish a real dialectic between theory and practice.

We are not unaware of the power of the scientific and positivist illusion. The semiologist claims not to offer the truth, or even the plural truths, of the text, but rather to establish the textual sign system or systems which can allow directors and actors to construct a signifying system in which spectators can find their place. The semiologist must keep in mind that meaning pre-exists his or her reading, that no one owns that meaning, not the author, and especially not the semiologist, who is neither a hermeneut nor a sorcerer.

The semiologist's goal is to explode, semiotically and textually, the dominant discourse – the acquired discourse – which places between text and performance a whole invisible screen of prejudices, of characters, and of passions.

We can readily see what enormous theoretical difficulties we face, not only because the semiology of theatre is still in its earliest stages, but also because the complexity of theatre practice puts it at the crossroads of the great quarrels that today cut across anthropology, psychoanalysis, linguistics, semantics, and history.

Of course, from a methodological point of view, linguistics occupies a privileged position in the study of theatrical practice, not only in terms of the text – principally dialogue – because the substance of its expression is verbal,[2] but also in terms of performance, given the relation (which we will have to clarify) between textual signs and performance signs.

We hope that our study, which is a modest attempt to cast light on a difficult area, will be of service to many different kinds of readers:

• first of all, among theatre people, to directors, who will find in it a systemization of what they do, either spontaneously or after reasoned consideration; to the dramaturge (in the German sense of the term) whose task – strictly semiological – is precisely to produce a reading of a theatrical text which can eventually be projected on an instance of performance;

• to actors, who seek to resist the real or supposed tyranny of directors through the freedom that knowledge will afford them, or who wish to make a substantive contribution to the creation of a new and revitalized reading;

• to high school and university students and teachers who feel annoyed or troubled by the inadequacy of their traditional methods of analysis when applied to theatrical texts, yet are equally sensitive to the difficulties facing poetics or story analysis when they are dealing with a literary object whose structures are greater than those of a poetic text, and even less linear than those of a story;

• finally, to all those who love the theatre and seek something that will mediate between what they read and what they enjoy on stage (albeit a difficult though necessary mediating exercise).

The framework within which this work is carried out makes it impossible to formulate a complete and fully developed discussion of the many problems facing the reader of theatre; we will have to settle for designating and locating those problems which we can neither resolve nor even articulate as rigorously as might be desired (for example, the problem of the communication-expression, sign-stimulus relation, or the problem posed by the non-arbitrary nature of the theatrical sign).

We are all familiar with the sometimes legitimate criticisms made of semiology. First, that semiology does away with history: but if semiology may be a convenient refuge for those who wish to do this, it does not mean that semiology cannot demonstrate that signs are historically determined products. 'Signs are in and of themselves units of social knowledge generalized to the highest degree. Arms and insignia, for example, are emblematically linked to the structure of society as a whole.'[3] Secondly, semiology is alleged to formalize the text, making it impossible to perceive its beauty. This is an irrational argument, belied by all branches of psychology that study aesthetic perception. A sophisticated reading that takes into account the multiple levels and components of a given object has an element of play, thus of aesthetic pleasure. Even more, it offers spectators a chance to be creatively engaged in deciphering signs and in establishing meaning. Finally, semiology is criticized for not being interested in psychology. True, it cuts off psychologizing discourse on characters and it puts an end to the autocracy of an eternal psychology of the human persona; but perhaps it also allows us to assign a legitimate place to the psychological workings of theatre with respect to the spectator. That is, it allows us to discover the legitimate status of the psycho-social function of performance.

Any work that reflects upon the theatrical text will without fail come up against the problematics of performance. A study of text can be linked only to the prolegomena, to the necessary but not solely sufficient point of departure of the totalizing practice or exercise that is actual theatre.

READING THEATRE

I. Text-Performance

1. The Performance-Text Relation

Theatre is a paradoxical art. To go even further, we might see in theatre the very art of paradox; it is literary production and concrete performance at the same time. Theatre is both eternal (indefinitely reproducible and renewable) and of the instant (never reproduced identically). It is an art involving instances of performance that are bound to a given moment or day and cannot be the same the next day. At the extreme, theatre may be an art whose creation involves only one performance, one fulfilment, as was Antonin Artaud's wish in *The Theater and Its Double* (Artaud 1958). It is the art of today, a performance taking place tomorrow but seeking to be the same as one that took place yesterday, acted by people who have changed and who perform in front of a new audience. A production that took place ten years ago, no matter how excellent, is as dead now as Roland's horse. But surely the text, at least in theory, is intangible and forever fixed.

Here, then, is the paradox: theatre is an art that involves highly refined textual creation, poetry of the greatest and most complex kind, from Aeschylus to Jean Genet or Koltès, with Racine or Hugo along the way – yet it is also an art that involves a practice whose strokes are broad, whose signs are vast, and in which redundancies are of the essence. Theatre must be seen, it must be understood by all. Again here we see the divide between the text, an object of an infinite poetic reading, and all that we understand by the term performance, an immediately read and readable phenomenon.

Another paradox: in theatre we see the result of a single 'great creator's' art – Molière, Sophocles, Shakespeare – but theatre as much and even more than cinema, requires the active and creative participation of many people, not to mention the direct or indirect intervention of spectators. It is an intellectual and difficult art whose fulfilment is reached only at that instant when its collective spectator – a crowd of people – becomes an audience for whom a unifying principle can be presupposed with all that is implied by way of shared credulity. Hugo saw the theatre as a means by which social contradictions could be reconciled. 'The transformation from a crowd to an audience, what a profound mystery!' (*Littérature et philosophie mêlées*, Hugo 1841). On the other hand, Brecht demonstrates in theatre a way of enhancing consciousness while profoundly dividing a given audience, exacerbating its internal contradictions.

The position of theatre is dangerous and privileged at the same time; theatre, more than any other art, because of its text-performance articulation, and especially because of its material and financial stakes, shows itself to be a social practice. Its relation to production can never disappear, although at times it may seem quite blurred, and theatrical seduction may transform it into nothing more than a means of entertainment for the pleasure of the dominant class. Theatre is a dangerous art. Censorship always has its eye on theatre, directly or indirectly – whether accomplished through economic structures, or by the police, or even in the particularly perverse form of self-censorship.

Theatre is an art that fascinates because of the participation it requires, a participation of which neither the meaning nor the function are clear, a participation that requires analysis. There is both the physical and psychological participation of the actor, and the physical and psychological participation of the spectator (and we will see the extent to which the latter is an active participation). Theatre appears to be a privileged art of capital importance, because more than any other art, it shows how the individual psyche invests itself within a collective relationship. The spectator is never alone; as his or her eye takes in what is presented on the stage, it also takes in the other spectators, just as indeed they observe him or her. As both psychodrama and a means to reveal and identify social relations, theatre holds both of these paradoxical threads in its hand.

1.1. The Text-Performance Opposition

The first contradiction inherent in the art of theatre is the *text-performance opposition.*

Of course, the semiology of the theatre must consider the totality of theatrical discourse as an 'integrated signifying event (form and sub-stance of content, form and substance of expression).'[1] We can quite rea-sonably apply the definition Metz gives for the discourse of film (Metz 1974, 13) to theatrical discourse. However, a refusal to accept the text-performance distinction will lead to all kinds of confusion since the same tools are not used for the analysis of both.

1.1.1. Classical Practice

A first possible way of seeing things is the 'intellectual' or pseudo-intellec-tual, classical way, which assigns privileged status to the text and views per-formance as no more than an expression and translation of a literary text. The director's job is to translate into another language a text towards which her or his primary duty is to remain faithful. This attitude presupposes an underlying basic idea of semantic equivalence between the written text and its performance. All that changes, according to this point of view, is the 'matter of expression,' in the Hjelmslevian sense of the term. Content and form would thus remain identical even as we move from the text-sign system to the performance-sign system.

This equivalence is very likely an illusion. The totality of the visual, audi-tory, and musical signs created by the director, set designer, musicians, and actors constitutes a meaning (or a multiplicity of meanings) that goes beyond the text in its totality. In turn, many of the infinite number of vir-tual and real structures of the (poetic) message of the literary text disap-pear or cannot be perceived, because they have been erased or lost by the actual system of performance. Indeed, even if by some miracle perfor-mance could speak or tell the whole text, spectators would not hear the whole text. A good part of its information is erased or lost. The art of the director and the actors resides largely in their choices as to what should not be heard. We cannot speak of semantic equivalence: if T equals the set of the entire set of textual signs, and P equals the set of performed signs, the intersection of these two sets will shift for each performance.

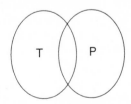

Depending on how the text is written and how the performance is delivered, the coincidence of the two sets will be greater or lesser. This gives us an interesting means of distinguishing between the various types of text-performance relations.

The approach that accords privileged status to the literary text and sees it as primary can be linked to the illusion of coincidence (one that is never realized) between the set of signs of a given text and the signs that are performed. If by some miracle this coincidence were brought about, the question of whether performance functions only as a system of signs would still be unanswered.

The main danger of this approach lies, of course, in the temptation to freeze or fix the text, to sacralize it to the point of making the system of performance impossible and thwarting the imagination of the inter-preters[2] (directors and actors). Further danger lies in the (unconscious) temptation to fill in any silences or spaces in the text, and to read the text as if it were a compact block or unit that could only be reproduced using tools external to it; in this way any production of an artistic object is pro-hibited. The greatest danger lies granting privileged status not to the text, but to one particular historical or codified reading of the text, a reading which, as a result of textual fetishism, will be granted eternal legitimacy. Given the relations (unconscious but powerful) that are established between a theatrical text and the historical conditions of its performance, the privileged status of the text, following a strange path, might lead to the further granting of privileged status to codified ways of performing that text. In other words, the result might be the prohibition of any advances in the art of staging plays. Thus traditional actors and directors thought that they were most assuredly defending the integrity and purity of a Molière or Racine text, when in fact they were defending a codified read-ing of that text, or perhaps even a given predetermined way of performing it. We can see not only the extent to which granting privileged status to the text can make theatre sterile, but also why, in theatre, it is so necessary to distinguish clearly between what is essentially of the text and what is essen-tially of the performance. Without this distinction, it is impossible to anal-yse the relation between the two phenomena and identify their common task. Paradoxically, the failure to distinguish clearly between text and per-formance leads those who defend the primacy of the text to indeed cause the effect of performance to revert upon the text.

1.1.2. Against the Text

The other approach, one that is much more common in modern or avant-garde theatrical practice, is a sometimes radical rejection of the text. Theatre is seen entirely in terms of the ceremony that takes place before or in the midst of spectators. The text is only one among several elements of performance – indeed maybe the least important element. The importance of *T* is minimal, indeed perhaps nil.

This is Artaud's thesis, probably not as he enunciated it but as it has too often been misunderstood: a radical rejection of text-based theatre.[3] This kind of illusion, inverse and symmetrical to the preceding one, obliges us to examine more closely the notion of text within theatre and its relation with performance.

1.2. The Distinction between Text and Performance

The main reason why confusion reigns here, particularly in the case of semiological analyses of theatre, is the refusal to distinguish between the domain of the text and the domain of the performance. André Helbo's book (Helbo 1975), which makes an important contribution, bears the misleading title *Sémiologie de la représentation* (semiology of performance) despite the fact that it deals primarily with the theatrical text.

1.2.1. Verbal and Non-verbal Signs
It is not possible to use the same tools to examine both textual signs and the non-verbal signs of performance. Syntax (textual) and proxemics[4] are different approaches to the study of theatre. These two approaches should not be confused, even (and especially) if it eventually becomes necessary to demonstrate the relationship between the two.

This confusion arises at the very heart of the notion of theatricality as defined by Barthes in the famous lines from *Critical Essays*: 'What is theatricality? It is theater-minus-text, it is a density of signs and sensations built up on stage starting from the written argument ...' (Barthes 1972, 25). An endlessly confusing definition. Where do we place theatricality when it is so defined? Must it be expelled from text and reserved for performance alone? Would the text then be no more than a writing practice that is subject to a literary reading, and theatricality a phenomenon proper to the domain of performance? If this is so, a semiology of the theatrical text makes no sense and any semiology of the phenomenon of theatre should be a semiology of performance.

Let us recall certain facts:

a/ The theatrical text is present within performance in its form as voice, as *phonè*. It has a twofold existence: first it precedes performance, then it accompanies it.

b/ On the other hand, one can always read the text of a play as if it were non-theatre. There is nothing about a theatrical text that prevents us from reading it as if it were a novel, from perceiving scripted dialogues as if they were dialogues from a novel and stage directions as if they were descriptions. We can always novelize a play just as conversely we can always theatricalize a novel. 'You can make theatre out of anything,' says Vitez, who created *Catherine* using Aragon's *Cloches de Bâle*. The textual transformation of a novel is analogous, but in an inverse direction, to the transformation brought by the reconstruction of the storyline of a play in a novel-like account,[5] setting aside the play's theatricality.

Our initial premise is that within the theatrical text there are matrices of 'performativity.' A theatrical text can be analysed by procedures that are (relatively) specific to it, procedures that bring to light kernels of theatricality contained within the text. This specificity is not so much of the text as it is of the readings that can be made of the text. Although we can read Racine as we do a novel, to do so will in no way enhance the intelligibility of Racine's text.

We should add another point, which will be demonstrated later: in theatrical writing, and more precisely in the presuppositions to such writing, there is a specificity that we will try to focus on, a specificity that must be brought to bear upon any poetic or novelistic text that one might seek to adapt for the stage.

1.2.2. The Components of a Theatrical Text

Just what is a theatrical text? It is made up of two distinct yet indissociable parts, dialogue and *didascalia* (stage or production directions).[6] The textual dialogue-didascalia relation varies according to the period in the history of theatre. Sometimes those directions are non-existent or almost non-existent (and thus all the more significant when by chance they do indeed exist).[7] On the other hand, they can occupy an enormous place in contemporary theatre. For example, in the works of Adamov and Genet, stage directions are of extreme importance, beauty, and significance. In

Beckett's *Act without Words*, the text is in fact one immense body of didascalia.

Even where didascalia appear to be non-existent, the textual locus for those directions is always present. Didascalia, after all, include the names of the characters, both in the initial list and within the dialogue, and indications of place, thus answering the questions of *who* and *where*. These directions set forth the context within which theatrical communication takes place. Thus they determine a pragmatics, that is, the concrete conditions in which *parole* takes place. The textuality of these directions is projected on their application in performance (where, of course, they do not figure as verbal utterances).

The fundamental linguistic distinction between dialogue and didascalia implicates the subject of enunciation, that is, it implicates the question of who is speaking. In dialogue we have a paper/writing creation (distinct from the author) that we call a character. In the didascalia it is the author who (a) names the characters, indicates who is to speak at any given moment, and assigns to each character a place from which to speak and a share of the discourse; and (b) gives directions, separate from the dialogue, as to the characters' gestures and actions.

This fundamental distinction allows us to see the author does not speak herself or himself in theatre, but rather writes so that another can speak in her or his stead – indeed not just one other but a whole group of others, through a series of speaking exchanges. The theatrical text can never be deciphered in terms of a confidence, or indeed as an expression of the personality, feelings or problems of the author. Those subjective aspects are expressly assigned to other lips. Here then is the first feature that is distinctive to theatrical writing: it is never subjective, to the extent that, of his or her own free will, the author refuses to speak on his or her own behalf and in direct reference to himself or herself. If there is a textual component of which the author is subject, it is the *didascalia*. Dialogue is always the voice of another – not only the voice of one other but of several others. If there were a hermeneutic way to decipher the voice of the writing subject, it would be in the superimposition of all of those voices. The literary problem of theatrical writing thus lies in the manner in which the voice of the writing *I* is covered by the voices of those others who speak. This is corollary to the fact of not speaking one's self.[8]

1.2.3. Performance and Textual Activity

The theatrical text, as we receive it in printed or manuscript form, book or folio, displays a number of characteristics:

a/ The substance of its expression is linguistic (while that of performance is multiple, verbal and non-verbal).

b/ It is diachronic communication that follows a linear reading, as opposed to the concretized polysemic nature of the signs deployed by performance. The theatrical text is a literary text, and as such it implies a reading that is ordered in time (even if re-readings or skipping back may reverse that order). Perception of the performed text implies a spectator capable of spatio-temporally organizing multiple, simultaneously-deployed signs.

This is why performance must effect its particular practice or treatment of the text, an activity that at the same time involves other signifying elements. This further processing of the text's material also implies a transformation into text of non-linguistic signs, a transformation effected by the practitioner of theatre that involves a certain reciprocity between text and non-linguistic signs. Hence we see the presence, alongside T the author's text (usually printed or typewritten) of T', another text that pertains to staging or mounting the play. Both are, of course, distinct from P, performance:

$$T + T' \rightarrow P$$

It must be understood that, like any literary text but even more so, for obvious reasons, the theatrical text has *gaps*, and that T' fits into the gaps of T. The simplest example can demonstrate the existence of these gaps and how they are necessary for performance. We know nothing about the age, physical appearance, political opinions, or personal history of such clearly presented characters as Alceste or Philinte.[9] Moreover, if we look at the first exchange between Alceste and Philinte, in the opening scene of *Le Misanthrope*, we realize that we know nothing of the relevant situational context. Are the two characters already there, on stage, or are they just arriving? How do they go there? Do they run? Who follows whom, and how? All these are questions are posed by the text with its necessary gaps. If these gaps were not there, the text could not be performed, for it is performance that bears responsibility for answering these questions.

In order to find these answers a treatment of the text must be carried out. We find this treatment recorded in staging notebooks; it can be written or unwritten. Whether oral or written, a T' text is necessarily interposed, mediating between T and P. It is by nature assimilable to T (because it is linguistic) and radically different from P (because its substance and codes are of a different order). The linguistic component of the phenomenon we call theatre is made up of the two sets of signs from $T + T'$.

2. The Theatrical Sign

2.1. On Theatrical Communication

To the extent that we define language as a sign system used for communication, it is clear that theatre is not a language, and that strictly speaking, there is no such thing as a theatrical language. Just as Metz rejects the notion that there can be a cinematographic sign, so we cannot correctly speak of a theatrical sign. In theatrical performance there is no isolatable element that can be considered the equivalent of linguistic signs with their twofold arbitrary character (relative) and double articulation (morphemes and phonemes).[10] As a consequence, any attempt to identify theatrical process with communicative process (sender-code-message-receiver) opens itself to an attack that Mounin has joined with passion (Mounin 1970).

However, we must note that:

1/ The theatrical text, while not an autonomous language, can be analysed just as any other object that is in essence a linguistic code; this analysis will follow (a) the rules of linguistics; (b) the communication process, since the text has a sender, etc.
2/ Theatrical performance is a set (or system) of signs of a diverse nature, concerned, if not totally then at least partially, with a communicative process; it involves a complex series of senders (closely linked with each other), a series of messages (closely linked in a complex way with each other and regulated by extremely precise codes), and a multiple receiver, all of which are in the same place. The fact that the receiver usually cannot answer using the same code, as Mounin notes, does not mean that there is no communication. A message that is sent out in Morse code or in an encoded language can quite clearly elicit an answer in the form of a gesture, an answer expressed in popular speech, or no answer at all. Having identical outgoing and incoming codes is in no way an absolute condition for communication.

If it is true that communication is not the entire function of performance and that we cannot ignore either expression or what Mounin calls the stimulus,[11] it is nonetheless possible to attempt an analysis of the way in which the text-performance relation can be organized. We can begin with the hypothesis that the phenomenon we call theatre can be viewed as a relation between two sets of signs – verbal and non-verbal.

2.2. The Saussurian Definition of the Sign

We must apologize for summarizing well-known concepts, but to omit this might risk leaving some readers in the dark. According to Saussure, the sign is a signifying element composed of two parts that are practically indissociable but which can legitimately be separated for methodological reasons (just as, although there is no such thing as an isolated system, we can nonetheless study, for example, the thermodynamic laws of an isolated system). These two elements are the signifier and the signified.[12]

One characteristic of the linguistic sign is that it is arbitrary (a relative thing); there is no visible relation of resemblance between the signifier and the signified, or more precisely between the signifier and the referent: the word *chair* does not resemble a chair.

Another characteristic is linearity; linguistic signs are decoded successively in time.

The third element in the triad of the sign is its referent – the element to which the sign refers in the communication process, and which cannot automatically be further referred on to some object in the world; there exist imaginary referents. Thus, the sign chair has as its signifier the morpheme chair (written or spoken) to signify the concept of chair, and as its referent the possibility of or the actual existence of an object chair (but not necessarily an object chair in the world).

The signs of the textual ensemble $T + T'$ in theatre correspond to this definition and can justifiably be treated according to linguistic procedures.

2.3. Non-verbal Signs

We include here some definitions, without going into all the discussion that they might suggest.

Luis Prieto identifies non-intentional signs that he calls *indices* (for example, smoke is an index of fire) and intentional signs that he calls *signals* (that same smoke might signal the fact that I am in the forest, if that is the agreed upon recognition code). Whether verbal or non-verbal, signs can be indices or signals: I can indicate or signal through speech or any other means (such as gesture). In the area of performance, all signs, verbal or not, in theory are signals, to the extent that theoretically they are all intentional. That, of course, does not prevent them from also being indices (they can indicate something other then their main denoted element).[13] Nor does it mean that there cannot be a whole multitude of indexical signs which directors and actors can ignore consciously and by choice, but which nonetheless come into play.

Peirce's terminology classifies signs as *indices, icons,* and *symbols:* the index has a relation of contiguity with the object (for example, smoke-fire). The icon shows a relation of resemblance to the denoted object (resemblance according to certain relationships, for example, as is the case with the portrait).

These concepts are subject to much discussion: in *Messages et signaux* (1966) Prieto shows that the index, far from identifying an obvious relation, requires a classifying activity based on the existence of a more general class, 'the universe of discourse.' Thus white is the sign of mourning in the sociocultural universe of Asia. Umberto Eco (1972, 174ff) has doubts about the icon as well. He notes that the resemblances between icon and object must be handled with a great deal of caution.

As for Peirce's symbol, it involves a pre-existing relation between two objects (for example, the lily and whiteness or innocence). This relation is subject to sociocultural conditions.

It is obvious that every sign is at the same time, more or less an icon, an index, or a symbol, depending on its use and its functions, as much as and even more than on its nature. In connection with the colour black, the colour of mourning clothes in the West (in Asia it is white), who is to say that we have an icon, index, or symbol? Generally speaking, in the area of literature, the index serves for the most part to announce or articulate the episodes of the story; it has to do with diegesis. The icon functions as a 'reality effect' and as a stimulus. As for the symbolic role of the sign, we will see it more clearly when discussing theatre.

It goes without saying that every theatrical sign is both index and icon, and sometimes symbol: icon because theatre is in a way the production-reproduction of human actions;[14] index because every element of the performance integrates itself within a succession from which it takes its meaning. The most innocent and seemingly most gratuitous item tends to be perceived by the spectator as an index of things to come, even if that expectation is never fulfilled.

2.4. Performance and Codes

Performance is made up of a set of verbal and non-verbal signs. The verbal message is contained within the system of performance and has its own acoustic substance of expression (voice). To this are added all of the *codes* by which the non-verbal signs can be decoded: visual codes, musical codes, proxemics, etc. Any theatrical message within performance, requires a multitude of codes if it is to be decoded. Paradoxically, this allows even those who do not possess all of the codes to hear and understand theatre: one can understand a play without understanding its national or local allusions, or without grasping a particular complex or outdated cultural code. For example, it is quite clear that neither the great *seigneurs* nor the lackeys who attended performances of Racine's plays understood his mythological references, both being as ignorant as fish. The Paris spectators who saw (and adored) the performances of Goldoni's *Il Campiello* presented by Giorgio Strehler in 1977 did not understand Venetian dialect; many of them were in fact unaware of the references to Venetian paintings and to Guardi's paintings in particular. It worked because all of the other codes in play allowed for sufficient comprehension of the signs.

To the comments above we must add mention of codes that are strictly theatrical. First there is the code that presupposes a 'relation of equivalence' between a play's textual signs and its performance signs. We can consider the theatrical code 'par excellence' the one which presents itself as a 'repertoire of equivalences' (Eco 1972, 56), or a 'rule of term-for-term equivalence between two opposing systems.' This theatrical code is as flexible, as mutable, and as culture-dependent as the code we call language. There are, for instance, the fixed systems of equivalence between an instance of speech (representing a situation) and a gesture in Japanese Noh theatre.

2.5. Remarks on the Theatrical Sign

Given the number of codes involved in theatrical performance, the theatrical sign is a complex concept which brings into play not only the phenomenon of co-existence, but indeed a superimposition of signs.

We know that any sign system can be read along two axes: the axis of substitutions or *paradigmatic axis,* and the axis of combinations, or *syntagmatic axis.* In other words, at any moment of performance, it is possible to substitute one sign for another sign in the same paradigm. For example, for the actual presence of the enemy in combat, one can substitute an object that emblematically represents that enemy, or a character who belongs to the same enemy paradigm. Hence the theatrical sign is flexible; it is possible to substitute a sign belonging to one code for a sign belonging to another. In Vitez's 1975 production of *Phèdre* the *tears* were represented by a bowl of water in which the actors washed their faces. The syntagmatic axis allows us to string together a succession of signs; one can see just how, without interrupting that string, such substitution makes it possible to play one code against the other, to cause the story to shift from one kind of sign to another.

We can see how a vertical accumulation of simultaneous signs in performance (verbal, gestural, auditory signs) allows for a particularly flexible interplay along the paradigmatic and syntagmatic axes. This is why it is possible for theatre to say several things at the same time, to construct several simultaneous and interlinked stories. The accumulation of signs allows for counterpoint.

As a result:

1/ The concept of sign loses its precision and we cannot identify a minimal sign; we cannot establish the minimal unit of performance. It would be like arresting a point in time so as to produce a vertical structure of all the codes involved: one is punctual or ephemeral (a gesture, a look, a word); another can be stretched out over the whole of the performance (a detail of the decor, a costume). The untangling of the many threads of these encoded signs can be carried out only with recourse to units that vary with the code, as we will see when we analyse the microsequences of the dramatic text.

2/ Any theatrical sign, even if it is only marginally indexical and purely iconic, can be involved in an operation we call 're-semanticization.' Any sign, even one created by accident, functions as a question asked of the spectator, a question that calls for one or more interpretations. A simple visual stimulus, for example, a colour, takes on meaning through its paradigmatic relation (reduplication or opposition), its syntagmatic relation (relation with other signs in the performance succession), or through its symbolism. Again here, the *sign-stimulus, index-icon* oppositions are constantly overtaken by the very function performance; the distinctive feature of theatre is the way it neutralizes oppositions.

2.6. Denotation, Connotation

It is clear that the principal difficulty in analysing the sign in theatre lies in its *polysemy*. This polysemy is of course the result of the fact that one and the same sign is present in sets belonging to different codes, although they come together on stage. Hence, the colour of a costume is firstly a visual element of what is seen on stage, but it also takes its place in a coded symbolics of colours. It is also part of a character's costume, and is identified with that character's social position or dramatic function. It can further mark the paradigmatic relationship of the wearer with another character whose costume has the same colour. But polysemy is above all linked to the process by which meaning is constituted: alongside the principal meaning – the denotative meaning (usually bound up with the principal storyline), a meaning that is generally obvious – every sign (verbal or non-verbal) carries secondary meanings that stand apart from the primary meanings.[15] Thus the 'red man' that Marion Delorme speaks of in Hugo's play bearing her name denotes Cardinal Richelieu (as does the colour of his costume); the colour red connotes the cardinal's duties, the power of a near- king, the cruelty of an executioner (red = blood). These connotations are linked to the sociocultural context. Red connotes not only the colour of a Cardinal's clothing, but also blood and cruelty (in Russia red connotes beauty, and since the October revolution it has also connoted revolution). In Asia, white connotes not innocence, but mourning and death; in India a woman dressed in white is not a virgin, but a widow. However, perhaps we do not have to restrict ourselves to the concept of connotation when dealing with theatrical signs, because instead of the denotation-connotation opposition, we can substitute the concept of a plurality of codes that underlie a whole host of performed textual networks. This will account for the possibility of giving privileged status to a secondary network at the level of performance, the principal network being the one implicated in the principal storyline. There remains the task of identifying the principal storyline – the task of the playwright-reader and the director. What is interesting in and specific to theatre is precisely the possibility to grant special status to a given sign system, to play various networks off against each other and thereby cause the same text-score to produce interplays of meanings with different resolutions.

2.7. The Sign Triad and Theatre

Starting with our semiological premise (the existence of two sign systems in theatre, one verbal, that of the text T, and the other verbal/non-verbal, that of performance P), we can see that there will be certain consequences for the relations between T and P. If T is the total group of textual signs, P the total group of performance signs, Sr the signifier, Sd the signified, R the referent of T, and r the referent for P, we end up with:

$$T = \frac{Sr}{Sd} \text{ referring to R}$$

$$P = \frac{Sr'}{Sd'} \text{ referring to r}$$

According to the classical hypothesis under which theatre is enacted in terms of a performance-translation of the text, $Sd = Sd'$ and $R = r$: the signified of the two totalities of signs are identical or nearly so (if they are not identical, it would be because of the weaknesses inherent in all 'performance') and they refer to the same referent. There would be a redundancy, a reduplication of meaning between text and performance.

But this hypothesis assumes that two totalities of signs, each with a different substance of expression, can have an identical signified. It assumes that the material make-up of the signifier has no bearing on meaning. Now, we can note the following:

1/ The totality of the textual networks cannot find an equivalent in the totality of the performance signs; there remains a Y part that is missing.

2/ If there is loss of information in the shift from text to performance (sometimes an entire part of the textual poetics is difficult to perform), there is on the other hand an increase in information to the extent that many of the performance signs can form autonomous systems X (X_1, X_2, etc.) that have no equivalent in the totality of the textual signs.

For the classical ideal of performance, the whole point is to diminish the value of X and of Y as much as possible in order to obtain a close coincidence of

$$\frac{Sr}{Sd} \text{ and } \frac{Sr'}{Sd'}.$$

This ideal presupposes that one can construct truly equivalent systems. Conversely, one might consider that the forming of performance signs

serves to construct an autonomous signifying system in which the totality of the textual signs has no part. This hypothesis is more fruitful and
is better suited to the reality of the theatre because the practical activity of performance consists of taking into account both signifying systems in order to combine them. However, it is also a reductive
hypothesis if the result is to diminish the role and importance of textual signs.

2.8. The Problem of the Referent

The referent R of the theatrical text refers us to a certain view of the
world, to a given contextual figure representing objects of the external
world. Thus the *diadem* in a tragedy by Corneille has to do less with a real
object, made of gold and perhaps encrusted with jewels, than it does with
royalty or the king: the referent of the diadem as seen by Corneille (and
his audience) is royalty. Even the real object that is the referent for the
lexeme *diadem* has only secondary importance.

In the area of performance, the referent has a twofold status:

1/ It is identified with the referent R of the theatrical text; the diadem in
Corneille's *Othon* is a referent for Cornellian royalty.
2/ It can also be materially present on stage in a concrete or figurative
form, a real diadem or a flesh and blood actor playing the role of king
with whom metonymically the diadem is identified. Thus we see the
unique status of the icon in theatre: it is identified with its own referent that is fixed like a sticker upon it.

Performance constructs for the text and, one might say, for itself, its own
referent. Here then is the semiotically monstrous paradox; a sign P (a
performance sign) appears to have three referents:

a/ the referent R of the dramatic text;
b/ itself $(P=R)$ *as its own referent*;
c/ its referent r in the real world.

This paradoxical situation marks the very way theatre functions because:

1/ The referent R of the text T is simultaneously: a system within the real
world (for example, royalty in Corneille's time); and the concrete
signs that represent T upon the stage. In other words, the textual signs

T are such that, and are constructed (by the author) such that, they refer us to two orders of reality – the real world and the stage.

2/ The totality of signs *P* is constructed as the *referential system for* T = *the reality to which the text refers*; but at the same time, as is the case for every sign, *P* has its own actual, contemporaneous, referent *r* (not to mention that indirectly, it also has *T's* referent *R*).

If we take the example of the *diadem* in Corneille, it is as if performance constructed a *king wearing a diadem* who is concretely present on stage as a referent of the Cornellian text. At the same time this king with his diadem functions as a sign that refers us to the historical referent of the seventeenth century. (What does the concept of a king mean to us, today?) We see how the very essence of the theatrical sign (*T+P*) in its totality conditions the status of theatre and its nature as an infinitely renewable practice and activity.

We hope that our thesis, a paradoxical one, can cast light on the historical functions of the theatrical sign. Each moment in history, each new performance reconstructs *P* as a new referent for *T*, as a new referential reality (necessarily a little unfaithful to exact historical time), with a second and different referent *r*, to the extent that this referent *r* is of the moment (as a function of the precise *hic et nunc* moment of performance).

Thus we see how and why theatre (even picturesque or psychological theatre) is an ideological practice, and even, most often, very concretely political.

We also see why we can neither wish for nor reconstitute a performance from the time of Louis XIV or even (not the same thing) present a referential image of Louis XIV's century (other than through play). Neither can we obliterate that historical referent in order, for example, to make a text from the 17th century brutally contemporary: *Le Misanthrope* in modern dress does not work well because it lacks its twofold reference. It is now clear that theatrical activity in performance is 'par excellence' a dialectical locus.

This is also one reason why attempts at naturalistic theatre are just an illusion: the formula for naturalistic theatre would be *R* = *r* – that is to say, the hope that the world presented on stage will coincide with the external world. The naturalistic solution is non-dialectical, and the danger posed by this coincidence between *R* and *r* is present also in so-called realistic performance.

There is also a corollary: theatre exists in order to *speak*, but also to *be*, and this is a problem we will meet again. It is too reductive of theatrical practice to view it only as a function of a sign system and to ignore its referential function. Theatre is a referent unto itself, and not all[16] of its elements can be rendered signifying; for the spectator it is a given: theatre is seen before it is understood.

However, if we speak of sign and referent, we can do so only in terms of the receiver of the message, the receiver-spectator so indispensable to the process of communication.

With communication that goes beyond communication, the paradox of theatre is not through with us yet.

3. Theatre and Communication

3.1. Two Sets of Signs

To sum up what we have tried to demonstrate so far (working hypotheses concerning the relations between text and dramatic performance), we can say that the theatrical performance is made up of a set of signs articulated into two sub-groups: text T and performance P.

These signs are contained within a process of communication whose message they constitute – a process that is indeed quite complex, but that, regardless, obeys the laws of communication:

Sender (multiple): author + director + others involved in mounting the play + actors.
Message: T + P
Codes: linguistic code + perceptual codes (visual, auditory) + sociocultural codes (social niceties, verisimilitude, psychology, etc.) + strictly theatrical codes (blocking, acting, etc. that codify performance at any given moment in history).
Receiver: spectator(s), audience

Mounin's basic objection to the hypothesis that includes theatre in the process of communication does not seem absolutely convincing; he says:

Linguistics ... sees the function of communication as central. This led Eric Buyssens and other linguists to identify clearly those phenomena that have to do with an *intention* to communicate, an intention that one can clearly point to (the existence of a speaker linked to a listener through a message which determines verifiable behaviours). These facts are to be distinguished from phenomena that do not demonstrate this characteristic, even if until now such phenomena have been called signs and have been included in the study of language. These phenomena, which Troubetzkoy calls *indices* and *symptoms*, ... have to do with information the speaker gives about himself, without any intention of communicating them (Mounin 1970, 68).

Mounin therefore sees communication as subordinate to the intention to communicate. Now surely this intention to communicate cannot be denied for theatre. Even if an actor states the intention of self-expression, it is not the self he or she seeks to express, but the self saying something. The intention to communicate cannot be reduced to the intention to communicate a science or some other delimited body of knowledge that is clear and distinct. Art generally distinguishes between the intention to communicate and the desire to say some specific thing; one can seek to communicate even though a large measure of the message is not born of any intentionality. We can say of theatre what we can say of other forms of art: the richness of the signs and the extent and complexity of the systems they form go infinitely beyond any primary intention to communicate. While there may be loss of information in relation to what was originally intended, there are also unexpected gains; even if we set aside the question of noise (involuntary signs which impede communication), there is in every act of communication information given involuntarily and unconsciously (but which only an abuse of language would call non-intentional), information whose reception is possible or even required of the listener. In daily life, gesticulations, a certain tone, slips of the tongue, abrupt changes of subject all come together to create a discourse that is perfectly comprehensible for the receiver. These observations, commonplace since Freud and probably even before him, allow us to understand the way in which theatrical communication is intentional in its totality, and even (this is the job of the director) in all of its essential signs. Theatrical communication merits the term communication in the restrictive sense, even if many of the signs emitted by theatrical activity cannot be accounted for in terms of a conscious plan, and even if the question of their intentionality is barely raised, because that question cannot be relevant to all the signs of poetic language. The playwright and the director can say, 'I wanted to *speak*,' even if at times they might also say, 'I didn't want to say *that*,' or if they cannot tell us what in fact they did 'want to say.'

3.2. The Six Functions

If one accepts the hypothesis that theatrical activity is a process of communication (even if it cannot be reduced to only that), one can then deduce that the six functions of language identified by Roman Jakobson (1964) are relevant not only for the signs of text but also for those of performance. Each of these functions is linked to an element in the process of communication:

a/ The *emotive* function, linked to the sender, is of capital importance to theatre: the actor exploits it using all the physical and vocal means available; the director and stage manager 'dramatically' deploy all relevant stage elements.

b/ The *conative* function, linked to the receiver, requires the dual receiver of all theatrical messages – the receiver-actor (character) and receiver-audience – to make a decision or to give an answer, albeit perhaps a provisional and subjective answer.

c/ The *referential* function never lets the spectator forget the *context* (historical, social, political, indeed psychological) in which communication takes place and its link to a given reality (see the discussion of the complexity of the theatrical sign's referential function above).

d/ The *phatic* function constantly reminds the spectator of the conditions under which communication is taking place and of his or her presence as spectator in a theatre: it interrupts or re-establishes contact between sender and receiver (whereas within dialogue it ensures contact between characters). Text and performance can fill this function concurrently.

e/ The *metalinguistic*[17] function, rarely found within dialogue since dialogue is not usually self-reflexive about the conditions of its production, functions fully in all cases where there is theatricalization, acknowledgement of theatre as theatre, or theatre within theatre – that is to say, 'My code is the theatrical code.'

f / The *poetic function*, which is linked to the message itself, can cast light on the relations between semic networks of text and those of performance. Theatrical functioning is, more than anything else, *poetic*, if by poetic we mean, as Jakobson would have it, a *projection of the paradigmatic onto the syntagmatic*, of textual-performed signs onto the diachronic totality of performance.

Far from being just a mode of analysis for theatrical discourse (and in particular of spoken text), the totality of the process of communication can cast light upon performance as a concrete practice.

3.3. The Receiver-Audience

It would be false to say that the role of the spectator in the process of communication is passive. No actor or director has ever thought that. But many settle for considering the spectator as a kind of mirror that sends back, refracted, the signs sent out to him or her. At most, such actors and directors might see the spectator as a kind of counter-sender, emitting signs of a different nature, relevant only to a phatic function: 'I hear you loud and clear' (as with radio messages), or 'I'm not receiving you at all' (as might be understood from hisses and hoots).

In fact, the receiver-function of the audience is much more complex. First, because spectators sort information, choose, and reject some of it, they push the actor in one direction, albeit through weak signs that the original sender can nonetheless clearly perceive as feedback. Second, there is no one spectator; rather there is a multiplicity of spectators who react to each other. Not only do we rarely go to the theatre alone, but also we cannot be alone at the theatre. Any message received by one spectator is refracted (upon fellow spectators), echoed, taken up, and sent off again in a very complex exchange.

Finally – probably the greatest paradox, and the most difficult to understand in the particular conditions and limitations of proscenium theatre – it is the spectators, much more than the director, who create the spectacle: they must reconstruct the totality of the performance, along both the vertical axis and the horizontal axis. Spectators are obliged not only to follow a story, a fabula (horizontal axis), but also to constantly reconstruct the total figure of all of the signs engaged concurrently in the performance. They are at one and the same time required to engage themselves in the spectacle (identification) and to back off from it (distancing). Probably there is no other activity requiring as much psychological and intellectual engagement. This is probably why theatre is irreplaceable and why it endures in various forms in so many diverse societies. Brecht did not invent the concept of the creative role of the spectator,[18] but he did discover the fundamental law of theatre whereby the spectator is a participant, an important actor (with no need whatsoever for the phenomenon of a happening).

Our task here is not to study the reception of the spectacle any more than it is to study the particular manner in which theatrical texts are read outside of performance – a reading that requires a very formalized kind of imagination. Suffice it to say that this reception seems to us to display three key elements:

a/ the need, given the torrent of signs and stimuli, to latch tightly onto the larger structures involved (narrative structures, for example – a point that implies the need to study the macrostructures of a text first);

b/ the function of theatre, not only as message, but also as expression-stimulation, inducing the spectator to possible action;

c/ the fact that we perceive the totality of theatrical signs as marked by negativity.

3.4. Illusion-Denial

3.4.1. The Status of Dream

The essential characteristic of theatrical communication is that the receiver considers the message to be unreal, or more precisely, untrue. Now if that is self-evident, or can be self-evident in the case of a written or re-told story, where the story is expressly denoted as being imaginary, in theatre the situation is different. What appears on the stage is a concrete reality – objects and people whose concrete existence is never questioned. Although they indisputably exist (they are the very stuff of reality), they are at the same time denied, marked with a minus sign. A chair on the stage is not a chair in the real world. Spectators cannot go and sit on it, or move it somewhere else; for them it is forbidden, it does not exist. Everything that happens on stage (however little that stage might be delimited and closed off) is marked with unreality. The modern revolution in theatrical space[19] (removing or adapting the proscenium stage, theatre in the round, bare theatre, trestle stage, booth stage, street theatre) attempts to blend the audience with the action on stage, yet none of this breaks down the fundamental distinction between spectators and actors. An actor could sit on a spectator's knee, and the two would be no less apart than if separated by an invisible ramp or blown apart by a 100,000-volt current. Even if a real event were to be staged (as in political theatre, or activist theatre), that reality, once theatricalized, would take on the dream-like status of unreality.

Octave Mannoni, in *Clefs pour l'imaginaire* (Mannoni 1969), forcefully analyses this process of denial. For Freud, dreamers know that they are dreaming even when they do not believe it or refuse to believe it. Likewise theatre has the status of dream: an imaginary construction whose spectators know that it is radically removed from the sphere of their daily existence. It is as if there were a dual zone for spectators, a two-part space. (We will encounter this problem again when discussing space and theatre.) In one zone they belong to everyday life and obey the regular laws of existence, the logic according to which they live in society; the other zone is the locus of a different social practice, a place where the laws and codes that normally govern their behaviour, while remaining in force, no longer govern them as individuals living out their particular socio-economic lives. They are no longer in the game (or victims of the game?). They can allow themselves to observe the laws that govern them in all of their constricting reality. This justifies the continuing presence of mimesis in theatre. There is imitation of people and their actions, while the laws that govern them appear, in that imaginary world, to be suspended. This is catharsis: just as dreams can in a way fulfill the desires of the dreamer by constructing a fantasy, so the creation of a concrete reality that is nonetheless denied insertion into reality, can liberate the spectator. The spectator sees his or her fears and desires realized or exorcised without becoming their victim, yet not without his or her participation. This function of denial is as present in ceremonial theatre, linked to festival rituals, as it is in the so-called theatre of illusion. Is there a contradiction between such a view of catharsis and Brecht's thesis? We do not believe so: the function of denial affects all forms of theatre.

3.4.2. Theatrical Illusion

We can go further: there is no theatrical illusion. The theatre of illusion is a perverse fulfilment of denial. It pushes the resemblance to the socio-economic reality of the spectator so far that eventually the whole of that universe teeters into denial. The illusion is turned back upon reality itself; more precisely, the spectator, faced with a reality that attempts a perfect, most verisimilar mimesis of that world, is forced into passivity. The spectacle says to him or her: 'This world, so minutely reproduced here, misleadingly resembles the world in which you live (or in which others luckier than you live). Just as you cannot join the magic circle of the world on that stage, you cannot intervene within the real universe you inhabit.' In a way that we might not have expected, Freudian denial has brought us to a rediscovery of Brecht's criticism of the process of identification.[20]

Now we can understand the absurd, meaningful story of the cowboy who, while attending his first theatrical performance, draws his gun and aims at the villain on stage. It's not that he doesn't know that what he sees on stage is not true (as Mannoni quite rightly notes). When you intensify the illusion and at the same time make it ever more impossible for people to do anything, revolt by a spectator who is uninitiated in the codes and is bowled over by this explosive contradiction can take this pathetic form: the cowboy, accustomed to taking immediate action, does not know that he is not allowed to intervene.

Here we come to the Brechtian paradox: it is at the point of the greatest identification of spectator with spectacle that the distance between spectator and spectacle is also the greatest; this in turn indirectly brings about the greatest 'distance' between the spectator and his or her own life and actions in the real world. This is where theatre, so to speak, disarms people even as they face their respective destinies. We say distance: there is no need to say that we do not mean Brechtian *Verfremdung* (distantiation), a dialectical process involved in all steps.

There is much to be said, more than we can fully treat here, on the meaning of mimesis as a 'copy' of reality. The entire analysis above expressly adopts the perspective that we are dealing with an illusion – the illusion, for instance, that naturalistic theatre copies reality, when in fact nothing could be further from the truth. Instead it puts on stage a certain picture of socioeconomic conditions and relationships between people, a picture that is constructed in conformity with the way a given social stratum sees itself. There is therefore no reaction on the part of the spectator. Of course denial comes into play; spectators know perfectly well that they are not seeing a true picture of the world. Instead, the illusion in its perfection offers them the model for a certain attitude towards the world. It is not objective relationships that are mimed, but rather a certain type of representation of those relationships and the attitude that flows from it.

3.4.3. Denial: Consequences

The phenomenon of denial is not without immediate ideological consequences. First, naturalistic theatre (based on the search for illusion) and the proscenium stage (with its premised fourth, transparent wall that isolates a bit of transposed reality) have their consequences. The spectator, having become a powerless voyeur, repeats in the theatre the role she or he plays or will play in real life; she or he contemplates without taking action, is implicated but not involved. Brecht is right when he says that this kind of drama is conservative and paternalistic. The spectator is like a child being rocked by an adult – nothing in the world will be changed because of her or his initiative; disorder must be attenuated. Melodrama and bourgeois drama express a dream of passional liberation that takes place only in the imaginary. So it is that thousands (millions if we include cinema) have seen and understood *La dame aux camélias*. How amazing! Passion will in no way change the world order. Spectators can identify with Marguerite or with Armand Duval with impunity. What they watch will never be changed by their actions.

Conversely, a historical-realistic theatrical mounting of a revolutionary event (such as Brecht's *Days of the Commune*) and any theatrical production that purports to recount historical events also runs the risk of sinking into unreality. How can denial be prevented from coming into play when all that is figured on stage is relegated to illusion? Too often, street theatre becomes non-realistic because it has not been understood that, come what may, the footlights are still there. The actor, although playing on the tarmac, brings them along, thus isolating a little corner of the street and transforming it into a magic circle where yesterday's arrest or strike becomes unreal. Theatrical realism cannot be created through textual and stage phenomena. It must follow another path. This is the reason for the many unfortunate misrepresentations we see. In what is now called *theatre du quotidien* (kitchen-sink drama) the danger is obvious: the daily reality of the poor and oppressed is made to seem unreal. It is rendered exotic, like the life of 'savages.' The theatre of the everyday can accomplish its goal only if its activity is one of language. It is everyday language that appears to be made unreal: a divorce is effected between language and the limiting forces of reality. What spectators see and hear is their own language, made unreal by denial.

3.4.4. Denial: Theatricalization

Although naturalistic realism is by nature unreal and produces passivity and although revolutionary naturalism has made no progress, because the same causes produce the same effects, and the illusory observation of reality rivets spectators to their seats, it is theoretically and practically possible to go beyond this stage of illusion. Artaud chose a regressive path – the term is in no way pejorative, we suspect, but rather simply historical – a path involving an infra-theatrical return to ceremony, where reality is not required to figure at all and where a deliberately fantastic ritual is constructed (Artaud 1958). Brecht, who is less revolutionary than he appears in this respect, rediscovered the majestic path of theatricalization. In other words, Brecht constructed a series of signs destined to remind spectators that they indeed are in the theatre. Ariane Mnouchkine's Théâtre du soleil or the Bread and Puppet Theatre have wonderfully understood this, as demonstrated in their use of all kinds of theatricalization: commedia dell'arte, circus, puppets.

As in Shakespeare, and indeed in Greek theatre there is within the confines of the stage a privileged zone in which theatre speaks of itself (trestle stages, songs, choruses, speeches addressed to the audience). According to Freud we know that when you dream that you are dreaming, the dream within another dream speaks the truth. Through a twofold denial, the dream of a dream produces truth. Likewise theatre-within-the-theatre does not convey reality but rather what is true, transforming the sign of illusion and identifying as illusion all that is mounted on stage.

Thus, although the message received by the spectator 'normally' (that is in theatre where illusion prevails) takes the form $m = -x$, the message received when theatricalization has taken place can be understood by placing certain signs in parentheses:

$$m = -x \ (-y) = x + y$$

This produces a complex situation for message-reception, one in which spectators are required to recognize the twofold status of the messages they receive and consign to denial all that belongs to the stage, except for the zone in which the reversal produced by theatricalization takes place. The actors' scene in *Hamlet* (like those in Corneille's *Illusion comique* or Hugo's *Marion De Lorme*) is a good example of unmasking through theatricality, of bringing the true to the fore. More generally, in Shakespeare and in Brecht, the role of songs, of clowns, of posters, already creates a play within a play. Those elements designate theatre as theatre. Here is an unexpected example: *The Caucasian Chalk Circle*, in which the staging attempted by the judge Azdak within the privileged space of the chalk circle is a Solomonic judgment that reveals the truth; this twofold truth solves the play's enigma (who is Michel's real mother?), but it also refers to the illusory, parabolic aspect of the entire representation – an aspect that has already been identified by the fact that the whole story is a staging of an exemplary tale.

A note: the mechanism of this sign reversal is very complex. In large measure it is a function of the fact that the actors on the stage are at the same time spectators, spectators who observe what is happening in the space where theatricalization is taking place and send back to the audience, after its inversion, the message they receive. This is why simple theatralization does not always presuppose inversion of message. Although the clownlike appearance of Beckett's characters indicates theatricalization, it only partially reverses illusion; one could analyse the particular effect of Beckett's theatricality in terms of a back-and-forth interplay between illusion and its inversion. For a true reversal of the sign there must be two stage zones conveying inverse meaning. In any event, even with a two-part disposition of space, one group of dramatic messages will come from the non-theatricalized zone therefore will be subject to denial. The playwright's job, and that of the director, is to create the phenomenon in which denial and theatricalization function together.

3.4.5. Theatricalization-Text

It seems that everything involved in denial-theatricalization belongs not to the text, but rather to performance. This belief is mistaken, however, because denial is already embedded within the text:

1/ Denial is present in the didascalia, which can be seen as textual figures of denial-theatricalization. The locus is indicated as a theatre-locus, not a real place, and the costumes indicate disguise, with masks. There is theatricalization of the actor's person.

2/ Denial is present negatively through the existence of gaps in the text, spaces necessary to performance that make it rather difficult to simply read a theatrical text. In particular, everything involved with the simultaneous presence of two areas of stage action runs the risk of being manifested only through the use of asides and by spaces or silences in the dialogue.

3/ Denial is present in the absurd and in textual contradictions. The presence of opposite categories in a single locus, a character's non-coherence with himself-herself – what classical (and pedagogical and academic) criticism calls lack of verisimilitude – are textual indices of the theatrical function of denial. As with dreams, theatrical fantasy allows for and indeed thrives on non-contradiction and the impossible, making them not only signifying but indeed operative. Where we note a lack of verisimilitude is the very locus for theatrical specificity. At the performance level, what corresponds to this is the mobility of signs:[21] an object shifts from one function into another, a ladder becomes a bridge, a treasure chest becomes a coffin, a ball becomes a bird, an actor slips from one role into another; any textual or stage-represented attack upon the prevailing logic of common sense is theatre.[22] We have long known that theatre makes it possible to say things that do not conform to the cultural code or to social logic. What is unthinkable logically and morally, what is socially scandalous, topics and themes that can be handled only in accordance with very strict procedures – in theatre, all of these are in a state of liberty, they are in contradictory juxtaposition. That is why theatre can constitute a locus for unresolved contradictions.

3.5. Trance and Knowledge

It is thus clear that the way theatre functions cannot be reduced simply to communication, even when envisaged not only in terms of its referenial function (the only function, it would seem, that Mounin considers) but also in terms of the totality of its functions, including the poetic function. To reduce reception of the theatrical message to the hearing or even the deciphering of signs would be, as we have seen, a sterile enterprise. But theatrical communication is not a passive process; if there is no impediment, it may convey a social practice. Maybe it is not quite right to set message in opposition to stimulus here. Advertising and the media as a whole are not only referential messages (concerning the quality of a product or the attraction of a movie) bu also stimuli designed to move people to buy and consume, which are social practices. In this sense theatre is not distinct from the media. According to Sapir, all languages have this same twofold function for signs; all linguistic activity presupposes an extremely complex interplay between two separate systems which he designates as referential and expressive.

But theatre, more than any other activity, requires an effort, a complex involvement, both voluntary and involuntary, in the process. This is not the place to examine the psychological and psychosociological role of the spectator. We should remember, however, that two competing elements are at play in the spectator's participation: on the one hand, reflection; on the other, contagious passion, trance, dance, and all those phenomena which come to the spectator from the actor's physical movements and which cause the spectator to experience physical and psychological emotions – all those things which cause the spectator of the theatrical ceremony to be induced by signs (or signals) to experience emotions, which are not the represented emotions but which are linked to them according to certain specific relations.[23] In this sense we note once again that theatrical signs are at the same time both icons and indices. What Brecht calls the *pleasure* of the theatre has a lot to do with the fact of a visible and tangible construction of a fantasy that you can live vicariously rather than in reality, which might be dangerous. There is, however, another element that is linked to the above: the spectator will reflect upon events in a such way that those events might cast light on concrete problems pertaining to his or her real life. Here we see identification and distanciation symbiotically playing out their respective roles. Thus, to take an example from history: in Turkish villages where malaria was rampant, the painter Abidine mounted a street play in which peasants successfully obtain restitution from a merchant who has been cheating them in the sale of quinine. Abidine tells us that subsequently, having participated in this theatrical victory in fantasy, his peasant spectators woke up and rushed off to find their own pharmaceutical dispensers. Naturally further performances were forbidden.[24]

Theatre does more than just awaken spectators' fantasies. It can also sometimes awaken their consciences, and perhaps the two go together. As Brecht says, this is brought about through the association of pleasure and reflection.

II. The Actantial Model in Theatre

1. The Larger Structures

Where might we begin? That is the key question asked by Barthes (Barthes 1970), the question which must precede all semiological research. Of course, it is theoretically possible to begin the study of the theatrical text with discourse analysis. However, given the length of a theatrical text, we would have to use a sampling from that text, and the use of a sampling would mean that any research into character-specific discourse would be an illusion. Further, it seems that the reading of a theatrical text by a reader and by a spectator is accomplished only at the level of the total spectacle, the total ceremony, or failing that, the script. Intellectual reconstruction and psychological catharsis take place only if the *fabula* has been understood as a totality.

It is therefore theoretically possible to start with the fabula; but the fabula, understood in the Brechtian sense of a reduction to zero of the diachronic aspect of the story's events, is, in the domain of theatre, precisely not theatre. To construct a fabula is to transform drama into a non-dramatic story and consign the conflict to history. That is a perfectly legitimate enterprise – one that Brechtian directors and playwrights consider indispensable – but it is a process of abstraction, a process that constructs abstract stories, rather than a search for structure. This may be an important stage, but it is a secondary enterprise. It is easy to demonstrate that fabula is an abstraction rather than a structure by reference to the fact that it is possible to give extremely different formulations of the fabula of a given dramatic text, particularly as concerns the order of events. Pure diachrony would make it impossible to formulate the fabula of a highly conflictual text. How might we construct the fabula for *Andro-*

maque? With what thread of the story should we begin? It seems that the operation of constructing the fabula of a given dramatic text is a secondary operation in relation to the operation whereby textual macrostructures are identified.

1.1. Macrostructures

We will base our study on the working hypothesis of text grammar (Ihwe, Dressler, Petöfi, Van Dijk), a hypothesis that is closely linked to the attempt by semantic researchers to construct a narrative grammar, from Propp (1968) to Souriau (1950) with A.J. Greimas at the head of the group. This basic hypothesis is formulated very clearly by Van Dijk:

> The central hypothesis of our textual grammar is the presence of a *macrostructure.* This hypothesis implies that there are also narrative macrostructures. The surface constraint of the presence of human actants and of actions can be determined only by deep textual structures: the story does not have the occasional presence (surface style) of 'characters,' but rather the permanent dominance of human actants (Van Dijk 1973, 204).

This means simply that beneath the infinite diversity of stories (dramatic and otherwise) we can discover a small number of relations between terms that are much more general than character, terms that we will call *actants* and that we will define more precisely later.

All of this presupposes certain conditions:

1/ that 'textual coherence be defined at a macrostructural level as well' (ibid., 189);
2/ (a corollary) that we can 'establish a homology between these deep structures of the text and those of the sentence' (ibid., 190) and therefore that the textual totality corresponds to a single long sentence (which means that from the text we can construct a sentence whose syntactic relations will mirror the structures of that text).

According to Van Dijk's hypothesis, macrostructures are in fact the deep structures of the text, rather than the surface structures. It would be necessary to make the theoretical choice between this hypothesis and the hypothesis that sees actantial structures simply as a way of reading and the actant only as a working concept. Here we can be tripped up by the philosophical debate inevitably set off when the very concept of structure is raised.[1] In our opinion, it is not even necessary to consider that the deep structures of a dramatic story can really be discovered. Probably it is sufficient that determination of the actantial structure allows us to dispense with confusing analyses (such as the classic psychological analysis of characters) as well as dubious analyses (such as the equally classic search for the dramaturgy of the theatrical text). This last method can legitimately be applied only to classical texts that were conceived within quite narrow constraints; it does not allow us to establish a relation between classical texts and other less classical texts.[2]

We should note that, by the very virtue of its link to semantics rather than to linguistics, actantial analysis, while extremely difficult to formalize, escapes the pitfall of formalism.

1.2. Surface/Deep

A twofold problem that Van Dijk does not avoid and which we found particularly difficult in our analysis of Hugo's theatre is the relation between 'surface' textual determinations and 'deep' structures.[3] How might we account for the twofold process, inductive and deductive, that proceeds from the surface to the deep structure and inversely from deep to surface? 'If this hypothesis is correct,' says Van Dijk, 'we must also be able to verify it, to find the (transformational) rules that link macrostructures with the semantic representations found at the textual surface' (Van Dijk 1973, 190). Van Dijk admits defeat. We did not get much further: this field of research is just beginning. We have only a few basic procedures that allow us to demonstrate certain details.

1.3. Structure and History

It goes without saying that, from the moment we begin to deal with structures that go beyond the level of the sentence (to a trans-phrase level), we are also beyond classical linguistics. We have gone beyond purely phonological-syntactic formalization to reach the level of content (form and substance of content) – that is, we are in the domain of semantics.

Even beyond semantics, the strict confines of the analysis of macrostructures is linked to other disciplines and can be tripped up, as we shall see, by the problem of ideology. Van Dijk himself says that 'a theory of narrative structures is part of a theory of man's symbolic practices and therefore is the object of anthropology as well as of semiotics, linguistics and poetics' (Van Dijk 1973, 191). This is not without its problems:

against this potential fragmentation of our efforts, there is the need for a totalized historico-ideological reading.

Maybe it is a Utopian dream for us to attempt an analysis of these textual macrostructures while at the same time trying to avoid severing them from the conditions under which they were produced, that is from their relation with history. But the potential gain renders the attempt valid. However simple and naive our research may appear, it may allow us to find, for theatre, that locus at which structure and history are articulated.

1.4. The Theatrical Story

Narrative analyses such as those that flow from the work of Propp and Bremond have to do with linear, relatively simple stories. Even most of Greimas's analyses are applied to non-dramatic stories. Certain modifications have to be made to the actantial model (Greimas) and the theory of narrative functions (Propp, Bremond) if we are to adapt them to theatrical writing. Probably it will also be necessary to ask a certain number of questions of ourselves and of the text: the tabular[4] nature of the theatrical text (a three-dimensional text) requires us to assume concurrence and conflict between several actantial models (at least two). Likewise the conflictual nature of dramatic writing makes it difficult, except in special cases, to uncover a fixed succession of narrative functions.[5] Here we may be able to apply what is specific to theatrical writing. Our attempt will be to show how theatricality is present even at the level of the textual macrostructures of theatre: the plurality of actantial models and the combination and transformation of those models are the principal characteristics that make the ultimate plural and spatialized signifying systems of theatrical text possible. Further – and we will continue to repeat this – theatricality in a theatrical text is always virtual and relative; the only concrete theatricality is that of performance. As a corollary, there is no impediment to making theatre out of anything because that same plurality of actantial models can be found in the texts of novels or even poetry.

2. Animate Elements: From Actant to Character

The first operation in any semiological analysis consists of determining what units are involved. We find that in the area of theatre, these units are particularly hard to grasp and indeed they may not be identical, depending on whether we consider the text or the performance. We know that if there is one element that is characteristic of theatrical activity, it is the presence of an actor:

But can the theatre exist without actors? I know of no example of this. One could mention the puppet-show. Even here, however, an actor is to be found behind the scenes, although of another kind (J. Grotowski, *Towards a Poor Theatre* (1969, 32).

The human body and the human voice are irreplaceable elements. Without them, we have only magic lantern, cartoons cinema, not theatre. It is therefore normal and indeed obvious that the basic unit for all theatrical activity is the actor – or, at the textual level, the script that contains the actor's particular role. This suggests a naive answer: the basic unit for the theatrical text is the character.

But we see that:

1/ It is impossible, for thousands of reasons, to identify a character or an actor: one actor can play the roles of several characters in a given play; conversely, the fragmentation of the character in contemporary theatre suggests the possibility that one character may be played by several actors, successively or simultaneously. We see this with Michel Tournier's *Vendredi* (staged by Vitez in 1974) in which the character of Robinson is multiplied on stage. Modern stagings play with the identity of the character by multiplying it or by melding several characters into one.

2/ As we shall see, the concept of character comes to us bearing a weighty and puzzling past – a further reason not to assign to it the overwhelming task of being the basic unit of theatre.

Greimas (1987, 106–20), following Souriau, provides some solutions by setting out a series of hierarchical articulated units: *actant, actor, role, character*. This allows him to deal with the same units at both the writing level and the performance level.[6] We will revisit these same units in an attempt to see how they function within a theatrical text and to what extent they govern the text-performance relation. In this sense, the deep structure of a text is the same as the deep structure of the performance, and we understand how a given deep structure can demonstrate, for various themes, completely different deployments of surface structures. This would explain how a fundamental skeletal similarity can produce different meanings and surface structures that convey similar semantic content although they differ in apperance. This research will undoubtedly bear fruit for the final purpose of our work, not so much as an attempt to bring the textual structures of theatre to light as to show how text and performance are articulated together as a concrete function.

On this point, actantial analysis, far from being rigid and fixed, appears to be, if one dialectalises a bit, a useful tool with which to read theatre. The main thing is to see in theatre not a pre-established form, a fixed structure, a Procrustean bed upon which all texts should be laid, but rather an infinitely diversified way of functioning. Strictly speaking, the actantial model is not a form; it is a syntax and is thus capable of generating an infinite number of textual possibilities. What we might try, the way having been paved by Greimas and François Rastier, is a syntax specific to theatrical narrative. In this we must not forget that each of the concrete forms produced by the model is: (a) inscribed in a theatrical story, and (b) a conveyor of meaning, and therefore in direct relation with the conflicts involved in that instance.

3. The Actantial Model

3.1. Actants

Ever since Greimas's *Structural Semantics* (Greimas 1983) and even before that, Souriau's *Deux cent mille situations dramatiques* (Souriau 1950), we have known how to construct a basic model using the units that Greimas calls actants. These units must not be confused with characters because:

a/ An actant can be an abstraction (the City, Eros, God, Liberty), a collective character (the ancient chorus, the soldiers of an army), or even a gathering of several characters (this group of characters can be, as we shall see, the opponent for a subject and his or her action).[7]

b/ A character can simultaneously or successively assume different actantial functions (see the analysis of *Le Cid* below).

c/ An actant can be absent from the stage, and its textual presence can be limited to its presence in the discourse of other subjects of enunciation (speakers), while the actant itself is never a subject of enunciation. Such is the case with Astyanax or Hector in *Andromaque*.

'[T]he actantial model,' writes Greimas, 'is, in the first place, the extrapolation of the syntactic structure' (ibid., 213). An actant is thus identified with an element (lexicalized or not) which assumes a syntactic function in the basic sentence for the story: we have the *subject* and the *object*, the *receiver,* the *helper,* and the *opponent,* all of whose syntactic functions are obvious. The *sender,* whose grammatical role is less evident belongs, so to speak, to another, earlier sentence (see below), or, according to the terminology of traditional grammar, to a 'complement of cause.'

Here is Greimas's actantial model of six functions:

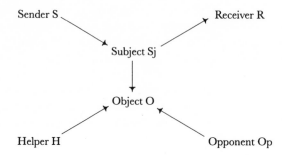

Note that at this stage Greimas has already done away (legitimately it would seem) with the seventh function of Souriau's model, the function of *arbiter;* no syntactic function can be assigned to the arbiter and a closer analysis always demonstrates that it is really part of other actantial functions – sender, subject, or helper.[8] Thus the king in *Le Cid,* whose role seems to be an arbitrating one, is successively the *sender* (= City, Society), the *opponent,* and the *helper* vis-à-vis the actions of the subject Rodrigue.

If we develop the sentence that is implicit in the schema, we find a force field (or a being we can designate as *S*); set in motion by the actions of *S,* the subject *Sj* seeks an object *O* that will serve the interests of a being (concrete or abstract) we designate as *R*; in this work, the subject has allies (*H*) and opponents (*Op*). Every story can be reduced to this basic schema, as Greimas demonstrates using the very clear example of *The Quest of the Holy Grail:*

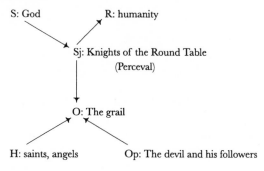

We see the abstract and potentially collective nature of actants quite clearly. Any novel that tells a love story, any love quest can be reduced to a similar schema, this time with individual actants, that might look like this:

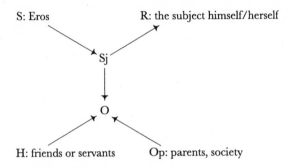

Here subject and receiver are melded into one. The subject wants the object of the quest for himself or herself, and instead of a receiver there is an individual force field (affective, sexual) that is in a way, melded together with the subject.

We should note that some positions on the schema can be unfilled in certain cases. Thus an unfilled *sender* position indicates the absence of a metaphysical force field or the *City*: we have a drama in which the individual character is especially marked. The function of *helper* may also be absent, indicating the solitude of the subject. We can also consider instances, as we shall see, in which a given function on the schema, that of *object*, for example, is occupied by several elements at the same time.

This raises a question as to the exact placement of helper and opponent with respect to subject and object. The arrows that go from helper and opponent could join up with the subject – that is Greimas's solution. In principle, I prefer to have them join up with the object, because all conflict involved is centred on the object. However, to be absolutely precise, we must distinguish the cases in which the helper helps the subject (friend or companion in the quest, Gauvain to Lancelot in the *Quest of the Holy Grail*) from the cases in which the helper helps the *object* (the servant woman to Juliet in *Romeo and Juliet*). Likewise we can distinguish cases in which the opponent is a radical opponent to the subject (for example, in the legend of Hercules, Juno opposes him in all his enterprises) from those in which opposition is focussed on the particular object of the quest alone (for example, in *Britannicus*, the hero opposes not the Emperor Nero but rather Nero's love for Junie).

Thus, from the outset, many questions suggest themselves when we set up the actantial schema; the answers to those questions are also manifold. We shall soon see how each element of the schema raises problems that can be resolved by several solutions.

At this point in our work we shall not distinguish between various types of dramatic and non-dramatic stories; the actantial model applies equally to all. However, it is our preference to take our examples from theatrical texts, while at the same time making it clear that we will have to refine models which at this stage are extremely general.

3.2. The Helper-Opponent Pair

Actants are distributed according to positional couples (subject/object, sender/receiver); the arrows of the oppositional couple (helper/opponent) can go in both directions, so that conflict often appears to be a collision, a combat between those two actants. There again we can distinguish between the cases in which the helper's aid touches directly upon the subject's actions and the cases in which the helper's effect is to make the object accessible. In Marivaux's *Les fausses confidences*, Dubois's actions are of direct importance vis-à-vis the object Araminte, whereas in a tragedy the confidant acts *upon the subject*, for example, comforting or counselling him.

The functioning of the helper-opponent couple is far from simple. As is the case for all actants, particularly with a theatrical text, theirs is a mobile function. At certain stages of the process the helper can suddenly become an opponent or, through the fragmentation of his or her function, be simultaneously helper and opponent. Thus, in *Britannicus* both Nero's counsellors are helper-opponents, conforming to a rule we shall have to make clear later.

What is remarkable, and what casts light on the relation of fable to actantial model, is the fact that we rarely deal with the conversion of an opponent who becomes a helper through some psychological process, a change in the motives of the character-actant. The change in function is a result of the complexity inherent in the action itself, inherent, that is, to the fundamentally important subject-object couple. Thus King Lear's two older daughters initially play the role of helper to their father in the matter of dividing up his kingdom, only to reveal themselves later as opponents. The change in their actantial role is not a function of a change in what they want but rather a result of the complexity of Lear's situation. This is true even in cases where we might think there has been a psychological change in a given character; for example, Lady Macbeth appears to be a helper to her husband in the matter of Duncan's murder, but in the end, when the king's tyranny goes beyond her field of action, she is unable to help him further. Actants that are both helpers and opponents (a much more common phenomenon than one might think), despite their very subtle relation with the totality of the dramatic action, generally have determining roles that are immediately perceptible to the spectator. In other kinds of action, the very identification of the helper-opponent functions represents the main puzzle for the spectator. This can be created through a deliberate ambiguity or illusion of the performance signs. Thus in Beckett's *Endgame* there is uncertainty as to the role of Clov in relation to Hamm. Finally there are cases in which the helper-opponent ambiguity marks not only a given character, but also his or her relation with the subject, as seen in the cases of Sganarelle in *Dom Juan* or Mephistopheles in *Faust*.

3.3. The Sender-Receiver Pair

This is probably the most ambiguous pair. The elements identifying it are the most difficult to grasp because they are rarely clearly lexicalized units such as characters or even collective characters. Usually what we see determining the actions of the subject are 'motivations.' Thus in Greek tragedy the City is almost always in the position of sender, even if at the same time it occupies the position of opponent, and even if it eventually becomes the receiver. Take the clear example of *Oedipus Rex*:

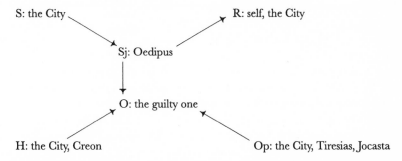

S: the City

R: self, the City

Sj: Oedipus

O: the guilty one

H: the City, Creon

Op: the City, Tiresias, Jocasta

It is the City that expressly assigns Oedipus the task of saving Thebes from the plague by finding Laius's murderer. But, contrary to Greimas's claim that the same element *X* is never found in both positions *S* and *R*, it is to itself that the City offers an expiating ritual when it requires Oedipus to pursue and convict a murderer who is none other than himself. In this sense, the City shifts from one actant to another, executing a circular movement by which it occupies successively the positions of sender, helper, opponent, receiver, progressively encircling the solitary man, the *subject* who had identified himself with it but whom it renounces and expels. The subject Oedipus can continue to identify with the City only if he adopts the City's campaign against him. Hence the strange events in which he blinds and exiles himself. It becomes obvious then that the City itself gives the dramatic performance of Oedipus's fate in *Oedipus Rex*.[9]

Here we see that the role of *sender* carries with it the ideological significance of the dramatic text. This holds true even in the case in which the occupant of the *sender* position is a force field that is related to the personal fate of the subject: Eros, for example.

Eros should not be considered as a simple equivalent of sexual desire or even of sublimated love, the Christian *agapè*. Eros is always related to the eminently 'collective' function of reproduction within society. Thus in John Ford's Elizabethan play *'Tis Pity She's a Whore*, society (the sender) wants Annabella and Giovanni to produce children, but at the same time, society, through the conditions it imposes on reproduction, is an impediment to it. The incest, a refusal to reproduce within society, results from a conflict at the level of that very society-sender. This individual revolt, incest, appears therefore not as some kind of bizarre desire, but rather as a social catastrophe. Likewise *Le Cid* will be completely misunderstood if we do not see that the Eros-sender that drives Rodrigue and Chimène together is also the Eros of reproduction within society, governed by all the attendant laws of feudal society.

There are consequences to all of the above:

a/ *The twofold sender*: the fact that the *sender* is at the same time an abstract element (values, ideals, ideological concepts) and a living element (character) results in the two being identified with each other. Thus in *Le Cid*, instead of a sender *S*, we have both feudalism (as a value system) and Don Diègue, the father. We do not have to elaborate on the consequences of this state of affairs, nor on the questions that arise when the king joins his predecessors in the sender position. Can the king be counted upon to maintain and preserve feudal values? Will the conflict taking place within the sender position result in the death of those values? In the classic example of the *Quest of the Holy Grail*, the failure of the quest represents the failure and death of King Arthur because both God and King Arthur occupy the sender position. As a result, the entire set of values is brutally cast into doubt and the function of a feudal king, *primus inter pares*, is dealt a fatal blow:[10] God has 'divorced' King Arthur.

b/ Sometimes the *sender* position is unoccupied or problematic. We could be spared a lot of useless speculation if we would just admit that the question asked of the spectator by Molière's *Dom Juan* is in fact the sender's question: *what makes Dom Juan tick?*

c/ In certain instances of the actantial schema we see that the City is located in two opposing positions – not successively as in *Oedipus Rex*, but simultaneously, as in *Antigone*:

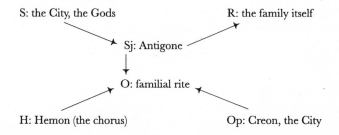

S: the City, the Gods   R: the family itself

Sj: Antigone

O: familial rite

H: Hemon (the chorus)   Op: Creon, the City

In this complex situation, the city figures twice, in two radically opposed positions – a sign of a crisis in the city, an internal division over values (that is in fact a result of a conflict of social dispositions, a conflict that the historian must keep in mind).[11] Here Sophoclean thought appears to be centred on the relation between city and tyrant, between laws and centralizing power. Thus we see how decisive the determination of the sender-actant is for the identification of the ideological conflict that underlies the fable.

d/ There is a corollary to the above: the sender-opponent couple is substituted for or combined with the sender-receiver couple. Sometimes the dramatic conflict takes place, so to speak, over the subject's head. In the Faust legend, as in Calderón's *Autos sacramentales*, the conflict is between the divine sender and the diabolical adversary.[12]

e/ As for the *receiver R* and its identification (or not) with the subject,[13] the presence, in the *receiver* position, of a hypostasis of the collectivity or group allows for a decision as to whether or not there is an individualistic meaning to the drama. Thus in Vichnevsky's *The Optimistic Tragedy*, the receiver of the drama is indisputably the fledgling Soviet Republic, in whose service the two opposing *subjects* (the sailors and the Commissar) toil. On the other hand, an absence of receiver connotes a void, an ideological despair (see Beckett), and the action unfolds without benefit for anyone.

f/ By virtue of the very way theatre functions, the *receiver* is also the element with which the spectator identifies. Whatever else, spectators know themselves to be the receiver of the theatrical message. Under certain conditions they might think that the action unfolds for them. A rough play on words, confusing the two meanings of the word 'destinatary' might well correspond to one of the psychological functions of the spectator. Insofar as the Brechtian spectator or the spectator of Greek tragedy is involved politically in the debate, she or he can identify with the actantial receiver (destinary), just as a Soviet citizen might well have identified with the receiver in *The Optimistic Tragedy.* The problem of identification is strangely complex.

3.4. Subject-Object

3.4.1. Subject and Hero
The fundamental unit in all dramatic stories is the two-part unit that links the subject and the object of his or her desire or wishes; the link is represented by an arrow that shows the direction the quest will take. Our first and greatest problem is to determine textually who the subject is, or at least who the subject of the main action is. Generally, in a narrative text (short story, novella, novel), there is frequently no question that the subject and the hero – the person who meets adventure, pursues a quest, undertakes a task – are one and the same. Of course it is not always that clear: if we say that Ulysses is the hero (and the subject) of the *Odyssey*, can we also say that Achilles is the hero-subject of the *Iliad*? At the very least this question can be asked. If, for a given dramatic text, we count the number of appearances of a character, the number of times he or she speaks, and even the total number of lines he or she speaks – even if the three numbers taken in balance propose an incontestable answer – we will still have done no more than to identify the main character, the hero of the play, but not necessarily the subject. An analysis of Corneille's *Suréna* might identify the eponymous character as the hero but not necessarily as the subject. Despite the importance of the role (and of the *discourse*) of Phèdre, although she is most certainly the heroine of the play that bears her name, it is not clear that she is its subject. The subject can be identified only in relation to a story's action and in correlation with the object. Strictly speaking, there can be no autonomous subject of a text, only a *subject-object* axis. We can say that the subject of a literary text is

the person or thing whose desire is the focal point of the action, the focus of the actantial model. The subject is the person or thing that can be seen as the subject of the actantial sentence, the person or thing whose success in overcoming obstacles moves the text along. Thus, to take an example from novels, it is Julien Sorel's or Fabrice del Dongo's successful realization of desire that makes them not only the heros, but also the *subjects* of *Le rouge et le noir* or *La chartreuse de Parme*. The heroic figure of Rodrigue makes him not only the hero, but indeed the subject of the action of *Le Cid*.

3.4.2. Consequences

a/ As we have seen, it is not just the presence of the subject, but the presence of the two-part subject-object unit that makes up the axis for a story. An actant is not a substance or a being, it is an element in a relation. A *welthistorisch* character (of this historical world), a grandiose character, as Lukàcs said, is not necessarily, or not at all the subject, if he or she is not set in relation to an object (real or ideal, but textually present).

b/ We cannot consider as subject someone who desires something she or he already has or someone who seeks merely not to lose what she or he has. The will simply to retain cannot readily set action into motion in the absence of the dynamic and conquering forces of desire. The conservative hero can be an opponent or even a sender, but not a subject. Indeed that is the status – and the drama – of Thésée in *Phèdre*.

c/ The subject can be collective – a group that desires its own salvation or liberty (these being threatened or already lost) or the acquisition of goods or property – but it cannot be an abstraction. The sender, the receiver, even the helper or the opponent can be abstractions, but the subject is always animate and presented as alive and active (animate vs. inanimate, human vs. non-human).[14]

d/ The object of the subject's quest can very well be *individual* (an amorous conquest, for example), but what is at stake in this quest always goes beyond the simple individual because of the links that are established between the subject-object unit (one that is never isolated) and the other actants. Romeo might well want Juliet, but the arrow of his desire implicates the enemy of his clan – a much greater stake.

e/ Whether the object of the quest is abstract or animate, it will in a way be represented metonymically on the stage. For example, in *Lorenzaccio*, Duke Alexandre is in a metonymic relation with the tyranny that is crushing Florence.

Note: There is a theoretical, more general, consequence: the whole actantial system functions as a rhetorical game (there being, of course, no pejorative connotation to either of these words); it functions as a combination of several paradigmatic positions. It is as if each *actant* were the locus of a paradigm. From this flows the potential to play out a whole set of possible substitutions. At the level of performance, a whole series of paradigmatic presences (characters and objects – see chapter IV, section 8 'The Theatrical Object') can be substituted for various actants. Thus in Hugo's *Lucrèce Borgia*, characters (la Negroni, for example) or objects (coats of arms) are part of the *Borgia-subject's* paradigm (Lucrèce). This is why the staging of a play can demonstrate the actantial model.

3.5. Sender and Subject: Autonomy of the Subject?

What is interesting about actantial analysis is the fact that we can avoid the danger of psychologizing the actants and their relations (the danger, that is, of hypostasizing characters into people). Above all we must see in the actantial system an integrated totality where all components are interdependent, and can therefore be isolated.

If we return to the basic proposition of the actantial model, we can perhaps formulate it more exactly and more precisely: *S wants that (Sj desire O) which will serve R.*

The proposition *Sj desire O* is embedded within the proposition *S wants that ... which will serve R.* Now this embedding of the proposition *Sj desire (or seek) O* has always been missing from classical theatrical analysis, which has always held that *Sj*'s desire is autonomous, with no need of a sender or even a receiver beyond itself. The proposition *Sj desire, seek O* is, in fact, a non-autonomous proposition that acquires meaning only through its relation with the social act *S wants that ...* For example:

God (King Arthur) wants the knights of the Round Table to seek the Grail.

The feudal order wants Rodrigue to seek Chimène and Rodrigue to avenge his father.

To the extent that there is true dramatization, the opponent is also the subject of a desire proposition, one that is similar but opposed to that of the subject. Likewise it is embedded in a proposition structure: *S wants that (Op, etc.).*

Each time there is confrontation of two desires, that of the subject and that of the opponent, it is because there has been division, an internal split of *S*, a sign of a historical or ideological conflict.

In any event, in theatrical conflict we can propose in principle that such an analysis excludes the autonomy of the subject: when such autonomy appears it can only be an illusion or a deception serving some reductive ideology.

3.6. The Arrow of Desire

If relations between actants are rather formal and inflexible, with a relatively limited potential for interplay of substitutions, the arrow of desire, an oriented vector, is even more clearly semanticized; we might say that psychology, banished from the relations between actants (who are not characters), takes refuge in the arrow of desire, the arrow that links the subject with the object. This poses a certain danger, the danger of going back to the categories of traditional psychology. We will try to impose relatively strict limits on the semanticism of the subject's arrow.

First we should note that, grammatically, the arrow of the subject corresponds to the *verb* in the basic sentence. However, the 'meaning' of this verb is already narrowly limited by the fact that the only verbs represented in this list are those that serve to establish a relation (and a dynamic relation at that) between two lexemes of which one (the subject) is necessarily *animate* and *human*: X wants Y, X loves Y, X hates Y. Right away we can see the arrow's semantic field shrinking: it is restricted to verbs of wanting, of desire. The arrow determines both a *wanting* ('an anthropomorphic classeme [...] that sets up the actant as subject, that is, as a potential operator of the doing' [Greimas 1978, 72]), and a decisive doing, since it determines the dramatic action.[15]

If the relation between sender and subject, or indeed between helper or opponent and subject, rarely needs motivation, the arrow of desire for its part is always positive; that is where a psychoanalysis of the desiring subject might properly be applied. This even further restricts the meaning of our terms. Contrary to Greimas' analyses, in which he lists the possible motives of the desiring subject (love, hate, envy, vengeance, etc.), we quite happily limit this desire to what is fundamentally the desire of the Freudian subject – that is, desire in the strict sense, with all its possibilities: narcissism, desire for the other, and perhaps even the urge to seek death.

However, what are usually understood as motivations, for example, duty or vengeance, cannot, it seems to us, be desires (semantically investing the subject-object arrow). They seem instead to be the inverse of desires, involving a whole series of mediations and metonymic transfers. Thus Lear's wish for the death of the daughters who betrayed him does not correspond to the arrow of desire. Perhaps if this analysis were to be carried through it would cast light on what is usually referred to as Hamlet's ineffectualness. The analysis could read as follows: the desire that drives Hamlet is not centred on murdering his father-in-law; that murder is for him secondary and mediate. And thus, in Musset's *Lorenzaccio*, Lorenzo's desire – a narcissistic attraction to a Florence identified with Lorenzo himself (or to the *mother*[16]), an almost sexual desire for Florence's liberty – turns, through a whole series of metonymic shifts, into a desire to kill the tyrant (Clement VII, then Alexander of Medici) and ends up melding with a desire for the tyrant himself. This passion for Alexander is not entirely ruse – it is also the temptation of death. In the final analysis, neither hate nor vengeance can ever in and of themselves semantically invest the arrow of desire. That arrow always represents the positive desire for someone or something. This is the only hypothesis that keeps us from falling back on our old psychological motivations – above all it is the only hypothesis that justifies expending the vital energy needed to drive the theatrical hero to perform his doing. Thus in Macbeth, the desire to be (a great person, a king, a man + the desire for his wife) is metonymically invested in 'desire,' or more precisely in the wish to kill Duncan.[17] After that, the desire to be, or rather to persevere mechanically or automatically engenders the inexhaustible wanting for the other murders.

3.7. Actantial Triangles

If we consider the actantial model, not in the totality of its six positions, but with emphasis on certain functions within those positions, we can identify a certain number of triangles which reveal (relatively) autonomous relations. In most classical scenes involving two or three characters, one or another of those triangles will be operative. We might see subject and opponent in a confrontation over an absent object, subject and object uniting against the opponent, or, as in a famous scene from *Le Cid*, the sender, Don Diègue, telling Rodrigue what the object of his quest is.

3.7.1. The Active Triangle
The arrow of desire orients the actantial model as a whole and establishes the *meaning* (*direction* and *significance*) of the opponent function.

Two solutions are possible (see the diagram on page 50):

a/ The opponent opposes the subject. For example, Snow White's step-mother opposes her person, not her desire for the Prince. In this case the active triangle (subject-object-opponent) takes the following form:

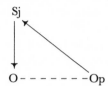

It is as if the subject were in possession of something the opponent wanted (supreme beauty, in the case of Snow White). In this case, the battle shifts in relation to the subject's desire (see section 3.8: 'Multiple Models'). We might say that the opponent is an existential, not a con-junctural, adversary. The very being, the very existence of the subject is threatened. The subject can satisfy the opponent only by disappear-ing; this is the case for Othello in relation to Iago.

b/ The opponent opposes the desire of the subject for a given object. The triangle will take this form:

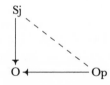

In this sense there is true rivalry (romantic, familial or political) with the collision of two desires centred on the same object. We see this in the case of Britannicus and Nero, rivals for Junie.

In *Suréna*, Corneille delicately advances both of the above solutions at the same time. King Orode is the hero Suréna's first opponent because he is afraid of Suréna's great glory. Suréna, by his existence alone, is a threat to his kingdom. My crime, says Suréna, is to be 'more known than my King' (act 5, scene 2). The Crown Prince Pacorus, Suréna's second opponent, is Suréna's rival for Eurydice. The two modes of opposition come together here.

We have called this triangle the active or conflictual triangle because it is of constituting importance to the action. All the other actants may be absent or only faintly present, but none of these three can be missing. Even in Beckett's *Endgame*, where all the actants seem to unravel and fade away, one can in a way say that Hamm's desire for death is countered by the other characters' desire for life. They function as a sort of collective opponent. 'It's going to end,' says Hamm, rather hopefully, but no one, apart from him, wants it to finish.

3.7.2. The Psychological Triangle
We call this form the psychological triangle:

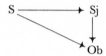

We call it psychological because it offers us a twofold characterization, ideological and psychological, of the subject-object relation. In an analysis it demonstrates how the ideological is reintegrated into the psychological, or more precisely, how the psychological characterization of the subject-object relation (the arrow of desire) is closely linked to the ideological. *Le Cid* is an especially useful example because the determinations are so clear. The presence of *Eros* in the sender position is linked with historical determinations: the presence in the Sender of both feudal values and monarchical ideals. These finally valorize Rodrigue's choice of Chimène as object. In particular, we can refer to the psychological triangle for the psycho-ideological determination of the object: the choice of the object cannot be understood in the traditional way, exclusively in terms of the psychological determinations of the subject (Sj). Instead it must be understood in terms of the sender-subject (S–Sj) relation. This is no more than common sense: the object of love, for example, is chosen not on the sole basis of the subject's tastes and desires, but rather on the basis of all the socio-historical determinations within which that choice is made.

As an example, indeed a dramatic one, consider the strange choice as object of love that Pyrrhus makes. Andromaque, his prisoner and victim, is the most 'impossible' choice he could have made. We can look to individual motivations – the relationship with the father (Achilles, who murdered Andromaque's husband Hector) allows Pyrrhus to make himself equal to (indeed, to become) the father by marrying Andromaque – but we cannot ignore the presence in the sender position of both Greece and the God that seeks to avenge Troy (the *deus absconditus* that re-establishes equilibrium between conquerors and conquered). Once more, we see how the actantial model serves not so much to solve problems as to pose and articulate them.

3.7.3. The Ideological Triangle
This triangle takes the following form:

It is the reverse of the psychological triangle and it marks the return of action to ideology. It allows us to see how the action, as presented throughout the course of the drama, takes place in a manner such as to benefit a social or individual beneficiary. At the other extreme of the action in question this triangle clarifies, not the starting point of the action, but rather the meaning inherent in its unfolding; this allows us to see that within the formal model there is a kind of diachrony, a *before* and an *after*. If we return to our previous example, we can ask this question: who benefitted from the action that was set in motion by Pyrrhus's desire for Andromaque? The answer is clear: although Pyrrhus's desire was his own, its consequences involve Troy – Andromaque becomes Queen of Epirus, a new Troy, *Troja rediviva*.

There is no example, at least outside popular theatre, of this triangle's failure to demonstrate a return not only to the City, but also to the idea men have of the sociohistorical situation in which they find themselves, a return to the ideological. The final problem posed by the dénouement of *Andromaque* is the problem of divine justice and historical reversal. An analysis of the ideological triangle requires us to examine the various mediations which permit movement from a given subject's action to the consequences of that action for the society in question. The ideological triangle shows us how the subject's action is involved in the resolution (or at least in the new position) of the problem. For example, the final question posed in *King Lear* can be formulated as follows: can the King continue to be a feudal king among everyone else (and solve his own problems in terms of that feudal situation) when feudalism is dying? The question posed by the ideological triangle concerns the relation between subject and receiver, between the individual action of the subject and its consequences, both individual and sociohistorical. Such an analysis, in its almost infinite variety, poses the key semiological question for the director: how to demonstrate both the individual meaning (for the subject) and the sociohistorical meaning of the dénouement? In mounting *Hamlet*, it is surely not enough to have a tear shed for the fate of the 'gentle Prince of Denmark.' We must also demonstrate the meaning of an action whose end result is to put Denmark back into the hands of Fortinbras, thus making the foreign king the receiver of the entire action.

3.8. Multiple Models

Up to now our examples have all come from theatre but we could have taken examples from other forms of narration without fundamentally changing our observations. At least up to this point, it is not at the actantial level that we can zero in on that which is specific to drama. We must go a little further: perhaps we can say that what distinguishes a dramatic from a novel, for example, is the fact that in theatre we are confronted not by a single actantial model, but rather by at least two.

If it is sometimes difficult to identify the subject of a given actantial phrase, it is because other possible phrases involving other subjects, or transformations of a single phrase, make it possible for the opponent or the object to become the subject.

3.8.1. Reversion

First, there is reversal of the *object*: in any love story a reversal of subject and object is possible. If Rodrigue loves Chimène, Chimène loves Rodrigue: an actantial model in which Chimène is subject would be every bit as legitimate as the opposite. If at first it was Romeo that loved Juliet, it is nonetheless true that Juliet ended up loving Romeo. Only social constraints and codes make it less possible for a female actant to become a subject. In performance it is never impossible to give privileged status to an actantial model that might seem less obvious than another, but that is more interesting and rich in meaning for us today. The semiological analysis of a dramatic text is never constraining: it allows another semiological system, that of performance, to play with its structures in terms of another code. Performance can construct an actantial model that is new or textually less obvious, by emphasizing certain textual signs, suppressing others, and constructing a system of autonomous (visual or auditory) signs, thus setting up the chosen subject as autonomous and triumphant in his or her desire.[18] Performance can produce a new actantial model by reversing a structure whose transformation is possible and already partially in play. There can be sequences which set up the object-character as subject of his or her own desire. So it is in the nurse scene in *Romeo and Juliet*.

3.8.2. Two Models

Another way roles can be reversed, which also is virtually inscribed in texts, is one that in certain cases, but not all, turns the opponent into the subject of desire. Thus Shakespeare's *Othello* is more easily read if one perceives Iago as the inverse subject, Othello's dark double.[19] In melodrama, the villain must be considered the real, active subject.[20] What can we make of this inversion? It can be given privileged status when the play is staged. But it is also possible, at the level of performance, to allow both actantial models to co-exist, to have both in play, to present them, linked together, with all their potential for conflict and competition. The plural nature of theatrical writing (more clearly than other kinds of texts) permits this twofold programming, which conditions the effectiveness of dramatic confrontation, in that the clash of two desires – that of the subject and that of the object – is governed by relationships with other actants that as a whole present social groups in conflict. We will encounter this notion of dramatic space again: actants are distributed within two zones, two conflictual or at least opposing spaces.[21] Thus the collision between the two shifted desires of Orgon and Tartuffe or of Alceste and Philinte appears as an antagonistic spatial relation.

3.8.3. Doubling or Mirroring of Structure

In certain cases the presence of two subjects is not an opposition between two antagonistic actants, but rather a doubling of one and the same actant. In *King Lear*, the Gloucester actant is a doubling and a shadow of the Lear actant with the same successive twofold function of subject and object. In *Lorenzaccio*, Marquise Cibo is a mirrored shadow of the subject, Lorenzo. What is even more surprising is that the opponent-actant Laërtes in *Hamlet* takes the exact place of the subject Hamlet, and, like Hamlet, he seeks revenge against a father's murderer.

This gives rise to a whole series of dramatic possibilities:

a/ There is counterpoint, as in *Lorenzaccio* where Lorenzo and the Marquise are implicated in the same action but never meet. The only relation between the two networks lies in the fact that the respective objects (and also the objects' relation to the subjects) are identical.

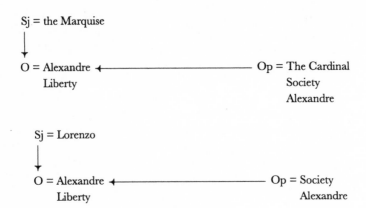

Sj = the Marquise

O = Alexandre ◄————————————————— Op = The Cardinal
  Liberty   Society
                                             Alexandre

Sj = Lorenzo

O = Alexandre ◄————————————————— Op = Society
  Liberty   Alexandre

The parallelism is very enlightening.

b/ Another possibility is the presence of two shifted schemas, as in *Hamlet*:

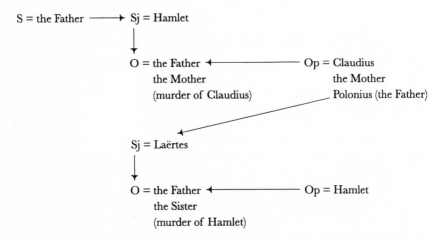

S = the Father ————► Sj = Hamlet

           O = the Father ◄———————— Op = Claudius
             the Mother   the Mother
             (murder of Claudius)   Polonius (the Father)

           Sj = Laërtes

           O = the Father ◄———————— Op = Hamlet
             the Sister
             (murder of Hamlet)

The reversibility of the action here prepares for the defeat and death of Laërtes and Hamlet, both combatants in a lost cause; the structure here calls for the integration of a new element, the young King Fortinbras, who is not caught up in the problematics of the death of the father, or more precisely, not disarmed by that death.

3.8.4. Multiple Models: Determination of the Principal Subject(s)

A simple method of determining the principal actantial model is to construct a series of models that start with the main characters taken as sub-jects. In the case of *Le Misanthrope*, we can construct at least two actantial models, one that takes the subject Alceste as its point of departure, and the other the subject Célimène:

S = Eros ⟶ Sj = Alceste ⟶ R = Self

O = { Célimène (transparency of the other/ of social relations) }   Op = Célimène everyone else

S = Eros ⟶ Sj = Célimène ⟶ R = Self

A = Eros ⟶ O = Self (through others) ⟵ Op = Alceste everyone else

Some observations:

a/ There is a similarity vis-à-vis the *sender*. In both cases the sender is Eros. There is also a certain relation to the group which might be a relation of domination, but the sociopolitical structure excludes any individual domination other than the King's.

b/ There is a similarity and an opposing relation in the object of desire, an object that is in contradiction with the relation of the desired group.[22]

c/ There is the curious similarity between the actantial schema whose subject is Célimène and the schema for *Dom Juan*, whose subject is Dom Juan. This similarity should identify the meaning of *Le Misan-thrope* within the series of Molière's plays: the story and structure should demonstrate their possible conjunction. After *Dom Juan* and *Tartuffe*, Molière wrote a play of desire and of a woman's will to power – a will that can be realized only within and through a social group that is close to the seat of power, within and through a (social) relation between desire and its masks. The actantial schemata indicate the two-fold (reversible) relationships of subject and object, and of subject and group, with the latter's helping and opposing roles. We see how a per-formance might give privileged status to the Célimène-subject. We also see how the relationship of the actantial models indicates the locus of dramatic conflict, seen here in all its complexity: on the one hand there is a twofold conflict between subjects, and on the other hand, a twofold conflict between each subject and the other opponents. This twofold conflict expresses the failure of the two subjects not only in terms of the confrontation between them, but also in terms of their fundamental conflict with the world.[23]

This failure brings about various consequences: Alceste accepts defeat and retires from the scene. Célimène does not accept defeat; as with Dom Juan, she awaits either a bolt of lightning from on high or old age.

A rapid analysis of this type, dealing with a well-known text, allows us to put a finger on the relationship between the construction of our model as a working process with no value other than heuristic and the construction of models claimed to determine structures inherent to the object. We should be leery of both these positions. One implies a relativism, an empiricism of knowledge, and the other projects the results of methods of investigation as objective truths; both arise from a scientific positivism. To the extent that theatre is a signifying activity, the (complex) analysis of the actantial model, or of specific actantial models, represents nothing more than a determination of some theoretical conditions for that signifying activity.

The presence of two subjects, a presence that is characteristic of the theatrical text, be it the result of either a textual investigation or the construction of the literary object, brings to light the fundamental ambiguity of the theatrical text. F. Rastier's excellent demonstration of this ambiguity for Dom Juan[24] is perhaps not linked clearly enough to the theatrical status of the text. Rastier reads the ambiguity at the level of the story; however, the example offered by Le Misanthrope (an example that is far from exceptional) allows us to place this ambiguity at the actantial level. A sequence-by-sequence analysis following the principle by which Rastier splits up the text of Dom Juan would show how Alceste the subject and Célimène the subject alternate in the unfolding of the story of the play. The spectator reads and/or constructs two stories (or perhaps, two fabulae) that are in competition: the story of Alceste and the story of Célimène. 'This would give us,' says Rastier, 'two descriptions of the deep structure of the story, descriptions that will account for the two possible readings' (Rastier 1973, 92).

We can go further: the presence of two actantial models revolving around two subject-object axes can have as a consequence, not only at the level of reading but also at the level of practice (performance), not a choice but a fluctuation that precisely sets out the dramatic problem of the text for the spectator. In addition to a univocal reading, there can be a twofold reading, a *dialogic*[25] one, which involves the spectator in this to-and-fro movement that constitutes theatrical activity.[26] Here again it is the production of performance which creates or destroys textual ambivalence, an ambivalence which never represents a non-differentiation of meaning, but rather a conflict of meanings.

3.8.5. Multiple Models: The Example of Phèdre

If there is a text that demonstrates the hugely predominant role of the hero (or heroine), it is Racine's *Phèdre*. The actantial model that sets up the heroine as subject is clear, complete, sharply formed:

S = Venus ⟶ Sj = Phèdre ⟶ R = Self
(Eros)   │   Death
Minos
(God)   ↓

H = Oenone ⟶ O = Hippolyte ⟵ Op = Thésée
Power   Good   Aricie

However, two other schemata taking Hippolyte or Aricie as subject, are textually possible:

S = Eros ⟶ Sj = Hippolyte ⟶ R = Self
Royalty   ↓

H = Théramène ⟶ O = Aricie ⟵ Op = Thésée
(Aricie)   Power   Phèdre (Oenone)

S = Eros ⟶ Sj = Aricie ⟶ R = Self
Royalty   ↓

A = Théramène ⟶ O = Hippolyte ⟵ Op = Thésée
(Hippolyte)   Power   Phèdre

These schemata are very interesting because:

a/ They correspond so precisely to the reversible twofold subject-object schema that the two schemata are really twins; the role of subject is actually assumed by Aricie (see act 2, scene 1 and act 5, scene 2), and there is a sort of virtual equality between the lovers.

b/The schema of Hippolyte's desire opens the text, and is clearly and precisely developed in Hippolyte's speeches as well as in Théramène's. Here we have one of those relatively rare cases where the discursive . level quite clearly elucidates the actantial structure.

c/ In the three schemata, Hippolyte is subject once and object twice, while Phèdre is subject once and opponent twice.

d/An essential fact: in all three schemata, Thésée is in the position of *opponent*, each time, linked with a woman. The love of Hippolyte and Aricie has as opponent (as is the rule) the parental couple. On the other hand – and this is very important – Phèdre's desire for Hippolyte, reversing an order held over generations, installs Aricie at the same actantial post as Thésée. This gives us a format in which only the Athenian 'indigenous' couple survives at the end, all 'foreigners' having been eliminated.

Thésée's position as opponent clearly indicates that all the protagonists share a desire to eliminate him. For Phèdre and for Hippolyte, he is the obstacle to their amorous desires. For Aricie he is, in addition, the (political or tyrannical) obstacle to her liberty and royal authority. Furthermore, the presence of the king in the opponent position gives the play a political meaning that is camouflaged by discourse, as if the commotion of passions were eclipsing political conflict. The conflict between father and son is not a simple Oedipal conflict, nor is it a simple generational conflict: it is a conflict between a king and his successor. *Phèdre* is a drama about royal succession, about failed succession.

There is a corollary to this: we cannot construct an actantial schema that has Thésée in the subject position. All he wants is to keep what he has: his wife, his power, his life, his son (his son as a son, not as a competitor or successor). Strictly speaking, he wants nothing, not even Hippolyte's death, which nonetheless he asks for. Only the dénouement of the play installs Thésée as actantial subject.

e/ If we note that Thésée is an opponent to the desire of both Hippolyte and Phèdre, we see the extent to which opposition to or by Thésée establishes the relations between Hippolyte and Phèdre, both of whom are 'censured' by the same authority. In a way, Aricie and Phèdre are, for Hippolyte, part of the same paradigm, the paradigm of the object (woman) that is denied by the father. Here we have actantial analysis working together with psychoanalysis.[27]

f/ The presence of Eros in the *sender* position (*S*), and the presence of the subject in the *receiver* (*R*) position is a sign of individual passional desire. But in all three schemata *power* occupies an actantial position and is in a kind of competition with the object of love (act 2, scene 2, the love scene between Hippolyte and Aricie, demonstrates the importance of the political object – power); power is a secondary object and a helper for Phèdre who seeks it as a type of currency (object) exchange with Hippolyte, the object of love.[28] For Hippolyte, power, like love, is the locus of revolt against the father. For Aricie, it is the locus of revenge against an oppressive tyranny.

The presence of a political being, both in symbiosis and in competition with the passional, and the absence of the City (state, society, monarchy) in the position of sender – all this signifies not only the explosion of desires and individual ambitions but also the transition from a tragedy of the City (albeit monarchical) to a bourgeois tragedy about individual will. The actantial model allows us to determine the historical place of the work: the evolution of absolute monarchy forces Racine to camouflage political problems (which can be precisely noted with the aid of the actantial model) behind the discourse of passions. The political is the unspoken element of the text at a time when individualism was reducing it to the smallest share.

We have seen how the story (and the ideology) invests itself in the text at the level of its macrostructures. We also see (looking at the same thing from a different point of view) how semiological analysis poses questions for performance that cannot be avoided. Which conflicts should be accorded privileged status? How should they be shown? For example, what role should be assigned to Thésée, to his presence on the stage? How can we establish the relationship between the semiological system of discourse and an actantial model that has different implications? How can we articulate the one and the other?

The problems faced by performance are the choice of an actantial model that warrants privileged status or the maintenance of several competing actantial models, and the clarification of the meaning and the function of the macrostructures for the spectator.

3.8.6. The Instability of Actantial Models
This is an even greater task than one might think because in most cases the model does not remain stable or fixed throughout the whole work. Often there will be shift from one model to another, or indeed a substitution in the course of the action.

Let us take the example of *Le Cid*. If we set aside a secondary schema,

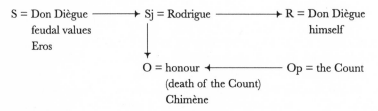

Sj = the Count

O = the position of Governor ◄——————————— Op = Don Diègue

we can identify a main model:

S = Don Diègue ——————► Sj = Rodrigue ——————————► R = Don Diègue
feudal values   himself
Eros

                                            O = honour ◄————————— Op = the Count
                                            (death of the Count)
                                            Chimène

This model has two different objects that are in occasional conflict (see Rodrigue's *stanzas*). After the duel and the Count's death, the model ceases to be contradictory and becomes in a certain way impossible. We have a non-contradictory model of the epic type (quest) which is maintained through successive episodes (sequences): trials, a battle against the Moors, a confrontation with Chimène, a battle against Don Sanche, new battles to come – a model for an epic story.

The dramatic, conflictual model which follows it has Chimène as subject and a double object: Rodrigue, and vengeance for the Father.

This shift from one model to another is in no way a sign of conflict between models; rather it marks the real convergence of the action of the two subjects (who belong to the same paradigm). The actantial construction indicates the unity of the two actants.

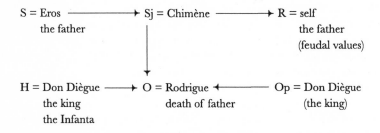

S = Eros ———————————► Sj = Chimène —————————► R = self
the father   the father
                                                                              (feudal values)

H = Don Diègue ——► O = Rodrigue ◄———— Op = Don Diègue
the king   death of father   (the king)
the Infanta

3.8.7. The Attenuated Importance of the Subject in Modern Theatre

Most of our examples are taken from classical theatre. The search for an actantial model appears to be more uncertain in a work by Beckett or

Ionesco – not to mention the attempts for theatrical works without text. What would an actantial model have to say about *The Bald Soprano?* Or even *Amédée ou Comment s'en débarrasser?* In a way, it is not the actants that have disappeared, but rather the subject's desire. In *Amédée* one might think that the (reified) subject is the cadaver that grows and whose desire is manifested in this overwhelming way, progressively expelling all opponents. In *The Bald Soprano* a series of micro-subjects develops a kaleidoscopic series of micro-desires, cumulatively creating a conflictual-repetitive, destructive situation. The weakening of the subject takes on a more rational form in the works of Adamov: in his early plays, the entire dramatic concern is a demonstration of the fruitless efforts of the hero to constitute himself as subject. The subjectivism of *Le professeur Taranne* or *Sens de la marche* is a kind of counter-check of the classical actantial model.

Genet's dramatic writing multiplies the actantial model by two or even three through the play of mirroring effects of theatricalization. In *The Maids* the subject Claire is simultaneously, through the effects of her own imaginary theatre, the object-madame. The way these embedded roles work casts doubt on classical actanial functions; the desires of the possible subjects constitute desires that are within the ceremony constructed to satisfy them. The model breaks up into partial subjects, all seeking integration into the same ceremony. Thus in *The Balcony,* we have the adjustment of the desires of Mme Irma, the Prostitutes, and the clients; here is the actantial model:

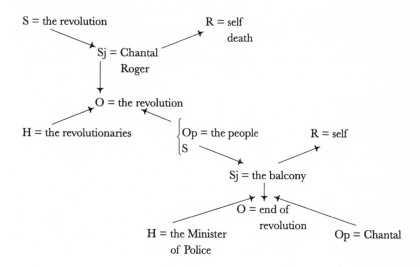

This twofold shifted model shows how the substitution of the balcony for the court (the bordello for the royal palace) makes it possible for the revolution to be crushed. But for this to happen we need this incessant metonymic shifting from bordello to revolution, then back to bordello, and from the Important Ones to their images on the balcony. But then, who is where? This displacement brings the spatial mechanisms of the actantial model into question. Here we are getting to the main point: the actantial model or models, because they are in competition or conflict, can be understood only if we bring in the notion of spatiality.

This is what we tried to demonstrate in connection with Hugo, and what Rastier demonstrates in his analysis of *Dom Juan*. He concludes by saying, 'The elementary, binary structure of meaning articulates each semiological system into two unconnected spaces' (Rastier 1973, 133). In order for the actantial system to work, there must be spatial disjunction.

3.9. Some Conclusions

Actantial analysis, as we have presented it, is incontestably a summary approach, but we can see how it can be refined by textual analysis:

a/ Our current methods for determining the actantial model are largely artisanal and intuitive. At times it seems that nothing more than intuition justifies the presence of a given character in a particular actantial position. One criterion is essential: the action or potential actions as they appear, and can be summed up, in the sequence of episodes of the fabula. Thus the helper is the one who helps the action. The criteria we borrow from discourse analysis (verbs of volition or action, for example) are sometimes useful, but must be subject to an important caution since a character's discourse can often be in contradiction with that character's actantial role.

Indeed it is useful to try out each character in the role of subject in an actantial model, as long as we are willing to give up immediately on impossible or fruitless combinations. Finally, we can determine the manner in which characters rotate between various positions on the model and the permutations resulting from these rotations.

b/ As a consequence, any increase in the precision of actantial analysis will depend upon the manner of examining it, not according to the text as a whole, but rather diachronically, in relation to the text's sequences of the text and the manner of their succession. For example, only a study of the way models evolve, sequence by sequence, will allow us to see the transformation of a model and to understand how combinations of models and conflicts between models evolve. This study depends on a textual analysis that proceeds sequence by sequence. Determining sequential units is the most difficult of procedures,[29] all the more so because, if we study the actantial model via units that are too small, we risk uncertain results. If we take the traditional, visible units (acts, tableaux, scenes) as a provisional base, we can identify a series of actantial models which, when superimposed upon each other as a reductive procedure, will give us one or more principal models.

c/ Rastier has developed a complex but very refined method for determining deep structures, through analysis of the actors' functions and the application of reductive analysis to redundant functions. This method also presupposes the identification of sequential units, but it has the disadvantage of ignoring the fact that actantial models can be in competition.

d/ Actantial analysis brings to light not only ideological significance but, more precisely, conflicts: this analysis allows us to identify, within the theatrical text, the locus of ideology and its related questions, if not the answers.

e/ A corollary: it is at the actantial level, and because of competition and conflict between models, that we can perceive the dialogism of the theatrical text; it is here that we note the fundamental fact that, because the subject of the scriptor-enunciation has been done away with or masked, the centralizing consciousness that normally unifies all discourses has been put to sleep. Furthermore, the dramatic action becomes a process in which the syntactic subject is never alone. He or she is not in a position (either as scriptor or as subject of the action) to claim that the whole scriptural system, a system that would then become his or her universe, is centered on him or her. The theatrical universe belongs to no one person. The subject's scriptural network enters into competition or comes into conflict with another network, another planetary system. Although the subject is at the centre, there are other centres. Actantial analysis demonstrates the polycentrism of theatre. Therefore, from the outset, there is no privileged voice in the theatrical text. By its very nature, theatre is decentred, conflictual, and at the extreme, anti-establishment. It is not that the dominant ideology does not often prevail: indeed official theatre must resort to singular restrictions, toning-down procedures, and strict observance of code in order to silence theatrical polyphony and safeguard the dominating importance of the principal voice. We should not be surprised to see censorship unleashed against theatre. The censors are right: theatre is indeed dangerous.

4. Actors and Roles

4.1. Actors

The actor is a 'lexicalized unit' of the mythical or literary story. '*Actants*,' says Greimas, 'have to do with a narrative syntax, whereas *actors* can be recognized in the specific discourses in which they are manifested' (Greimas 1987, 106). In other words, actors usually have a name; they are the discrete units that theatrical discourse is able to specify quite simply – an actor (in the story) = an actor (a play actor). This of course does not mean that the notion of actor is limited to theatre. According to this point of view, an actor is a particularization of an actant. He or she might be seen as the (anthropomorphic) unit that manifests, within the story, the notion (or force field) that is covered in the concept of actant. Thus the sender-actant is lexicalized under the type of *king-actor* at the end of *Cinna*. In *Phèdre*, the helper-actant is lexicalized under the type of *nurse-actor* who bears the name Oenone.

But Greimas, who as we have seen first believed that the actor is a particularization of the actant, eventually had to admit that 'if an actant (*A1*) can be manifested in discourse by several actors (*a1, a2, a3*), the converse is equally possible: just one actor (*a1*) being able to syncretize several actants (*A1, A2, A3*) (Greimas 1987, 107).

The actant is an element of a syntactic structure that can be common to several texts. The actor is in theory an actor in one specific story or text. A single actor can move from one actantial position to another, or indeed occupy several at a time. Thus in all love stories, the same actor is both subject and receiver. In turn, it is impossible to construct an actantial schema (especially for a theatrical text) without putting several actors in a single actantial position.

But this feature is held in common by both actor and character. How can we distinguish one from the other?[30] Both are elements of surface structure, not deep structure, and as such they correspond to a lexeme. As lexeme, an actor corresponds to a certain number of semes[31] that characterize her or him. But not individuality: the actor is no more a character than is the actant. Of course the distinction is not simple: in a way the notion of actor includes Propp's idea of the executing character (noun + predicate). Greimas, from the beginning, defined the concept of actor 'based solely on the naive concept of it as a "character" who in some way remains constant throughout a given narrative discourse' (Greimas 1987, 111). But this view is still inadequate. It would be possible for several characters to be the same actor. For example, suppose there are several pretenders to the hand of a princess: they are not the same actant (only one will win her hand), but rather the same actor – the actor who is claiming the princess for himself. In *Le Misanthrope*, the minor courtiers are not only the same actant, but indeed the same actor. It is impossible to confuse actor and character.

The actor is thus an animate element characterized by an identical functioning, sometimes, as necessary, bearing different names and operating in different circumstances. Thus in *Les Fourberies de Scapin*, Scapin, whatever his actantial role (sender, subject or helper, depending on the model of that moment and the sequences involved), is the actor-who-produces-fourberies, the one whose repeated action is to dupe others. Hence the repetitive recounting of the 'fourberies' [deceits] he has committed against Léandre. He can be quite similar to any other character who might have the same actorial role as his, the role of trickster or deceiver.

The actor is characterized by: (1) a *process* which is proper to him or her – $NS + VS^{32}$ – in which he or she plays the role of a noun phrase in relation to a fixed verb phrase (Scapin *dupes X*); (2) a certain number of differential features demonstrating a binary functioning. In a manner analogous to Jakobson's phoneme, the actor is a package of differential elements, similar to what Lévi-Strauss called *mythemes*.

[I]n a tale (and, we might add, in a theatrical text) a 'king' is not only a king, a 'shepherdess' not only a shepherdess, but ... these words and what they signify become tangible means of constructing an intelligible system formed by the oppositions: *male/female* (with regard to *nature*) and *high/low* (with regard to *culture*), as well as all possible permutations among the six functions (Lévi-Strauss 1976, 142).

We see this likening of mythemes to semes only in terms of a comparison; we do not view them as identical. Nonetheless Lévi-Strauss adds (and this brings us back to our field of inquiry):

[mythemes] result from a play of binary or ternary oppositions (which makes them comparable to phonemes). But they do so among elements which are already full of signification at the level of language and which can be expressed by words of the vocabulary (Lévi-Strauss 1976, 143).

An actor is defined, then, according to a certain number of characteristic features: if two characters possess both the same characteristics and perform the same action, they are the same actor. For example, an actor is one who plays a fixed role in a religious ceremony: whoever plays the same role is the same actor if he has the same characteristics (a priest, for example). The difference of a characteristic feature marks the opposition between one actor and another, for example, between a male actor and a female actor (two actors whose process is the same can be differentiated by such a characteristic feature). Actors belong to a certain number of paradigms; the feminine *vs* the masculine paradigm, or the king *vs* non-king paradigm. Being a unit of the story, the actor is at the crossroads of a number of paradigms and of one or more narrative syntagma (his or her *process*).

Thus Cornelian characters represent a certain number of actors characterized by distinctive features. Let us take the example of *Cinna*: the three characters – Cinna, Émilie, and Maxime – are three conspirator-actors; they have the same process (the same action) – conspiracy – and the same distinctive features – they are young, closely linked to Auguste, and hostile to his tyranny. Of course they are not identical in all of their distinctive features: Émilie is a woman, and Cinna is loved (a feature that distinguishes him from Maxime). We can thus see that the actor is an abstract element that allows us to perceive relations between characters, because the 'actorial function' is identical. In Corneille's later plays, the main feature of the actorial function revolves around the *king/non-king* opposition. We can see how the analysis of this function serves mainly to identify characters and the relations between them. In Racine, we no longer have a king/non-king opposition but rather a *powerful/not powerful* opposition. Power is no longer 'royal' power, legitimate, and accorded by divine right; instead it is a simple matter of force. Therefore, the interplay of actors is very simple:

loving/not loving:	a
loved/not loved:	b
powerful/not powerful:	c
man/woman:	d
exiled/not exiled:	e

Take the example of the trio of characters in *Bérénice*:

Antiochus	= a	(–b)	(–c)	d	(–e)
Titus	= a	b	c	d	e
Bérénice	= a	b	(–c)	(–d)	(–e)

Note that the king/non-king feature is not relevant because they are all chiefs of state, kings. What opposes Titus and Bérénice, although the two are linked by love,[33] is the situation of power and exile. On the other hand everything (except, alas, love) should bring Bérénice and Antiochus together. The decisive structural element, the one that determines a Racinian actor, is the exile + non-power situation characteristic of such *actors* as Junie, Andromaque, Bérénice, Britannicus (deprived of his inheritance), Atalide, and Phèdre; there is an added split between Junie, Andromaque, Monime, Atalide, and Bajazet, who do not love the powerful one, and Bérénice or Esther who do love him. We also see how the presence of identical distinctive features does not necessarily mean that the actors will be identical. The processes must also be identical. Here, for example, we have the following process: loving the non-powerful *vs* loving the powerful one.

a/ We see that it is not at all easy to distinguish a given quality that is specific to one actor (for example loving/not loving), from the process of that actor's process; both can be legitimately called predicates. The notion of actor has still not been clarified.

b/ We see how this concept serves to elucidate the way in which characters work and, more precisely, we see the way it clarifies relations between characters.

c/ We see that what characterizes the animate material of an author is his stock of actors – what we commonly call type-characters. The women in Corneille or the children in Maeterlinck are actors, that is characters endowed with a number of common distinctive features. This concept helps to cast light on the universe of a given dramatic author.

4.2. Roles

Under this point of view, the term *actor* runs the risk of being confused with the term *role*.

What is a *role*? Greimas and Rastier use the term frequently in the sense of function (actantial role, actorial role, the role of *aggressor*, for example). We use the term in the sense employed by Greimas (Greimas 1987, 106–120), that is in the sense of a coded actor that is limited by a predetermined function. Like actor, role is one of the mediating elements that allow us to move from the abstract actantial code to the concrete determinations of the text (characters, objects).

Thus in the *commedia dell'arte* all actors are roles, determined by a function that is imposed upon them by the code. Harlequin has a predictable and unchanging functional behaviour. In the circus, the Augustus is an encoded role. In a religious ceremony *roles* are (or can be) occupied by several actors.[34] This view of the concept of role is like the traditional meaning of (encoded) role in the theatre, and it is also close to the meaning of role as that which someone does, his or her function. The Matamoros (killer of Moors) is not an actor, but rather a role, although he is also determined by differential features that are more precise than his killing function. Strictly speaking there can be no role unless there is a narrowly encoded story (a religious ceremony or a very tightly defined form of theatre). Thus the characters in melodrama (classical melodrama, for example Pixérécourt) are, not strictly speaking actors, but rather roles – the Noble Father, the Pure Young Girl, the Villain, the Young Hero, or the Simpleton.

In less tightly encoded forms of theatre (or even outside theatre), a character can play a role for which he or she is not intended. The young hero in a sentimental novel can play the role of father to the orphaned heroine: here we see a blurring of actor-role. In romantic drama we frequently see a shift from actor to role. For example Ruy Blas, not only an actor marked by a number of distinctive features, but also an actor in a determined process (lover of the Queen), plays the objective role of villain (masked, false identity, laying of traps). This process involves a shift from actor to encoded role, then a shift back from encoded role to actor. At the level of performance a whole process can be set up to pull characters out of their original code in order to re-encode them differently; a given role (a melodramatic one, for example) can be subverted at the textual or staged level. For example, Bernard Sobel's adoption of a hyperbolic melodramatic code for Lenz's *Le Précepteur* (Théâtre de Gennevilliers, Spring 1975), exploded the melodramatic roles one might expect of such characters. Alexandre Ostrovski, on the other hand, decodes melodramatic characters in order to re-encode them differently: the role becomes a character (in *The Storm* [1860] for example). An entirely contestatary process can be set up by constructing performance signs which demonstrate the opposition and deepen the divide between actor and role. On the other hand, that process can mock the expected norm by fusing actor and role. We can, for instance, construct Racine's young heros (actors) by encoding them, in performance, according to norms for the young hero of popular sentimental drama.

The approach that distinguishes carefully between actor and role (as a function of code) must be carried out at the level of performance by the director and actor. They will also distinguish the actor (and her or his process) from the encoded role and decode the character in order to re-encode it differently, or instead they may establish actor and process in a (theatrical and sociocultural) code. All semiological analyses of text end up bringing to light the code that underlies the writing process and informs the animate elements of the story by assigning its historicity and its ideological character to that code. Likewise, all instances of performance have an effect on the *actor/role* relationship (in the semiological sense of the terms) and thereby clarify or suppress the historicity and ideological determinations of the twofold code – that of the text and that of the performance. A text that is written with performance on a proscenium stage; in mind can be decoded then re-encoded for a different kind of performance: actors and roles can be rewritten as a consequence and the relationship between them will have to be reconstructed. Thus, we see that however necessary it might be, a purely textual analysis of theatre is deceptive because it can always be struck out or overturned by the signifying exercise of performance.

Note: As for the particular point of theatrical roles, some of their determinations do not come only from dialogue, or even didascalia; rather they are the product of an unwritten (but traditional) code, a product of, for example, a fully encoded gestural system. Thus the role of Matamoros is determined to a much greater extent on stage (costume, gestures) than it is textually. In this case the text-performance relation is reversed. Now the text is dependent upon performance and seems secondary to it. The stage determinations of the role not only complete the determinations of the text, they also condition and, one might say, predetermine them. There is a simple and entirely material reason that concerns the very conditions of theatrical writing: the writer of theatre has in mind not a commercial success in the bookstores, but rather the socioeconomics of the stage. It is a practice that presupposes the stage, actors, a public, money for initial expenses, and various material requirements which have an effect upon that writing. Rarely is anything written for the theatre that, as far as material circumstances (including reception) are concerned, could not be performed or heard. And when people do indeed fail to write with performance in mind, obvious textual distortions result: the (historically determined) performance code is openly violated and subverted (for example in *Lorenzaccio* or in *Mangeront-ils?* which is part of Hugo's *Théâtre en liberté*).

Here we have put our finger on the limits of any semiological analysis that is not based upon an analysis of the textual story. Although the text-performance distinction is a necessary methodological given, a semiology of the theatre will ultimately succeed in demonstrating the articulation of the two, by virtue of its reversal of the theoretical text-performance order (see *Lire le théâtre II*).

In any case – and here historical studies are required – we must draw up the inventory of distinctive features that constitute the encoded roles of the theatre, their evolution and the relationship constructed between the actor's process and the functioning of the role. Thus we need to analyse the relationship between the actor Scapin (a producer of deceits) and the encoded role of valet (particularly the deceitful valet) in Latin and Italian comedies. Likewise it will be interesting to see how the actor Scapin moves from one actantial position to another – from helper to sender, and even to subject. Here is one example from among many: the Fool in *King Lear*, whose actantial position is very uncertain (is he the helper or a doubling of the subject-object Lear?) is an actor whose function is, among others, to speak derisively of royalty and of Lear's paternity, but at the same time as he acts within the encoded role of Court Jester (costume, behaviour, gestures, and a vulgar, popular, sexualized vocabulary).

4.3. Procedures

The determination of actors and roles in the text and in theatrical representation is relatively easy at the level of intuitive and artisanal study. It is a simple thing to identify the main action (or successive actions) of such and such a character: Hermione loves Pyrrhus, then Hermione has Pyrrhus killed – two very obvious successive actions. Likewise it is a simple matter to identify the characteristic features that make Hermione a specific and clear-cut actor (woman, young, powerful). However, we must consider *role* in terms of the contemporary (or earlier) theatrical code; this is where notions of the *history of theatre* and of *genre* come in (*commedia dell'arte*, comedy, tragedy, melodrama, drama, etc.). This type of investigation is something that actors and directors do spontaneously; it is a rough and ready research into questions of actor and role.

Some remaining observations:

a/ The actor is as little isolated and isolatable as the actant. Just as there is an actantial system, there is an actorial ensemble whose distinctive features form an oppositional system (as we saw in the simple example from *Bérénice*). The important point about the determination of the actorial ensemble is that it provides the direction that makes it possible to read performance through an interplay of a few simple determinations and oppositions.

b/ More refined research would require a sequence-by-sequence study (see chapter V, section 4 'Time and Sequences'), with (1) a list of the actor's actions in their succession; (2) from the lexical perspective, a noting of the verbs of which the actor is the subject of enunciation; (3) a list in order of appearance, of the semic features that figure in the didascalia and in dialogues (even those in which the actor does not figure). A more precise analysis would eventually come down to a study not of the actor but of the character. When all is said and done, the analysis of actorial functioning is an integral part of the analysis of characters. The actor offers us a clarifying and simplifying point at which to see into the whole complex phenomenon that we know the theatrical character to be.

III. The Character

The theatrical character is in crisis. This is not new. But it is not hard to see that the situation is getting worse. Càrved up, exploded into pieces, scattered among various interpretations, its discourse brought into question, reduplicated yet dispersed, the theatrical character has been spared no mistreatment at the hands of dramatic writing or directing.

1. Criticism of the Concept of Character

1.1. Character and Meaning

Even when we are dealing with character in classical theatre, whose existence (at least virtual) no one denies, an analysis of character results in its atomization. Whether we see *actant, actor,* or *role* in the concept of character, contemporary semiology sees character as the locus of *functions,* and no longer as a substance-copy of a human being. Can we, in theatre, do away completely with the notion of character?

The concept of *character* is not only one of the central issues among all the textual and methodological uncertainties reflected in today's discussions about theatre, it is in fact the battleground for these discussions. Beyond problems involving method, what is at stake is the Self, in the autonomy of its substance, its very soul – very tired concepts after eighty years of thinking and re-thinking in psychology. Is it possible that what can scarcely be said any longer about human beings in their daily existence can still be said about literary characters? We should not be surprised by the enormously amusing cliché that such characters are more real than some people, more real than reality. It is as if we could place the idealist notion of person, now in such utter disrepute, in the domain of the fantasma of literary creation.

So it is that we see a whole tradition of discourse focussed on the concept of character, in the novel and in theatre – substance, soul, Kantian transcendental subject, universal character, eternal Man, infinitely renewed hypostasis of consciousness, culture's supreme flower. The literary character has been seen as eternal, yet modern: this concept goes back at least as far as the second half of the twelfth century.

The refusal to give up on the idea of literary character is also connected with the desire to preserve the idea of a meaning pre-existent to dramatic discourse. The ensuing benefit is twofold: on the one hand we save the concept of intentionality for literary creation (as opposed to the concept of creation of meaning by the spectator); on the other hand, we protect dramatic literature from the contagion of performance. The character's autonomy and pre-existence vis-à-vis its performance guarantees the autonomy of the literary object (in relation to its lesser avatar in material and concrete performance, in theatrical production itself); in this respect we have scarcely made any gains since Aristotle. The pre-existence of character is one way of assuring the pre-existence of meaning. The task for literary analysis would then be a discovery of meaning linked to the massive essence of the character, a hermeneutics of consciousness – rather than a construction of meaning. The work of semanticists today is directed against these amazingly tenacious concepts.

1.2. The Textual Character

Let us go further. Perhaps we can indeed say that, literally speaking, there is no textual character. The textual character we discover when we read is never alone. It is always accompanied by the set of all the discourses already held about it. These discourses present an infinite variety, depending on the text in question. Thus, we cannot know or understand Phèdre (we might say we cannot read that character) independently of a knowledge of all discourse on Racine (and *Phèdre*), a discourse that goes back more or less to the eighteenth century (a discourse of Voltaire and his *Siècle de Louis XIV*, if you will, that was confirmed and enlarged throughout the nineteenth century and during the first half of the twentieth century, along with a few variations): Phèdre, the image of passion; Phèdre, a soul torn apart, a Christian abandoned by grace; Phèdre, consciousness in evil, a fascinating person, etc. We can no longer read *Phèdre* as a text, but rather as the sum of text + metatext.[1] Indeed, this sum of text + metatext underlies the sacrosanct classical notion of character, as well as all the analyses of a given character that are particularly representative of that notion. It seems that the most urgent task for analysis is to deconstruct this totality (text + metatext). We cannot hope to attain a pure, ahistorical look at the text (and the textual character) – that is, of course, impossible – but if we eliminate the metatext we can at least reach the textual layers otherwise hidden by it. There can be no innocent reading or production of a given play; this is all the more reason not to clutch at a reading that seems obviously true only because it comes to us from the tradition of a given acquired discourse.

As Rastier demonstrates, deconstruction of the 'classical' character was already undertaken by Propp, whose work emphasized *action* over *agent*: 'The question of *what* a tale's dramatis personae do is an important one for the study of the tale, but the questions of *who* does it and *how* it is done already fall within the province of accessory study' (Propp 1968, 20). But that is not enough. Of course it is of paramount importance to know that Thésée has his son killed, but can we separate the murder from the father/son relation? In most cases, as in this example, action cannot be separated from the fundamental relationship between the protagonists: a murder involving rivals is not necessarily a case of infanticide.

Rastier correctly notes that it is difficult to distinguish between the quality and the action of a character: for example, how can we establish the distinction between the feature loving (X is one who loves) and the process (X loves Y)? 'The opposition between action and quality has no scientific basis in linguistics,' points out Rastier, and he adds (as every theatre specialist knows) that 'inventories of the qualities and actions of an actor vary correlatively throughout the unfolding of the story. Beyond the fact that this obviates the possibility that the character is identical to itself throughout, it follows that ... the opposition between qualifications and functions ceases thereby to be operative' (Rastier 1973, 215).

1.3. On the Character as Locus

Although all of the above critical thoughts are perfectly relevant and sufficient to destroy the classical meta-discourse on the character, they are not entirely adequate to our needs in the area of theatre, for the following reasons:

1/ Something remains even beyond a demonstration of all the variations in qualifications and functions, beyond and within the question of passage from one actantial role to another: it is the actor, the existence and physical unicity of the actor. We will soon see the importance of this question.

2/ Although Rastier believes that the ontological definition of characters is part of what he calls the 'referential illusion' (and he is right), theatre by definition is in part referential illusion since the theatrical sign has the twofold status of being the semiotic set and the constructed referent of the theatrical text (see chapter I, section 2.8. 'The Problem of the Referent'). In theatre it is not possible to escape entirely from a *mimesis* that results from the fact that the physical reality of the actor is a mime of the text-character. This physical nature of theatre guarantees a (relative) permanence for the text-character, with all of the possible shifts, changes, and paradigmatic substitutions.

3/ To the extent that the theatrical text is *tabular* rather than linear, the character is a decisive element in the verticality of the text. The character allows for unity in the text's simultaneously dispersed signs. In textual space, the character figures prominently at the point where paradigm and syntagma meet, or more exactly, where paradigm overlays syntagma; the character is a strictly poetic locus. In performance, the character appears as the point at which we can anchor and bring together the diversity of signs in a given text.

Thus we believe that the notion of character (textually staged) in its relation to the text and to performance is one that any semiology of the theatre must consider. This holds true even if we have to take character not as a substance (a person, a soul, character type, a unique individual), but rather as a geometrical locus made up of different structures and having a mediating function. Instead of seeing, in character, a truth that would allow us to construct an organized discourse or meta-discourse, we must in fact take character as the point at which relatively independent functions meet.

1.4. The Character Lives On

a/ The character (in theatre) is not to be confused with the psychologizing or even psychoanalysing discourse that we can construct about it. This type of discourse, however brilliant, is never of much help to practitioners of the theatre. There is a good reason for this. The risk is that such discourse will form a mask, hiding the true function of the character. It isolates the character from the text as a whole and from the other semiotic ensembles that the rest of the characters represent. Finally, there is always the risk of making the character appear to be a thing, or at best a being to be discovered by a linguistic procedure of unmasking; thus the character will be frozen or 'transfixed.' Once the character has become an object it can no longer be an infinitely renewable locus where meaning is created. This is also why that other theatrical practice is rather dubious – the practice, especially common in the early part of this century and still followed by some actors, of reconstructing a set of extra-textual sentiments, an extra-textual biography, and a set of hidden or obvious motives for a given character. All this reminds us of the dubious nature of the practice by which the actor identifies with the fantasmatic construction that his character, as discussed above, in fact is. The character in theatre is not be to confused with any of the various discourses that can be constructed about it.

b/ We should not think that today's questioning of the status and nature of the theatrical character comes in full panoply from a new scientific theory. Neither should we think that instances of an illusion-character felicitously representing a real character cannot function effectively in the theatre. This practice was the glory of bourgeois theatre and of performances of classical theatre until quite recently. Indeed, the scientific practice by which we distance the character cannot be understood without the historical developments that make it possible. We could only see character as an object, not of intuition or affective communication, but rather of analysis, if character had already been desacralized, if it had already been understood to be the product of the myth of the absolute person. The theatrical character is a historical construct and its deconstruction is also historical. As Brecht says, 'What do we do now, since the true, unexchangeable individual is disappearing from life?' The task of any semiology of the character is to demonstrate precisely its nature as divisible and exchangeable but at the same time articulated into elements and an element itself of one or more paradigmatic sets. Any character that remains a possible semiological unit is never anything more than a temporary unit. It is as indivisible as the atom, and like the atom, it is made up of even smaller units and it combines with other elements.

c/ The character is not to be confused with the other units or systems within which it can figure. The character is not to be confused with the actant, even though characters usually have an actantial role. The actant is an element of syntactic structure, the character is a complex aggregate grouped under the unity of a name.

d/The character is not to be confused with the actor: several characters can be just one actor (the messenger-actor, for example). 'Can we take as two characters,' says Rastier, 'the two angels who appear before Mary Magdalene (John 20:12)? Since from the functional point of view nothing allows us to distinguish between these two angels, the analysis of the story should list only one actor, just as in Matthew it lists the Angel of the Lord' (Rastier 1973, 214). This clear example allows us to understand, in spite of Rastier, how and why we can never completely do away with the concept of character. We can admit that we do not know why John writes 'two angels,' but it is obvious that the meaning of this biblical story will be different, depending on whether there are two angels or only one. The duplication of the angel is a signifying factor. We can allow that presupposition even if in this case its exact significance escapes us. This should make it all the more obvious that in theatre, dividing an actor into several characters (for example the many 'fâcheux' [bores] in Molière's *Les Fâcheux*), whether in the theatrical text or the performance, is a signifying writing procedure.

We could consider the character as an abstraction, a limit-setting phenomenon, a crossroads at which series or independent functions meet. Alternatively, we can take the character to be an aggregate of non-autonomous elements. In any event, the character will not be denied. To say that a notion we can call a is the relation, sum or product of two elements, b and c, does not mean that a does not exist ($a = b + c$ or $a = b \times c$ or $a = b/c$). Even if we say that the character is not a substance, but rather a production found at the crossroads where various functions meet – or more exactly that it is the intersection of several sets (in the mathematical sense of the term) – that does not mean that we can ignore it. We have to take account of the character, even if only from the strictly linguistic point of view. It is a subject of enunciation. That character is the subject of a discourse which is marked by its name, a discourse spoken by the actor bearing the character's name.

Although the character is neither a being nor a substance, it is an object of analysis. What then are the discernable elements that should represent the main lines of inquiry in our analysis of character? The first and incontestable element, as we have just seen, is the fact that the character is the subject of a discourse. The second element is the fact that, since the character is part of many structures that we can call syntactic structures, it can be viewed as a word, a lexeme. It functions as a lexeme within syntactic structures: the actantial system (deep structure), the actorial system (surface structure). As a lexeme, it functions within the totality of textual discourse and can thus be inscribed within a given rhetorical figure (metonymy or metaphor). Finally, by means of its own textual determinations we can construct a semiotic totality which the actor, at the moment of performance, can bring forth. At this point, the actor can allow herself or himself all kinds of transformations, on the understanding that: (a) she or he will not be able to restore all of these determinations; (b) for historical reasons she or he will often have to seek equivalents; (c) conversely, the physical and psychological person of the actor will bring unforeseen determinations to the character in question.

2. The Character and Its Three Main Themes

There are three lines of inquiry open to those who seek to study a theatrical character, along with several conditions: (a) these three lines of inquiry must be followed at the same time; (b) the importance of any one will vary according to the moment in the history of theatre; (c) no character should be studied in isolation except as a provisional, working, strategy.

2.1. The Character and Its Figures

The character grid on page 79 shows that:

a/ Any semiological analysis of the theatrical character is an extremely complex operation. It is very difficult to latch on to a single line of inquiry and follow it through without coming up against one of the other lines of inquiry: one constantly encounters links between themes.

b/ An analysis of a given character will meet up with all the analyses of other characters, whether in terms of similarities or of differences. This takes place at all levels. The isolated analysis of a given character is never more than a provisional step. Each feature of a character is marked in terms of its opposition to another feature: if a character is marked with the feature of *king*, this will always be opposed to a *non-king* character or to an *other king* character. A king is not a king except as opposed to non-kings or as another version of another king.

c/ The referential aspect as such is missing from the character grid. In effect, the semiology of character places the referent at a distance, whereas that same referent is always the foremost element in discourse or metadiscourse on character.

The Character Grid

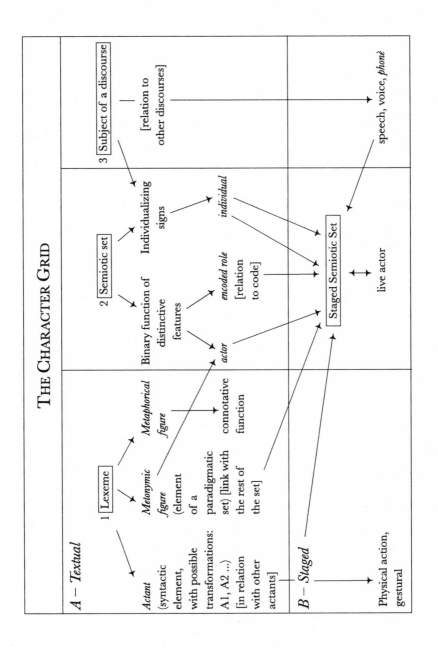

d/This referential element is necessarily involved in the staging of any given character: the character portrayed by an actor necessarily resembles someone or something. Thésée portrayed on stage in 1995 will necessarily resemble someone or something – Louis XIV, a Minoan figure, a statue of Phidias, a king in a deck of cards, or the King of Spain. The director, with the help of the semic textual totality of the character in the pages of a book, creates a concrete figure. In other words, the semiological analysis of a character does not account for the whole of that character: he or she is always a complex and constructed figure. We should note that it is impossible, within the practical activity of staging a play, to take all elements involved into account: there is indeed a risk that textual elements and staging signs will come into conflict. The character can thus be seen as the intersection (in the mathematical sense) of two semiotic sets (text and stage). Beyond that intersection, those signs should be seen as noise: this is true not only for textual signs (which for various reasons the actor cannot always include in her or his accounting) but also true for signs that are involuntarily produced by the actor. The set we identify as p – the intersection of the two sets – will thus be constructed through a process of selection.

2.1.1. The Character and the Actantial System

Although character can be included in the concept of lexeme, it is also implicated in a syntactic structure and as such demonstrates its grammatical functioning: Hamlet as subject of an action portraying a father's revenge, Rodrigue as object of Chimène's love. A character can occupy the same actantial position as another character (in *Hamlet*, Laërtes occupies the position of subject in the father's revenge action, along with Hamlet). However, a character may occupy a different actantial post in another actantial model (for example, Rodrigue is also a subject in the father's revenge action). Here we see how the determination of these various syntactic functions allows us to clarify the actantial profile of a given character. This is especially significant in cases where the actantial function of a given character is in contradiction with the importance of that character's discourse or his or her central role in the action. Phèdre's importance as subject of the action is uncertain and conflictual, even though it is clear that hers is the most important discourse in the play. We see this also in Adamov's early plays, where characters (such as Henri in *Le sens de la marche*, and Taranne in *Le professeur Taranne*) who are indisputably heroes and are constantly on stage but who can never reach the point of constituting themselves as subject of the action.

2.1.2. The Character in the Actorial System

The character's encoded role and functions as *actor* have long since been identified and analyzed. What is important here is not so much to identify the deceiver in the character of Scapin (actor action function) or the valet originating in Latin comedy (encoded role), as it is to demonstrate how these elements combine with a syntactic function or with semiological features that are not necessarily consonant with this actorial or encoded role. The importance of this kind of analysis can be seen if we compare, for example, the role of *deceiver* in a character such as Scapin with that same role in a character such as Dubois in Marivaux's *Les fausses confidences*.

2.1.3. The Character as a Rhetorical Element

As a lexeme, a character can be implicated in the total textual discourse, and there he or she will figure as a rhetorical element. A character can be the metonymy or synecdoche (a part for the whole) of a paradigmatic set, or the metonymy of one or several other characters. Thus, in a tragedy a guard will appear as the metonymy of the king's might; a counsellor or a minister can appear as the metonymy of authority; the nurse Oenone is the metonymy of Phèdre's desire. A series of metonymic exchanges can occur around, or through, a given character. Thus the Fool in *King Lear* appears as the metonymy of Lear in his madness. The Fool says 'Prithee, nuncle, tell me whether a madman be a gentleman or a yeoman,' to which Lear replies, 'A *king*, a *king*!' (act 3, scene 6).

Beyond this metonymic function, a character can be the metaphor of several orders of reality. Phèdre appears as a metaphor for the conjunction of desire and the repression of that same desire: *Minos vs Pasiphaé*. Thus, one and the same character can take on both a metaphorical and a metonymic role: Phèdre is a metonymy for Crete in that she refers us metonymically to all that is included within the Cretan paradigm, of which Minos and Pasiphaé are part.

We can go further. A character can appear as a unique figure of discourse, a basic figure of theatricality, an essentially dialogical figure – namely an oxymoron (a co-existence, within the same discourse, of contradictory categories: life-death, light-night, law-crime). A character can be a kind of living oxymoron, a locus par excellence for dramatic tension, because it metaphorically brings together two opposite orders of reality. Phèdre is the locus at which we find the confrontations of Minos vs. Pasiphaé, desire vs. repression, individual vs. society, and Crete vs. Greece. Likewise in *King Lear* Cordelia appears both as daughter (metaphor of life, of fecundity, of the future), and as a mute (metaphor for death, according to Freud). Cordelia can be seen as a life/death oxymoron, a figure representing Lear's impossible desire to be reborn, to be loved; but in place of life, there is death. Such is the character oxymoron.

2.1.4. The Character in Relation with the Referent

It is at the rhetorical level that the relation to the referent becomes part of the analysis of character. The character can be considered as the metonymy and/or the metaphor of a referent and, more exactly, of an historico-social referent: Phèdre, a textual metonymy of Crete, can also be seen as a metonymy for the Sun King's court. Hence, through that character, today we are able to make the connection between the seventeenth-century referent and our contemporary referent. It is clear that here we have gone beyond the textual level, into the area of performance: we are able to grasp the constructed nature of character. The seventeenth-century referent according to which the character is developed is not a given, but rather a construct of director and spectator. Hence the character as metonymy of that referent is also constructed out of textual and extra-textual elements that can be listed. This construct depends not only on the above-mentioned textual inventory, but also on the story as it is known or constructed by the director or actor, and on the past and present story as it is known and lived by the spectator. The character's rhetorical and, more precisely, metonymic function allows for its mediating function between historical contexts that are foreign to each other.

2.1.5. The Connotative Network

Here it might be useful to refer to the concept of connotations (see chapter I, section 2.6. 'Denotation, Connotation'): as a lexeme, a character denotes a historical or imagined figure, a set of 'semes.' It will also, however, connote a series of related meanings. Thus a heroic character or a character from antiquity can connote all those elements of the legend surrounding him or her that are not in the actual text of the play. With this adaptable and extendable system of connotations, a whole series of constructs on the part of the reader or spectator can be invested in a given character, using extra-textual, historical or legendary elements, or elements that have been brought into play in the course of performance. A series of semantic fields can function in relation to the character even in the absence of the slightest textual reference: thus the character of Nina in *The Seagull* can connote 'Slavic charm.' A whole vaguely defined set of meanings can be brought into play by a character, as long as it is confirmed throughout the reading or performance by redundancies.

At the textual level, it is more difficult to distinguish between the denoted level (action and discourse) and the connoted level. Thus for example, the semantic system for death, or more precisely for the kingdom of the dead, is found in Racine in connection with Phèdre and Thésée; we can see Thésée's relation to that kingdom as connotative. A whole connotative system for death underlies Gubetta's text and song in *Lucrèce Borgia*. A series of elements that normally are not heard or perceived by the spectator can be set into play as a result of the manner in which a character is presented on stage. Thus the totality of the connotative network set up around a character can be integrated into a constructed system of meanings. The character's connotations can help in the construction, for and through performance, of a new way for a given theatrical text to function.

2.1.6. The Character's Poetic Function

As a lexeme, a character, because of his or her links with several semantic fields and his or her inclusion in several paradigms, is an important element of theatrical poetics. It is in large measure through character that the paradigmatic can be projected upon the syntagmatic. The relative permanence[2] of a character in effect allows for the projection, through the whole of the narrative syntagma, of the paradigmatic units with which that character is associated. Thus the Lorenzo character in *Lorenzaccio* makes it possible to apply the death-of-the-tyrant paradigm or the prostitution-paradigm to the whole syntagmatic narrative. It seems clear that any articulation of a textual poetics or a poetics of performance must be centred upon the character. Once more we see the character as the guarantor not only of textual polysemy but also of the vertical functioning of polysemy.

2.2. The Individual-Character

The second axis along which a character functions makes a character into a bundle of (differential) semiotic determinations. There are two kinds of determinations:

a/ First there are determinations that make the character not an actant, but an *actor* (see chapter II, section 4 'Actors and Roles'), with a certain number of characteristics that she or he shares partially or totally with other characters of the same text or of other texts. Thus in Brecht's *A Man's a Man*, the English soldiers share certain features (in a relationship that is in opposition to the central character's features) that make of them a single actor. Yet one of them, Fairchild, has further determinations which make him a privileged actor, whose nature and functions are different from the rest of the English soldiers.

b/Another set of determinations makes an individual of the character. For instance, Brecht adds individualizing determinations to the actorial determinations; first among these is the name. The modern view that character is dubious starts with the view that names are dubious. In *The Good Person of Szechwan* – a fabula that typifies the phenomenon of the divided character – the heroine (the subject of the action) has two names: Shen Teh and Shui Ta, the invented double. According to another perspective, it is not by chance that in *The Bald Soprano* Ionesco explores the limits of the individual determination of the character; he subjects the couple to a game of unknown identity, and has Mrs Smith recite the *Bobby Watson* saga of various characters of different age and sex, despite their having the same *name* (which is linked to an illusory blood relationship). Other individualizing elements are physical determinations; sometimes these elements cannot be avoided because they are part of a code (that might, for example, describe the beauty of the heroines Célimène or Nina) or because they are linked to a historically unique character (for example, Napoleon, Louis XIV, or Nero). We know that not all forms of theatre pay equal attention to individual determinations of characters. A given character may act behind a mask (which by nature is de-individualizing), be reduced to an encoded role (*commedia dell'arte*, clowns, etc.), or simply be defined by a network of abstract sociocultural determinations which turn a character into a figure in a deck of cards (the King, the Queen, the Hero, the Servant) so that only the primary oppositions of sex, strength, and the role of power remain.[3]

All individual determinations of a character can play a twofold role. (a) They identify the character as an individual with a soul, a hypostasis of the ideal person, in relation with the whole area of idealistic thought concerning the transcendental subject. (b) They can also identify the individual as a highly determined element in an historical process; in other words, the role of the individual is not only to refer us to a historical referent using the reality effects of his or her concrete individuality (marked, for example, by a known name), but also to demonstrate the insertion of the individual into a determinate sociohistorical context.

In a way, both bourgeois drama and historical tragedy require individualized characters: Lorenzaccio, Goetz in Sartre's *Le Diable et le bon Dieu*, or Anouilh's characters, and indeed Becque's characters in *La Parisienne*. The whole interplay of text-performance, especially modern forms of performance, is involved in this individualization/de-individualization of character. A sort of brutal inversion involving textual elements and signs of performance can appear, including disguises and the use of actors whose physical appearance belies what the play supposedly represents. This divide that separates textual images and signs of performance can, as far as a character's individual features are concerned, confuse or distort the accepted meanings of a given case and substitute new meanings. Such was the case with Vitez's almost childish Phèdre (at the Ivry theatre, 1974), or the tonsured Phèdre that Michel Hermon put on stage to demonstrate her ravaged femininity (at the Petit Odéon, 1974).

2.3. The Character as Subject of Discourse

Finally – what is most often studied at schools and universities and indeed most commonly seen in classical theatrical practice – the character speaks, and in speaking, she or he says of herself or himself things that can be compared to what others say of her or him. We can draw up the inventory of the character's (mostly psychological) determinations by analysing the (psychological) content of her or his discourse that defines the character's relations with interlocutors or other characters. This is a well-known procedure: we can take at face value Hermione's statements about her jealousy and the stages in her love for Pyrrhus; we can also test the truth of these statements by comparing what we learn from her directly with what other characters say in the same regard. This is how the classical analysis of a character's discourse proceeds. We can also take a more modern approach; we can consider a character's discourse as being able to and indeed intended to be the object of a hermeneutics that would bring to light the subconscious content of the character's psyche.[4]

2.3.1. Discourse and Speech Situation
Discourse analysis is traditionally carried out in order to clarify something other than the discourse itself and to enhance our knowledge of the fictive object that the character's psyche represents. It is a fictive object, in the exact sense of the term, to the extent that the sentiments and emotions the character is supposed to feel are in fact felt by no one: not by the character (a being created on paper), nor by the actor (who experiences other emotions and feelings), nor by the spectator (who is not

directly involved and whose emotions, linked to a reflective participation, differ radically from what is mimetically represented). However difficult it might be to accept, in a performance of the scene in *The Trojans* where Andromaque weeps for Astyanax, nobody suffers – not the actress, nor, the character (and for good reason!), nor, of course, the spectator. The emotions of the actress and the spectator are not those of a mother.

In order to understand the relationship between the character and his or her discourse we have to reverse our approach. We no longer view a character's discourse as a stock of information that will allow us to decode the psychological character or psyche of that character; instead we examine the entire set of that character's distinctive features and his or her relations with other characters (his or her speech situation) in order to clarify a discourse which is in effect indeterminate. Speech does not signify outside of its conditions of enunciation. Pure 'meaning' is reduced to equivocation or nothingness. 'I haven't loved you, cruel? What then have I done?' (*Andromaque*, act 4, scene 5); these completely ambiguous words (*love, cruel, done*) are not made any clearer by the verb tense. The dictionary is no great help. Only the speech situation can clarify the meaning of this discourse, and the main element of that speech situation is the character as a semiotic totality in relation with other semiotic totalities.

Note: Does this mean that the character's discourse does not ever refer to something that might be 'psychological?' That would be absurd. The character's discourse does, of course, refer to a psychological referent, but that referent is not of the order of the individual psyche. Hence the need for more precise and specific tools than those of traditional psychological analysis. If we put our trust in a psychological hermeneutics of the character's discourse, we will never discover a single being, but rather a situation.

Take the most paradoxical example – Molière's *Amphitryon*, act 1, scene 3: Jupiter, throughout a seemingly infinite night, has possessed the desired Alcmène in the guise of her husband; in the morning he delivers a hair-raising speech to his lover, insisting that she declare herself pleased with the lover, not the husband. Alcmène rejects the *distinguo*. The spectator vaguely understands that the god has not been satisfied. (Yet, why not? He was refused nothing, and he is assured a brilliant posterity in the person of Hercules.) Jupiter's non-satisfaction is strange yet all too easily explained. *Who* possessed Alcmène? Not Jupiter in any case; the god Jupiter received nothing. What is in question is not the uninteresting divine 'individual' but rather a situation where someone is master and the psychological fallout from that situation. If the king's favourite utters a wholly submissive or a wildly enthusiastic *yes*, who is thereby loved? The King, the man, or no one? Tyranny progressively sterilizes all that surrounds it; in depriving master and servant of his or her 'I,' tyranny also eradicates all interpersonal relations. That in fact is the referential truth of Jupiter's discourse: the king, the master, moves through a world that has lost all affective reality. He has indeed become a 'god.' A being, an *I*, a psychological existence of the character of Jupiter does not even have the reality of a phantom; it is less than a soap bubble, pure illusion. Psychology, in the theatre, should be sought elsewhere than in the internal causalities for which a given character is the locus.

2.3.2. The Character: Subject of Enunciation or Twofold Enunciation

The character is that which enunciates a discourse (usually a spoken discourse, with phonic reality, sometimes mimed, and with an accompanying series of gestures). A discourse constitutes a regulated stretch of spoken words which can be studied, as we shall see, from a linguistic point of view (as an instance of continuous speech), or from a semiological point of view (as a sign system, in relation with other sign systems). A character's discourse is thus a *text*, a determinate part of a greater whole, the totality of the play (dialogue and didascalia). But a character's discourse is also, and above all, a message with a sender-character and a receiver (interlocutor and audience), in relation with the other functions of any message, in particular a context and a code. As we have seen, the message takes on meaning only in relation with what the receiver knows about the sender and the conditions under which the message is sent. Hence the ambiguity inherent when we read a theatrical text: it is a literary text and it is also a message of another order. This brings us to the following corollary: all discourse in theatre has two subjects of enunciation – the character and the writing self (just as it has two receivers, other characters and the audience). This law of the twofold subject of enunciation is a main element of the theatrical *text*; this is where we find the inevitable gap that separates the character from his or her discourse, that prevents the character from being constituted as the true subject of his or her speech. A character never speaks alone; the author speaks at the same time, through the character's lips. Hence we see a dialogism that is constitutive of the theatrical text (see chapter VI: 'Theatrical Discourse').

3. Procedures for the Analysis of Characters

From the character grid on p. 79 and our discussion, we can deduce a certain number of procedures for the analysis of characters. If, as we have tried to demonstrate, it is difficult in theatre to dispense with the notion of character, and if our concept of character will dictate the procedures to be applied to it, then the very nature of those procedures and the relationship between them will influence any theory of character. The relative importance of these various procedures for analysis depends on the type of theatrical text and performance envisaged. We should bear in mind two important precautions: (a) these procedures can scarcely be adopted in isolation, except perhaps provisionally; (b) each procedure presupposes analysis of the relation of the character under study with all other textual elements, particularly with the other characters. The necessarily successive nature of any analytical operation should not lead us to forget the synchrony inherent in all theatrical phenomena; nor should we forget the nature of theatre as an organized whole.

3.1. Establishing an Actantial Model

Determining an actantial model, or rather several actantial models, allows us to establish the syntactic function of the character. A number of methods can be used, with very similar practical results. The first is intuition and approximation. A relatively summary analysis of both the discourse of which a character is the subject of enunciation and the discourse of which he or she is the subject of the utterance (the discourse of others about him or her) allows us, by superimposing the verbs concerned, to determine precisely enough the object of the character's *desire* or *wanting*.

A summary analysis of the stages of a dramatic action (or of the *fabula*) allows us determine the main action and to write the basic sentence that constitutes the formulation of the actantial model or one of the actantial models. Thus, we can easily write *Phèdre wants Hippolyte* (opponents: Aricie, Thésée – see chapter II, section 3.8.5. 'Multiple Models: The Example of Phèdre'); starting with that basic proposition we can construct the actantial model, and place all the characters concerned (even characters who are off-stage or non-lexicalized, such as Minos, Pasiphaé, Pirithoüs, Neptune, the Monster) within it. The next step will be to test each character as subject of an actantial model so that we can identify the models whose simultaneous existence indicate the locus of conflict and eliminate any unsatisfactory models. After that, we need to see how any given character fits simultaneously or successively into the various positions of the model.[5]

3.2. Character and Paradigms

A fruitful and indispensable procedure is one that determines paradigms, or more precisely sets of paradigms, to which a given character belongs (in relation and/or opposition to other characters or other elements of the theatrical text). The *inventory* of these sets allows for the analysis of a character on two different levels:

a/ It allows us to account for both the referential functioning of the character and his or her poetic function (sustaining a metonymic and/or symbolic relation with several networks of meaning). For example in Racine's *Andromaque*, Andromaque belongs to the following paradigms:
>   *Troy* (vs. the Greeks)
>   *prisoner* (vs. all those who are free)
>   *war* (victim thereof vs. all conquerors, especially Pyrrhus)
>   *woman* (widow, mother in conjunction-opposition with Hermione)
>   *antiquity* (vs. seventeenth century)
>   *poets* (a heroine for Homer, Euripides, Virgil, Racine).

All of these paradigmatic sets justify the way she functions, both referentially and poetically, as pathetic victim (mother, wife in mourning, prisoner) in a situation of solitude, of exile (displaced person), and in her twofold relation with Antiquity and with the seventeenth century. These things are obvious, of course, but it is useful to formulate them as exhaustively as possible.

b/ At the same time, this inventory allows us to draw up at least a partial chart of the distinctive features of the character, not only in and of himself or herself, but in his or her relations of conjunction and opposition with other characters. The inventory thus helps to constitute the character as a semiotic totality.

This type of inventory serves not only to juxtapose obvious truths (which sometimes acquire new meaning as a result of the juxtaposition), but also to help us discover unobserved meanings. It allows us, if not to fill in all textual blanks, at least to ask questions which might lead to filling them in. Let us take two simple examples:

Nina, Chekhov's 'seagull,' whom we might be tempted to set apart from others in the play, has the same distinctive feature as Arkadina or Treplev; like them, she is the child of landowners, and she has the same largely superficial relationship to love and art as the rest of her social caste. However, she does not have the money needed to prevent that relationship from becoming destructive. The list of Philinte's distinctive features provides another example; we find him to be the structural twin of Alceste. He is the only one who, according to the text, is *not* in love with Célimène. If we fill in that textual blank, presupposing ambivalent relations resulting from a hidden rivalry between friends, we would clear up many of the oddities of the text – particularly the sustained aggressiveness of Philinte's discourse with Alceste, from the first scene on, that involves Célimène and even takes place in her presence. This is an exciting hypothesis, a question to be asked about *Le Misanthrope* by drawing up the inventory of the distinctive features of the character Philinte. We do not claim to offer new or compelling analyses, but we can demonstrate how a methodical inventory can draw together and clarify what the director and the actor, using their intuition, accomplish with a close, professional reading of a play.

3.3. Analysis of the Character's Discourse

Any concrete analysis of theatrical discourse must take into account the fundamental fact of theatre's twofold enunciation: the character speaks under the name of his or her character, but the author causes that speech, requires that speech, and chooses the words that are spoken. Thus we should not speak of the character's speech (individual usage in a situation of real communication), but rather of his or her discourse as a constructed process: even when, in forms of naturalistic theatre, the character's discourse simulates speech, it is still fundamentally separated from speech by virtue of the fact of twofold enunciation. A character's discourse is always twofold. This explains why, in a semiological study of a character, his or her discourse is always the object of the final analysis: the entire inventory of the character and the situations of his or her speech allows us to sort out what comes from the author's writing and what comes from the character's speech (see chapter VI: 'Theatrical Discourse').

We would like to remind readers that the modern devalorization of theatrical speech, following Artaud, is a singularly paradoxical attitude when we consider the efforts of thinkers today to demonstrate how most important human activity is dependent upon language. Maybe it is worth reminding ourselves that it is in theatre that we can see, analyse, and understand the relationship of speech to gesture and act.

3.3.1. Analysis of the Character's Discourse as a String of Words

a/ The quantitative (number of lines) and qualitative (number and nature of a character's speeches) has always, for many different reasons, including financial, been a concern for actors. They often judge the weight or importance of their roles in absolute and relative terms. Along with actors, we will count the number of lines and speeches of each character, and examine the relationship between the two. We see that the eponymic-hero character of Racine's tragedies is generally the least talkative of all (with some notable exceptions). We note that the role of the mute Cordelia in *King Lear* is longer than that of her sisters, even in the scene in which she eloquently refuses to speak – a point that makes her silence problematic.

b/ It is of course necessary to note the place of the character in the general economy of the play (presence and discourse); we will not dwell upon classical analyses but they are particularly useful for establishing the tableau of a character's speech relationships with all the others.

c/ The above observations clarify the kind(s) of discourse of a given character (monologues, dialogues, multiple scenes), the average length of speeches, and the types of intervention: for example, it would be interesting to study the variety of modes of speech in Molière's *Dom Juan* (brief speeches, strongly pressed questions, or a stream of words, depending on interlocutor).

3.3.2. The Character's Discourse as Message

Within the analysis of theatrical discourse (see chapter VI) we will be able to identify clearly what the notion of character in fact means for theatrical discourse. Conversely, we will also be able to see how the character is determined by her or his discourse. There is a unity of discourse which we can identify as the discourse of a character upon the stage – the discourse concretely uttered by an actor, of which the character is the subject of enunciation.

We discover the following:

a/ a message in which we can see the six functions of communication at play;

b/ in some cases, a character's idiolect using that term in its precise sense

of linguistic particularities: language of a given social class (such as
Molière's or Marivaux's peasants, the simpleton in a melodrama, or
the argot in 'popular' theatre) or language of a given province (*patois*);
c/ in most cases, as we shall see, a discourse that has its own determinations, a 'style' that may or may not correspond to other facts that determine the character and his or her functions;
d/in all cases, a message that is not isolated but is instead related to the
totality of the text and its speakers (dialogue).

4. Theatricalization of the Character

We must return to the obvious fact that the character has a concrete existence through concrete performance alone; the textual character is only
virtual. Moreover, a brief examination of the character grid demonstrates
that there is a reversion of performance upon the text. It is as if the text-
character was read in a different way, modified by the signs that accompany
the corporeal presence of the actor. There was a well-known phenomenon
in the nineteenth century, less common in today's theatre but still found
in cinema, that the set of roles previously played by an actor leave a mark
on any new role through creative superimposition. Thus Hugo preferred
to have his leading male roles played by Frédérick Lemaître, an actor
known for a role marked by the 'grotesque' effects of Robert Macaire,
because Hugo wanted his romantic hero to have a grotesque aura.

The theatricalization of the character, which is the fruit of the concrete
elements of performance, is already marked textually in a great many
cases. Textually the character can be theatricalized by her or his theatri-
calizing speech, that is, by directly addressing the receiving audience: 'I
am ... Sosie' or '... Harlequin': the spoken identification of the twofold
receiver theatricalizes the character. The character can also be textual-
ized by the theatrical mask she or he takes on (not a concrete mask as in
the theatre of antiquity, *commedia dell'arte* or Japanese theatre). Here the
name is the mask, a name such as that of:

• an already encoded character – the name of the leading man or the
  valet in classical theatre (Dorante or Basque), or the name of a character in Italian comedy, which is even more rigidly encoded;
• a legendary or historical character that has been theatricalized through
  that single reference (Theseus, David, or Napoleon);
• a character that is recognized as already theatrically encoded (requisite
  figures of melodrama);

- a character in the disguise of a borrowed identity of which the spectator knows the secret;
- a character whose identity remains problematical (Don Sanches of
Aragón, Hernani).

Aside from the particular workings of what we commonly call theatre-
within-the-theatre, many characters are the object of a fundamental theatricalization. Jean Genet's theatre is based upon this transformation of
characters into roles. In all probability, that very writing mode explains
why his theatre is considered the most theatrical literature of today. The
great theatrical heroes are theatricalized either in their own right (if we
can say that) or as a result of the other protagonists with whom they come
in contact. Hamlet and Lorenzo are theatricalized through their murders; Tartuffe and Dom Juan, on the other hand, are theatricalized by
themselves or by others. Ruy Blas is theatricalized by Don Salluste. Indeed
the Dame aux camélias herself, that most referential of all characters, is
theatricalized by the myth of the courtesan. No study of the theatrical
character can afford to ignore the linguistic and dramatic processes by
which characters are theatricalized.

If this survey has convinced the reader of the complexity of the concept of the theatrical character, the intention has been less to demonstrate the usefulness of minutely detailed analyses than to indicate the
great creative opportunities afforded to practitioners of theatre, as well as
the non-constraining nature, the flexibility, and the almost infinite adapt-
ability of both the theatrical text and the character-object. Each of the
procedures we envisage will ultimately propose meanings. The construction of meaning is the moving, shifting task of performance. The indeter-
minacy of the character, the essential instability inherent in twofold
enunciation, in twofold speech, allows the character to fill his or her role
as mediator: mediator between text and performance, between writer
and spectator, and between pre-existing meaning and final meaning. This
mediator bears within himself or herself the fundamental contradiction,
the unanswerable question, without which there would be no theatre: the
character's speech is a speech behind which there lies no person, no subject. That very absence, and the expectations so created, force the spectator to involve and invest his or her own speech.

IV. Theatre and Space

If the primary characteristic of theatre is the use of characters played by human beings, the second characteristic, indissolubly linked to the first, is the existence of a space within which those living beings are found. The activity of these humans takes place within a certain locus and creates among them (and between them and the spectators) a three-dimensional relationship.

1/ In this respect, theatre is unique and should not to be confused with recitation or story. In this respect also, text and performance differ the most and the specificity of the theatrical text and theatrical practice is most obvious. We can read the adventures of a theatrical character as if we were reading a novel and reconstruct in our mind the adventures of Lorenzo de Médicis, the hero of the play-novel, but the theatrical text, in order to exist, must have a locus, a spatial dimension in which the physical relationships between characters unfold.

2/ Because theatre represents human activities, theatrical space is the locus of those activities – a locus that necessarily has a relationship (of mime or distance) with the referential space of the human actants. In other words, theatrical space is the image (indeed the reverse, the negative image) and the counterproof of real space.

3/ The theatrical text is the only literary text that absolutely cannot be read according to a diachronic succession of a reading, and that opens itself to understanding only through layers of synchronic signs tiered in space, spatialized signs. Whatever spatialization is produced by a literary text, whatever spatializing a reader accomplishes when reading a novel (a novel localizes the activity of its characters through description), it remains true that the space of a novel is flat, even materially flat. The poetic activity that establishes a poem according to a non-linear, but tabular, reading is nonetheless two-dimensional; even a poetic text whose blanks and marks occupy a whole page remains flat because it still lacks depth.

4/ In this sense (at the textual level, of course) the theatrical text is even flatter than any other: it does not describe its own spatiality. (Place descriptions are always quite sketchy and, with rare notable exceptions, found only at specific places in the text.) Also, place descriptions serve a functional, rarely poetic purpose involving not an imaginary construct but rather the practice of performance, arrangement within space. On the other hand, the poetics of the page – the visual effect of a text's spatial arrangement upon a page – is foreign to the theatrical text. A spatial poetics of the text, to the extent that it can be found in theatre, is no more than an accidental effect (see, for example, Racine).

5/ It is at the level of space that the text-performance articulation is played out; this is because space is, to an enormous extent, an unspoken element of the text, a unique weakness of the theatrical text. Indeed space is uniquely lacking in the theatrical text.

1. The Stage Locus

1.1. Text and Stage Locus

Space is a given that is immediately received as we read theatrical text. This is because concrete space is the (two-fold) referent of all theatrical texts.

1/ Theatrical space is, first of all, a stage locus that must be constructed; without it, the text cannot find its place, its mode of concrete existence.

2/ The essence of this spatiality – the elements that allow us to construct the stage locus – is found in the *didascalia*, which provide:

a/ place directions that are more or less precise and detailed, depending on the individual text;

b/ the characters' names (which, we should not forget, are part of the didascalia) and simultaneously a certain anticipation of the way these characters will use space (the number, nature, and function of the characters);

c/ indications concerning gestures and movements (sometimes rare, or even absent) that, if present, allow us to understand how space will be occupied (for example: 'taking long strides,' or 'making himself very small,' or 'standing still').

3/ Spatialization can be created from dialogue: in Shakespeare most stage directions are simply derived from dialogue by deduction (a phenomenon called 'internal didascalia').

1.2. A Locus to Be Constructed

Stage directions are of use to the director (and the imagination of the reader of a theatrical text) in the construction of a locus in which the action is to take place. But the status of this locus is entirely different from the imaginary locus of a novel: the reader of La chartreuse de Parme, with the help of books, illustrations, memories of trips taken or films seen, has the pleasure of imagining the citadel from which Fabrice escapes; the reader of Lorenzaccio connects the play's Florentine location not with the city where perhaps he once strolled, but rather with a twofold locus – a theatre stage (with a constructed Florence),[1] and its referent, the historical Florence of the 16th century. In other words, the textual locus implies a concrete spatiality, that of the twofold referent characteristic of all theatrical practice. This means that theatrical space is the very locus for mimesis: constructed from textual elements, theatrical space must at the same time project itself as representational – a figure for something from the real world. But a figure for what? That is what we shall be searching for. Stage space is itself the locus for concrete theatricality, that activity which creates performance. The stage locus is like a mirror both for textual directions and for an encoded image.

1.3. A Concrete Locus

The stage locus is a unique locus with its own characteristics:

a/ It is limited or circumscribed – a delimited part of space.

b/ It is twofold: the stage-hall dichotomy, which we barely perceive at the textual level (except in certain modern texts where that relation is indicated), is pre-eminent for the text-performance relation: the theatrical locus confronts actors and spectators in a relationship that is closely related to the shape of the hall and the kind of society[2] (circus, proscenium stage, theatre in the round, etc.) with or without movement from one location to another, or intrusion of one locus upon the other.[3]

c/ The stage locus is encoded in precise ways that are dictated by the stage traditions of a given era and place, although modern spectators are less aware of this because they are accustomed to a diversity of stage loci and the violation and scrambling of codes. The narrow and shallow classical stage scarcely allows for crowd movement, and this was exacerbated by the presence on stage of aristocratic spectators. Conversely, the vast Elizabethan platform allowed for crowd scenes and combats; its succession of different areas for dramatic action (platform, chamber, recess) allowed for alternation between open scenes involving many people and interior scenes with only a few people. The encoding of stage loci is one case in which performance imposes its own constraints upon the text. Witness the role played in romantic theatre by the stage locus and its multiple possibilities: vertical arrangements, open scenes, horizons and backgrounds, multiple furniture pieces, quick changes, painted decor, and the advent of the stage designer (such as the famous Ciceri) – all of which had an effect on the text in its role as creator of space.

d/ The stage locus always represents something. Spectators have come to believe that the stage locus reproduces a real location. This idea – that the stage locus represents a 'real,' concrete space with its own limits, surface, depth, and objects, a fragment of the world suddenly and integrally transported onto the stage – is relatively recent in theatre and is encountered only in the West, or more precisely in bourgeois Western culture (see chapter IV, section 7 'Theatrical Architecture and Space'). However, the spatial structures reproduced in the theatre define not so much a concrete world, but rather the image people have of spatial relationships and the conflicts underlying those relationships in the society in which they live.

Thus the stage symbolically represents sociocultural spaces: space divided into 'mansions' in mystery plays of the Middle Ages symbolizes hierarchical yet horizontal spatial divisions – not feudal society but rather the image people have of that society. In one way, theatrical space is the place of history.

e/ The stage locus is independent of any mimesis of a concrete space that reproduces, whether transposed or not, symbolically or realistically, a particular aspect of our real universe; stage space is an area of dramatic action (or a locus for ceremony), it is a place where something happens that does not refer to some elsewhere. That something that happens defines the stage space in question according to the physical relationships between actors and the deployment of physical activities – seduction, dance, battle.

Whatever the mode of performance, these last two characteristics are simultaneously present in any act of performance; stage locus is always both an area of dramatic action and a locus where, in transposed form, the concrete conditions of human lives are represented.

2. Towards a Semiology of Theatrical Space

2.1. Space and the Social Sciences

The vocabulary of space fills all the metalanguage of the sciences; the mathematicization of the social sciences has been accomplished with the aid of spatialized terms and procedures. We find graphics (coordinates) and sets (topological spaces) in historical metalanguage, as we do in anthropological, sociological and economic metalanguage. This spatialization of language in the social sciences allows both for richer analyses of theatre in relation with the totality of human activities (in particular anthropology and history), and for an extension of the field of theatrical activity itself, since it is by nature spatial. All metaphors that underline the spatial nature of human activity can fruitfully be applied in the area of theatre. Broadly speaking, we can say that to spatialize the world is not only to make it comprehensible, but also to render it 'theatricalizable.'

These relationships are particularly close with two sciences: linguistics – because the theatrical text, like any other text, is a linguistic object – and psychoanalysis – because theatre is not only an artistic (literary) object (and thus the legitimate object of an interpretive reading) but also a unique psychological (imaginary) activity.

2.1.1. Space and Linguistics
One of the basic oppositions in linguistics involves the syntagmatic and paradigmatic axes. The syntagmatic axis indicates the linear succession of discourse (the horizontal axis); at every point along this discourse there is grafted a paradigmatic axis (the vertical axis) that indicates possible substitutions.[4] We find, in fact, that this opposition is particularly relevant in the area of theatre, which is characterized by the richness and complexity of the operations of its paradigmatic axis. We mention this only to remind the reader of all the work done in modern linguistics to spatialize grammatical relations. Likewise, we note Chomsky's metalinguistic metaphor for grammar: *deep structure/surface structure* is a spatial metaphor indicating a vertical dimension.

2.1.2. Space and Psychoanalysis

Freud's first task was to substitute, for the classic idea of the soul (a substance without extension, the old Cartesian idea), the concept of a *psyche* that functions like an 'apparatus' and therefore according to the categories of extension. A famous note by Freud reads: 'The *psyche* is extension. It doesn't know it.' Freud, and after him Lacan, have both given a whole series of spatial formalizations to the psyche. In particular, the *first topography* divides the ego into zones (conscious, unconscious, preconscious). Pontalis refers to this in *Clefs pour la psychanalyse*, using a pleasing metaphor, 'the geographical aspects of conflict.' Of course, Pontalis himself also warns against envisioning those localizations in too 'realistic' a way. In the second topography Freud refers less to localizations and more to instances, the *ego*, the *id*, and the *superego* being instead anthropomorphic characters of a kind. However, we should not forget that localizing remains a practice, because each of the above instances has its own field of action, its own space. A kind of layering or stratification marks the relationship between these instances. The topological nature of the Lacanian metaphors – the Moebius loop, the overturned bouquet – is extraordinarily obvious. We will see how these spatial structures can shed light on theatrical activity (text and performance).

2.1.3. Space and Literature

For several years the idea that literature is not only linked to time (duration) but that it also demonstrates important connections with space has been an important aspect of criticism. Blanchot devotes an influential essay to the subject (*Espace littéraire*). Genette, in a few decisive pages ('La Littérature et l'espace,' in Genette 1969) summarizes the various relationships involved in the space/literature question. He writes: 'Literature, among its various "subjects," speaks of space and describe locations, habitats, or "landscapes," but above all, there is an active rather than passive, signifying rather than signified literary spatiality that is proper to literature, specific to literature, a representing and non-represented spatiality' (Genette 1969, 43). What constitutes this spatiality? First there is the spatiality not only of language itself, but also of visual resources such as graphic markings and page layouts,[5] and above all the resources offered by meaning and its polysemic multiplicity,

with the semantic space between the apparent signified and the real signified abolishing the linearity of discourse. It is precisely this space and nothing else that we identify by a word that bears a felicitous ambiguity. The word is *figure*: a figure is at the same time the form that space takes and the form that language assigns itself; it is the symbol of the spatiality of literary language in relation to meaning (Genette 1969, 47).

The two basic figures of literary language, and more specifically of poetic language, are metaphor and metonymy, and both refer to an activity that takes place within a space. Metaphor is a phenomenon of condensation (of two referents or two images), and metonymy is a displacement. Note that these are the two fundamental movements in the activity of dreaming, as described by Freud and as theorized by Lacan with express reference to a relationship between dreams and linguistics. We will see how the role of space in the area of theatre is also the activity of these two fundamental figures, with dramatic space (textual-stage) appearing to be a metonymy for a certain number of non-theatrical realities and a metaphor for other textual and non-textual elements that may or may not be part of the sphere of theatre.

2.2. The Spatial Sign in Theatre

If we analyse the spatial sign not as textual sign, but as a performance sign, we are led to make certain observations:

2.2.1. Definitions of the Iconic Sign
The stage sign (stage space as the totality of spatialized signs) is by nature non-arbitrary. It is iconic; it maintains a relation of similarity with what it is supposed to represent. For Peirce, an icon 'may represent its object mainly by its *similarity*' or 'by virtue of characters of its own.'[6] For Morris, 'a sign is iconic if it *possesses some of the properties of the represented object.*' This definition is not without its difficulties, as Morris himself admits when he adds, 'An iconic sign is a sign that is similar in certain aspects to the thing it denotes. Therefore iconicity is a question of degree.'[7] Of course, we quickly realize that there are fundamental differences between the portrait of a human being and that human being in the very matter of which they are constituted, but there are also certain similarities that are difficult to place and clarify. Umberto Eco, who asks pertinent questions about the concept of *iconicity*, points out that it can be assigned meaning only through the process of perception, and only by using the notion of code. He concludes that: '(1) iconic signs do not possess the properties of the represented object; (2) they reproduce some conditions of perception common to both the iconic sign and the represented object, accord-

ing to normal perceptual codes' (Eco 1972, 176). He adds, even more precisely, 'Iconic signs reproduce certain conditions of perception of the object, but only after having selected those conditions according to recognition codes and having noted them according to graphic conventions' (ibid., 178).

2.2.2. The Twofold Status of the Stage Sign

We note that these definitions can be applied to stage space signs only if they are adapted somewhat. First, we are dealing not with graphic conventions but with other types of encoded conventions. Second, unlike painting and cinema, stage signs do not need material support such as canvas or film; their material support is the object itself, the space itself. The theatrical object is an object in the world; in theory it is identical (or functionally similar) to the object belonging to the non-theatrical real of which it is the icon,[8] and it is situated in a concrete space, that of the stage. If it is true that every iconic sign is non-arbitrary but motivated, the stage sign is doubly motivated because it is both a mimesis of something (the icon of a spatialized element) and an element within an autonomous, concrete reality.

From the above we can say that, in the activity of staging a theatre piece, a subtle play between those two aspects is set in motion with an emphasis, depending on staging and performance, on either the construction of an autonomous (non-iconic) ensemble of signs or the semblative reproduction of elements of the world. The field of performance covers everything from naturalism to abstraction without losing iconicity or even reducing it. If iconicity were lacking, that which is unique to the way theatre works would be prevented from functioning. After all, theatre is the performance of a mode of activity (however aberrant that activity might appear) that the spectator recognizes, or in which he or she recognizes certain elements. Thus stage space is both the icon of a given social or sociocultural space and a set of signs that are aesthetically constructed in the manner of an abstract painting.

2.2.3. A Double Referent

The stage sign, as we have seen earlier (see chapter I, section 2.5. 'Remarks on the Theatrical Sign'), functions in an extremely complex way. As is the case for all signs, it has a signifier S' and a signified s'. It brings together (as a set of phonic signs) the text T and its signified s'. It has a double referent: the referent R of the text (in *Phèdre*, the referential universe is Athens, Crete, etc.), and the referent R' (the stage, the referential universe constructed in the dramatic setting). If we start with the text, we can say that the text has constructed its own referent upon the stage, and the stage space presents the text's referential space. The stage sign has the paradoxical twofold status of signifier and referent.[9]

2.2.4. Functions of the Stage Sign

If we start with performance P, we can say that the stage sign S'/s' has as referents R (the referent of the text) and R' (its own referent). In other words the spatialized stage universe R' mediates between the (real) referent R of the text and the referent r of the instance of performance. Thus we see the historical (*ideological*) function of theatre confirmed. In Racine's *Phèdre*, the text refers us to a historical referent from antiquity (which is also, to a certain extent, contemporary). At the time of Racine, performances indisputably referred to the historical referent Louis XIV. Performance mediates between two different historical referents to which, in another era such as ours, a third is added, that of today's performance. The stage space that is represented brings together several referential fields between which it sets up a whole series of complex mediations.

This produces a curious inversion of the sign triad: it is as if the double referent (text and performance) presupposes a system involving the signs S^1 (the stage system) and conveys its signified s' $(R + R' \rightarrow S' \rightarrow s')$. The spatialized stage universe *is constructed in order to be a sign.*

2.2.5. A Spatialized Universe

Corollary: theatre constructs a space that is not only structured, but in which structures become signifying – a spatialized universe in which chance becomes intelligible.

In *Writing and Difference* (1978), Derrida defines theatre as 'an anarchy that organizes itself,' and if we accept that definition we will note that the activity of space takes on a considerable part of that organization. If theatre, as we have seen, constructs its own spatial referent, the activity of construction causes (referential) space to change from a set of unordered signs that cannot immediately be grasped intellectually, into a system of organized, intelligible signs. Theatricality constructs a signifying totality out of what, in the world,[10] is in-significance. This reversible signification, so to speak, is perhaps the principal task of theatre. The networks of signification that are established within the stage space and are read and ordered by the spectator, revert on the reading of the external world and make it understandable. As we shall soon see, the didactic value of theatre has to do with the creation of an ordered space within which the spectator can observe and experience the hidden laws of a universe normally experienced as chaotic. The articulation of Brechtian didacticism with a type of semiology of structure, so clearly observable in his work, undoubtedly hinges on the above.

The task of the semiologist in the area of theatre is to find, within the text, the spatialized or spatializable elements that will provide a mediation between text and performance. To affirm the relationship between textual structures and spatio-temporal structures represents a postulate that can scarcely be justified theoretically, but which must be our starting point, provided we are willing eventually to construct (or analyse) 'non-Euclidian' performances, performances that completely subvert or reverse textual structures. If textual structures are to be subverted, there is all the more reason why they must be the starting point.

Thus we have to find the spatialized-spatializable elements in the theatrical text: semio-lexical fields, binary paradigms, syntactic structures (actantial models), textual rhetorical elements.[11]

3. Theatrical Space and How to Approach It

Theatrical space is an autonomously constructed, complex reality and a mime (icon) both of non-theatrical realities and of a theatrical (literary) text; theatrical space is also an object of perception for the audience. It can be approached from three points of departure:

a/ *The text*: We prefer this approach because the object of our study is precisely the theatrical text. We will therefore first see how theatrical space is constructed *starting from* or *with the help of* the theatrical text.

b/ *The stage*: Here we will examine the construction of theatrical space, starting from a number of performance codes and using a stage locus whose concrete determinations pre-exist the specific, given instance of theatre.

c/ *The audience*: We begin here with the spectator's perception of stage space, and the psychological functioning of his or her relations with that 'special zone' of the world we know the stage to be.

3.1. Space and Text

Once we accept the fundamental idea that theatrical space is always in a performance relation with something else, that it is the icon of something, we must ask what it is the icon of. Theatrical space can have an iconic relation with: (a) the historical universe of which it is part and which, in a more or less mediated way, it represents; (b) psychological realities in the sense that stage space can represent the different instances of the *ego* (see section 2.1.2. 'Space and Psychoanalysis'); (c) the literary text. In all three cases, stage space maintains a relationship with its text-support, but in the first two cases the text appears to be the element that allows for mediation between the stage space and the sociocultural universe of which it appears to be the image. We see this in Greek tragedy: if we analyse the direct relationship that the stage materiality of Greek theatre maintains with the Greek city, we see that the text exists also in order to speak that relation. For example, the textual functioning of the chorus establishes a link between its stage space and its relation with Athenian democracy. Likewise, textual analyses allow us to see how a particular split of space can correspond to a split of the ego in a Claudel or Maeterlinck text. The text here is mediation, but it can also be the starting point that then represents the key element of which stage space is strictly speaking the icon (see section 3.4. 'Stage Space as Icon of the Text').

3.2. Text, Space, and Society

It is commonplace to demonstrate how spatial relations among characters (for example the background position of the confidants in classical theatre) correspond to a material hierarchicization, how the classical 'vestibule' – that simultaneously closed and open space, socially protected and undifferentiated – corresponds to the sociopolitical workings of the court, and how the bourgeois salon, shut off, isolated from nature, with a strict code governing access, is the mime of the social relationships among the upper bourgeoisie. The mimetic possibilities and the semiological nature (open, closed, etc.) of stage space are both at play here. In other words, the space in bourgeois drama or naturalistic theatre is not only an imitation of a concrete sociological location, but also a topological transposition of important characteristics of social space inhabited by a particular social class. For example, the country setting of act 3 of *La dame aux camélias* by Alexandre Dumas fils demonstrates a strange split *vis-à-vis* nature: the salon veranda, from which the garden can be seen only through the windows, represents a perverted relationship with nature that might be experienced by a nineteenth-century courtesan. A considerable creative effort goes into connecting important categories of stage space with categories of the spectator's perception of social space.

There is no need to point out that things become complicated because of the fact that the director is required to spatialize not so much the social space of the age or historical moment when the text was written, but rather his own social space and that of his spectators. Once again, the text functions as a mediate element.

3.3. Space and Psychological Elements

Stage space can also appear as a vast psychological field in which psychological forces of the self confront each other. The stage is then comparable to a closed field in which elements of the divided, split self confront each other. The second topic on the self could be considered as a type of model that allows us to read stage space as the locus of internal conflicts whose instances (*ego*, *superego*, and *id*) include the principal characters. The stage then would be that Freudian 'other stage'; it would be pointless to say that we cannot read pre-Freudian texts in that way, because those 'instances,' although named and described by Freud, serve as operative tools that allow us to read conflicts of the psyche. What is important is not that Racine wrote before Freud, but rather that we read Racine *after* Freud. Nonetheless this mode of reading stage space is particularly interesting when applied to authors such as Maeterlinck or Claudel who are more or less contemporaries of Freud. Claudel himself asserts, with reference to *L'échange*, that the four characters are four parts of his own self.[12] As for Maeterlinck, if we were to choose a psychoanalytical reading of his textual space, it would probably be more fruitful to place the spectator in the position of psychoanalyst: the spectator would discover, beyond a reconstructed image of the psyche, a series of related phantasms (analogous to a series of dreams) that the spectator-reader would have to decipher. Here again we can say that although the text is not the origin of spatial representation (whose *origin* should be sought in a certain spatial nature of the psyche, in a topography of the mind, or in already spatialized phantasms), it functions as mediation: it is in the recurrence of certain spatial images, in the permanence of elements from the didascalia or the dialogue that we can find the spatialization elements for an eventual performance. In this case there is also a triangular reading that moves from structures of the mind to textual structures and, conversely, from both of these to the materials of stage space.[13]

3.4. Stage Space as Icon of the Text

In a general way, we must bear in mind the status of the text within performance. First, the text (dialogue) figures in performance as a linguistic sign system whose substance is phonic: the text of the dialogue is understood as an instance of speech (addressed to a twofold receiver) and at the same time as a poem (poetic object). But performance is also the plastic and dynamic visual image of textual networks – an aspect that, although less obvious than another aspect, is no less important. We will set aside the (already addressed) problem of the visual translation of stage directions, both when they appear as such, and when they are deduced from dialogue. It is clear that the text suggests (if indeed it does not impose) a certain stage locus with concrete determinations and co-ordinates, but we also know how easy it is to disregard those indications at the moment of staging, how easy it is to subvert them, or ignore them completely. (Although Hugo included a bewildering mass of stage directions for *Ruy Blas*, he asserted at the same time that for the play to be staged, a table and some chairs would be sufficient.) The relationship of performance to textual structures is even more restricting, although less obvious.

3.4.1. Spatiality and Totality of the Text
Beyond the spatiality prescribed in the didascalia and implicit in the dialogue (expressly denoted spatiality), spatiality can be part of the code of objects in an unexpected way. The director who wishes to use the objects that Racine calls for to furnish the space in his tragedies cannot really do so because the text specifies very few objects (or even items of clothing). Once a director has taken into account 'Que ces vains ornements, que ces voiles me pèsent!' (How these empty ornaments, these veils, weigh down upon me) and the walls and vaults mentioned in the text of *Phèdre*, there are no more details. The list of terms that refer to a concrete object in the world is very short. For example, in the first act of *Andromaque*, almost all of the terms indicating objects have to do with parts of the body: *mouth, heart, hands, eyes, tears*. Thus in Racine's semio-lexical field for objects we find a problematics of the body seen in terms of its different parts, a dispersed body; that problematics can serve as a point of departure for the setting into space of a given work.

3.4.2. Space and Textual Paradigm
Theatrical space at the level of the text can be defined according to a certain number of lexical determinations. What concrete steps must we take in order to try to determine the semio-lexical field or fields of space in a given text?

The first step is to take note of everything that might have a role in the identification of locality – place names (common nouns, geographical names) as well as lexical items indicative of spatial disposition. Everything that might be considered part of the spatial lexicon should be noted: not just *Spain*, but also *Paris, the ramparts, the room, the palace, the street, the countryside, the west, the roof, below, hell, heaven.* The main thing is that the initial inventory should not be drawn up according to any differentiating principle.

a/ There should be no distinction between semantic fields or usage.

b/ There should be no distinction between didascalia and dialogue (although that distinction will have to be made at a later stage); that is, the entire textual surface should be taken into account.

c/ There should be no distinction between what is or might be a stage element and what is or might be off-stage. For example, in *Andromaque,* what concerns Troy and the Trojan universe must be taken into account just as much as what is relevant strictly to the stage locus, namely Epirus; if we set aside all the off-stage factors, we would make it impossible to lend (spatial, geographical) reality to the Troy-Greece conflict and to the opposition between a Trojan universe and a Greek universe.

The second inventory is not just lexical but rather what we might term semantico-syntactic: it consists of listing all locality determinants (what traditional grammar calls 'locatives'). Everything, absolutely everything, must be taken into account: the above-mentioned locatives, in which the noun belongs to spatial semantics, as well as any others (spatial pronouns and adverbs have a role, along with what they represent). We must also take into account phrases such as *in the palace* and *in her or his bed,* as well as *in his or her heart,* since affective localization is an important inclusion; the 'shifters' such as *there, from* or *in there, above* must also be noted, along with their substitutes.

Since theatrical space is not a void, a third inventory must be added: the list of objects – everything that might be included in the broadest sense of the word object. We can see how parts of the body of a given character can be counted as objects (see section 8 'The Theatrical Object').

These three lists can be considered the raw material that will then allow us to construct one or more space paradigms for the text under consider- · ation. Thus in *Lorenzaccio* we have the Florentine paradigm, in Racine's *Phèdre* the edge-shore paradigm.

3.4.3. Space and Syntactic Structures

a/ Because the actantial model is an 'extrapolation from syntactic structure' (Greimas), syntactic structure can be made up of a type of network of forces, a chess game; we can spatialize the structures just as a chess board spatializes the relationship of forces. Then we can demonstrate on stage how the actantial pawns evolve. This is possible primarily because what is active in a dramatic text is the functioning not of one actantial model, but rather of a multiplicity of actantial models, whose polyvalence and simultaneity in space permit the enactment or presence of a given moment. Dramatic conflict then might be spatialized not only according to the model of a single game of chess, but rather according to several games of chess played simultaneously. For example the polyvalence of Elizabethan space makes it possible for Shakespeare to advance many threads of plot and simultaneous actions representing a multiplicity of actantial models (as we see in *King Lear* with the actants Regan-Goneril, Cordelia, Edmund, Edgar). Likewise we might understand *Phèdre* in terms of a reinvestment of all of its space by the off-stage actant Thésée.

b/ All narrative syntax can be understood in terms of the investment or disinvestment of a given space by the principal character or characters. We can understand *Tartuffe* in terms of the investment and ultimate disinvestment of the Orgon-space (house, family) by the hero Tartuffe. The story of *Hamlet* can be understood as representing the simultaneously effective and destructive efforts of the subject-character to recover his own space in its totality. In a way, the structure of almost all dramatic stories can be read as a conflict between spaces or as conquest or abandonment of a space.

c/ The main feature of what we might call theatrical poetics concerns the definition of the poetic function according to Jakobson – that is, the folding of syntagma over paradigm (Jakobson 1963, 220). The simultaneity of space allows for the presence of substitutive elements side by side, whereas narrative syntagmatics will space out the elements of the paradigmatic set that had been grouped together in a single location. Thus the two members of the fraternal paradigm 'César de Bazan' find themselves together in the first act of *Ruy Blas*; later the presence of one will automatically exclude the other. Not only is the paradigm projected on the syntagma, as if everything seen to be symbiotic within the stage space were projected upon the 'axis of combination,' but also a kind of reversion allows for a regrouping, in the form of a paradigmatic set, of all that the story had dispersed. Thus the final scenes of classical plays bring together the dispersed elements. From another perspective, in the last scene of *Lorenzaccio* the Florence spatial paradigm is brought together and grouped around the enthroning of Côme de Médicis. The Borgia paradigm, projected all through the action of the narrative syntagmatics of *Lucrèce Borgia* (particularly in act 3, scene 1) is centred again in the final scenes. This produces a complex interplay that is made possible by the simultaneous nature of space.

The paradigm-syntagma opposition is not the only phenomenon that functions in a unique way with regard to theatrical space. The *synchrony-diachrony* opposition can also be noted. Thus, the phenomenon of simultaneity that allows a multiplicity of Elizabethan loci gives rise to a whole historical interplay. The division of space allows a demonstration of the multiplicity of historical forces at play. For example, Gloucester's 'suicide' at the cliffs of Dover coincides with Lear's rebirth in the arms of Cordelia. Also, the multiple nature of the Florence-space in *Lorenzaccio* makes it possible to stretch the limits of time (see chapter V). In Salacrou's *L'inconnue d'Arras*, the polyvalence of space allows the author to evoke the hero Ulysses' entire past simultaneously. Even in classical tragedy an evocation, through discourse, of off-stage elements allowed authors to extend tragic temporality: all of Roman and Oriental history, the death of Vespasian and the sack of Jerusalem are evoked for the spectator by poetic spatial discourse in Racine's *Bérénice*.

3.4.4. Space and Figures

We see, therefore, that stage space can be the transposition of elements of textual poetics. The entire activity of staging a play consists in finding spatial equivalents for the great rhetorical figures we know, first of all, metaphor and metonymy. For example, the vast expanse of tent canvas delineating the stage space in Giorgio Strehler's production of *King Lear* was an image for the theatre-metaphor that runs through the dialogue between Lear and his Fool: *le gran teatro del mundo* is a circus that suddenly rends the (heart-rending) pain of the King bearing his child in his arms. The concrete poetics of space plays a part in the transposition of textual rhetoric, unless (and this can happen) it represents its antiphrase. As for the way metonymy works here, it is truly a law of staging a play: the waxed parquet upon which the characters in Vitez's *Phèdre* slide is the metonymic image of the closed-in nature of the court and the poetics of . Versailles. In particular, nothing about the way objects work can be understood unless they are seen as the concrete figuration of the poetic workings of the text. Thus in Hugo's *Lucrèce Borgia*, the woman-trap, the girl-poison, the Princess Negroni (with her meaningful name) can appear to be what she indeed is – a metonymy for the Borgias. Stage space can be an image for the text's metonymic and metaphorical networks. Recall J. Lotman's observation: 'The structure of the space of the text becomes a model for the structure of the space of the universe.' We can in turn observe that theatrical activity can renew that proposition, creating a stage space shaped by textual space.

3.5. Space and Poetics: Consequences

It is clear that, among all possible projections, among all applications (to use a mathematical term) of the textual object within stage space, there are substitutive crossovers. In other words, by virtue of the multiplicity of its concrete networks, stage space can simultaneously convey the image of a metaphorical network, a semantic field, and an actantial model: in *Phè-dre's* space, we can show the interplay of the separate parts of the body and actantial functioning at the same time. Likewise, once stage space can be simultaneously the figure of a given text, of a sociocultural or sociopolitical network, or of a topography of the mind, we can be sure that there are substitutive crossovers between these different shaping structures. Once stage space can be the image (in the mathematical sense of the term) of these different sets, we can be sure that stage space indeed establishes a relationship between those models. From that it follows that concrete stage space appears as a mediation between different ways of reading the text; moreover stage space (pertaining to performance) allows us to read both the poetics of the text and the relation of that poetics to history at the same time. Since stage space has become the locus of combination for networks, the spectator's reading of it is turned back upon the text. Reading the textual space of a dramatic text is decisively influenced by the stage space of performance.

Between these various analyses, there are substitutive crossovers, vertical combinations. Theatrical space appears to be a symbolic structure to the extent that the functioning of those substitutive crossovers is nothing less than symbolism at work. In this sense, stage space is the point of conjunction of the symbolic and the imaginary, of the symbolism that everyone shares and the imaginary of each individual. The active role of the spectator in the theatre is nowhere more obvious than it is in connection with space – space invested with the phantasms of each of us but necessarily reconstructed. The simultaneous presence of different networks can bring conflicts to the fore, just as it can cast light on the theory of theatre. Brechtian distancing (*Verfremdung*, a spatial metaphor) becomes clear at the level of space: it can appear as the simultaneous functioning of two spatial networks in a dialectical relationship. The stage space before us is simultaneously presented as an elsewhere (made distant or foreign). Staging a play involves choosing between the different spatial networks, or keeping them together in a relationship of conflict: the text and the staging clarify each other when this point of view is chosen.

Let us return to the example of *Phèdre*: we can spatialize *Phèdre* in terms of conflict between several spaces, in terms of the problematics of the body divided, or in terms of various other 'matrices' of spatialization. The choice depends on the relation, at the time of performance, between the staging of the play and the play's contemporary referent and with the code currently in force. It becomes uniquely interesting for us to make note of the choice made by the director among the various matrices of spatialization in the text.

4. The Stage and Its Point of Departure

4.1. History and Codes

The theatrical point of departure is always sociohistorical. We will not emphasize here elements that are just as important as spatialization to the very origins of theatre, of rite, or of the cultural element. Perhaps the circular structure of Greek theatre is not unrelated to its link to Dionysian dances, which, we can surmise, from the outset created a circular form, a circular movement. A study (not to be undertaken here) might be made of the spatial code of the stage and of 'stageography,' in which stage space appears as a doubly encoded space – encoded both by earlier structures from the history of theatre and by the historical determination of a given moment in time. For example, consider ceremony in France during the second half of the classical seventeenth century: there is a whole dialectical (and conflictual) play between the birth of the Italian style of theatre (with the distancing of an audience deemed nonetheless necessary) and the presence of courtiers seated on the stage.

4.2. The Concrete Space of the Stage

How is space constructed on the stage? It is not created solely in relation to the theatrical locus as it is culturally constructed. It constructs itself essentially through the physical movements and the *phonè* of the actors. This is the source of the principal questions asked of the actor: Where is your voice directed? From where do you speak? What spatial relations structure your body and your voice?

Obviously we cannot consider research into these questions to be independent from research whose starting point is textual. The two areas of research are linked: the shaping of space by physical movements and by *phonè* can be determined or informed by a reading of textual structure, but those physical movements can also have a history, a precedence against which textual structures (syntactic, for example) might be applied (or not). Physical, gestural activity (mime or other) can construct, finally, a space that develops in a parallel or indeed even opposite direction to that which might arise from the imaginary of the text. And that text could after all be a non-text, an exploded text, or a text that has been put into question *qua* text – texts that contemporary drama offers in abundance.

Even if, from the outset, what is constructed on a stage appears to be solely gestural and voiced elements that pre-exist textuality, we must nonetheless never preclude the phenomenon whereby the written text rejoins pre-existing oral elements; in other words, reverse textual activity begins only once the text has been constructed.

Here we should note the presence of a spatial element which, although it is not strictly theatrical, is in direct relation with the stage – the presence of an audience. The establishment of physical relationships between actors cannot be done without the intervention of the attending public. What is presented on stage is never merely a binary or triangular relation between actors; it is always a complex relationship in which the spectator plays a part. This brings us to the last constitutive axis of theatrical space: the audience.

5. Space and the Audience

Although it is not our topic here (see *Lire le théâtre II*, chapter II, section 7), it would be interesting to study the way theatrical space functions when the point of departure is the audience, since the audience is both physically and psychologically involved in theatrical space. We will limit ourselves to a few observations.

5.1. Space and Perception

The first problem is that we must resist the temptation to think of the perception of theatrical space as we would a painting. It is hardly possible (with some notable exceptions) to conduct an iconological study of stage space using the same methods as for a painting. That can only be considered in the sense of a space determined by the theatre (the proscenium stage). Indeed, even in that case, perception varies (and what is worse, it varies in a hierarchical way) according to the location of our seat in a proscenium theatre. The orchestra seats and the gallery (the gods) offer singularly different images of the same show: we have all made that cruel discovery.

As for the complexity of theatrical perception in its totality, a quote from Christian Metz concerning cinematographic images will give an idea. In *Language and Cinema* he classifies the problems inherent to the perception of the image in cinema according to five categories:

(1) visual and auditory perception itself (systems for constructing space, figures and backgrounds, etc.), to the extent that it already constitutes a threshold of intelligibility which is *acquired* and variable according to different cultures; (2) the recognition, identification and enumeration of visual or auditory subjects which appear on the screen, i.e. the capacity (which is cultural and acquired) to appropriately manipulate the material that the film presents; (3) the ensemble of symbolism and connotations of the diverse orders which are associated with objects or with relations between objects even outside of the film (in the culture), but within films as well; (4) the ensemble of principal narrative structures (in the sense of Claude Bremond) which are at present within a given civilization and which occur in all sorts of filmic or non-filmic narratives; finally – and only finally – (5) the ensemble of properly cinematic systems (i.e. proper to films alone and common to all films) which serve to organize into a special type of discourse the diverse elements presented to the viewer by means of the preceding four elements (Metz 1974, 33–4).

Even if we transform these systems proper to cinema into systems that are proper to the theatre, we cannot forget that in cinema the substance of expression, to use Hjelmslev's term, is homogeneous (an image on a negative); this is not the case in theatre, and that fact gives rise to an infinitely greater complexity.

There is an additional problem, specific to theatre, posed by the neutralization of information. The theatre, especially in the sphere of stage construction, and consequently of space, produces a certain amount of information that we can ignore, even though we perceive it easily. A classic example comes from opera, where we see an overweight singer but we do not have to pay attention to her monstrous proportions. When we attend a failed staging of a play we are deluged with parasitic signs – called 'noise' in communication theory. What functions parasitically in one kind of stage space might be precisely what is called for in another kind of stage space. Thus clown gesture is badly received on a prescenium stage, and conversely, a superabundance of objects seem to be parasitic or redundantly useless on a circular stage.[14]

5.2. The Audience and Theatricalization

Much research could be devoted to investigating how the spectator might become implicated in performance and even have an effect upon it. That would require a study of various forms of theatre to investigate the concrete relationship between stage space and spectators for a given type of performance.

A particular case is that of theatre-within-the-theatre, because it involves the audience's perception of a unique zone within stage space in which the story played out is in fact theatre in relation to everything else happening on stage. The theatre-within-the-theatre effect is not limited to Baroque drama; it can be found everywhere in various forms – in Shakespeare as well as in Brecht. It is as if one segment of the stage space were to say, 'I am theatrical space, I am not a world referent,' and further, to consider the other part of the stage and the people upon it to be its audience. A study of this triangular action of stage/audience/theatre-within-the-theatre would be very important.

5.3. Denial

Theatre-within-the-theatre can cast light on the mysterious phenomenon of denial in theatre and the possible reversal of that phenomenon (see chapter I, section 3.4.1. 'The Status of Dream'). This question of denial is important if we are to understand how theatre functions and its pedagogical and/or cathartic role. That is in fact what we attempted to demonstrate in chapter I when we emphasized the relation of theatre to dream.

Stage space exists, period! It exists, with all its content of concrete beings and objects of the world. Of course it exists, but it exists under the minus sign.[15] A negative number exists in the same way, but we cannot use it *to count*. On the other hand, in the loci of theatre-within-the-theatre, within this stage space that exists under the minus sign, we find something that says: '*I am theatre.*' There, denial is reversed, since it is in fact true that *we are in the theatre*. Thus the main phenomena involved in that reversal, the phenomena by which theatricality asserts itself, must be studied.

Consequences: we should be able to demonstrate the unreality of naturalistic theatre, a theatre in which there is no space proper to theatre, no sense of Brechtian *Verfremdung* as marker and focus of theatricality.[16]

6. Spatial Paradigms

We are reminded by J. Lotman that 'historical and national-linguistic models of space become the organizing basis for the construction of an "image of the world" – for an entire ideological model that is proper to a given type of culture' (Lotman 1973, 311). The spatial model is organized, and therefore articulated. Independently of Lotman's research we reached the same conclusion when we identified 'two dramatic spaces' ..., two zones of meaning, an *A* zone and a non-*A* zone, such that at any moment, non-*A* is defined by its relation with *A*. [There are] non-symmetrical spaces that do not function in a homologous manner' (Ubersfeld 1974, 408). To be a little more precise, we can identify two paradigmatic sets in any given dramatic text, sets that do not (in the mathematical sense) intersect. These sets can be called spaces not only because their elements are spatial (or can be made spatial) but also because the essence of dramatic action can be identified by observing changes in the relations between dramatic elements and the two sets. The action is the voyage of the elements of one space to another space. In Hugo's theatre it is as if, for example, the main characters were travelling from one space to another, thus determining a play's dramatic movement. J. Lotman asserts:

A border divides the text's space into two sub-spaces, which do not overlap. The main aspect of that border is that it is impenetrable. The way a text is divided by its border is one of that text's essential characteristics. There can be a division into 'those of the same group' versus foreigners, living versus dead, rich versus poor. What is important is something else: the border between the two must be impenetrable, and the internal structure of each sub-space different (Lotman 1973, 321).

Lotman's analysis seems correct, except on one point – the permeability of the border. If no movement between spaces is possible, there can be no story, and in theatre there can be no drama. While we acknowledge that some simple forms of story are constructed according to this impenetrability, and also that, particularly in short stories, the hero is not considered to belong to either of the two spaces (and that seems difficult), in theatre the border is crossed constantly.

6.1. The Content of Dramatic Spaces

These spaces (logical sets or subsets of binary functioning) are sign collections in which we can find all the signs of the text and the stage: characters, objects, props, various elements of the stage space. In this sense we cannot separate and contrast phenomena that are essentially relevant to dramatic space and phenomena that are essentially of the character. Indeed even temporal categories are part of dramatic space when we understand that term in its broadest sense.

6.1.1. A Disjunctive Functioning

Each of these signs functions in opposition to another sign in the same or another space. Take the example of the king: he is king within his own space and non-king in another space.[17] Thus Theseus, King of Athens, in Epirus is a persecuted and imprisoned non-king. To the binary functioning of the king sign (the king/non-king opposition within the same space) is added a binary functioning from space to space: thus king X is in opposition to the king of space Y, or king X is a non-king in space Y, or the royal space X' is dramatically opposed by a non-royal space X'' (these last two are obtained by dividing space X into two subspaces).

6.1.2. Semanticized Features

The above spaces are distinguished from each other and contrasted in terms of a certain number of distinctive features and spatial semes that are also binary and are limited in number: closed/open, high/low, circular/linear, depth/surface, continuous/broken. For each of these categories there are, beyond the indication of a geometric location, semanticized features which in fact can be extraordinarily variable according to cultures: thus the valorization of high, a sign of spiritual (and social) elevation, is linked to a culture and to an image of the heavens as source of value and authority. The functioning of space is always semanticized in a rather complex way, and the staging of a play has scenic equivalents of the textual semanticism. Thus one staging of *George Dandin* always placed the hero at the lowest level and arranged the titled characters in ascending order as if on a ladder; a rather simplistic but eloquent spatial figure.

6.1.3. Organized Sets

These features, which are at the same time geometric and semanticized, combine with each other to construct two facing organized sets that do not function symmetrically since one is privileged both textually and in terms of staging. Thus in Hugo the privileged stage space is a closed, constructed, solid, hierarchical, elitist space that is always clearly denoted (castle, palace, fortifying walls, great hall, etc.). In opposition to this privileged space, there is an unformed, open, indeterminate, sometimes broken space (streets, squares, ruined houses, etc.). Added to both spaces we find a whole series of related elements, objects or temporal determinations: night, moon, celebratory torches, the master's or the king's key or arms.[18] All these elements come together to provide a network of stable significations. Thus, in opposition to the uncertain, plural, ravaged world of 'the Spains' in Corneille's *Sertorius* there is the geometric, monolithic rigour of Sylla's Rome. In Shakespeare's *Henry IV*, *King Lear*, or *Macbeth*, the open and obscure lands where the future of royalty is decided are in opposition to the feudal forts. A major part of the analysis of space, for the critic as for the playwright or the director, consists in identifying those spaces that are in opposition to each other and the tight interplay of their binary networks of meaning. They can be identified:

1/ by establishing the spatial paradigm or paradigms of the text (see section 3.4. 'Stage Space as Icon of the Text');
2/ by drawing up a list (especially from the stage directions) of the major semic categories that determine stage space;
3/ by drawing up a list of characters and signifying objects, and organizing them according to opposing categories.

The purpose is to determine whether the textual space is organized, and to see how it is organized into oppositional spaces, either by splitting up the stage area or by creating an on-stage/off-stage opposition.

6.2. The Stage and the Off-stage

Binary opposition can be created between two sub-sets that are intended to be part of the totality of the staging. In other words, several dramatic spaces can function in the same stage locus. Such is the case, as we have just seen, with romantic drama, and also, for example, with Beaumarchais, or later with Chekhov. Or we might consider that the totality of the text is intended to be applied to the totality of the staging, as is the case with Racine and all of classical theatre, even though there is a whole other textual totality alongside whose referent is necessarily off-stage. Thus there are two layers to the text: one designed to be performed on stage, and another that merely refers to an imaginary off-stage. This is a decisively important distinction that may allow us to understand what we mean when we speak of unity of place in classical tragedy and that clarifies the dramatic workings in Racine: how an off-stage character enters the stage space (with the status of an exile) and how that intrusion sows disorder and disorganization among the order of the tragedy's space, independently of the character's qualities or virtues. We can construct a whole problematics of the textual off-stage (temporally and physically off-stage) whose metonymic role is implicated in the rhetoric of stage space. We see this in the case of Troy in *Andromaque*, Crete in *Phèdre*, and in the events of Claudius' reign in *Britannicus*.

6.3. Transformations

The construction of these sets and/or sub-sets implies that they can be transformed in a way that is governed by laws, and these possible transformations must be researched: the movement of an element from one set to another; the shattering of a set because of the invasion of a non-conforming element or a foreign body, or because of the removal of one of its elements, such as the death or expulsion of the disruptive element; the re-ordering of dramatic groupings into other configurations through the addition or loss of an element. A whole possible geometry of dramatic spaces can be created. One example in Genet's *The Balcony* might be Chantal's movement from the space of the balcony to the space of the rebels, with the resulting destruction of the latter.

7. Theatrical Architecture and Space

Perhaps we might hope to attain a typology of theatrical spaces, a typology that we could try to develop further:

a/ Spaces constructed with the spectator as starting point: These spaces depend on a geometric view of space, a 'geometrization' of the stage, even if that geometry is based on entirely different models (the perspective of proscenium theatre, classical theatre, theatre of antiquity, Elizabethan theatre). The important factor is the relationship between the various areas in which the play unfolds and the movement of characters implicated in those areas. Stage architecture is a determining factor for the way in which these spaces work for the spectator.

b/ Spaces constructed with the referent as starting point: The stage, necessarily closed upon three sides, is homogeneous (that is, we do not distinguish segments of the stage or places where action occurs, although they are by nature different) and space reproduces a referential locus (that has potential divisions) on the stage. Unlike the theatre of the Middle Ages (which is almost totally non-referential) bourgeois theatre after the early eighteenth century, naturalistic theatre, realistic and neo-realistic theatre, or Chekhov, all presuppose a purely referential space that is a copy of a real location or one that is supposed to be real. Space is seen and understood in relation not so much to the action, but rather to an autonomous stage reality, whose manner of functioning is essentially iconic, or in the extreme case, mimetic (see *Lire le théâtre II*, chapter I, section 2 'Forms of Theatrical Space').

c/ Space constructed *in relation to the actor*: This type of space is more difficult to identify, because it is relatively recent and it has an informal character; it is constructed in relation to the space the actor defines around himself or herself, in relation to the ways in which actors physically react to each other. Grotowski's contribution has been to rewrite classical texts (Calderón's *The Constant Prince*, for example) or to construct textual groups (*Apocalypsis cum figuris*) that allow for the creation of an informal space that is entirely constructed by the movements, gestures, and physical relationships between actors. One might say that while Genet, for example, needs a more 'geometric' space, Beckett can make do with an undefined space that is perpetually reshaped by the actors. Paradoxical as it might seem, Brechtian space is closer to this last than to anything else.

These distinctions should not be taken as absolute: they presuppose a whole possible interplay among different forms, as well as transitional forms such as *Le Mariage de Figaro*, a play that is halfway between stage constructions *a* and *b*. These two forms presuppose that staging a play can involve playing one form against another: for example, staging a classical play but transposing it to fit a spatial form for which it was never intended. In the nineteenth century *Phèdre* was staged with the referential space of a palace; now we prefer to use solution *c*: this was done, albeit in a different way, in the productions of *Phèdre* by Michel Hermon and Antoine Vitez (see chapter III, section 2.2. 'The Individual-Character').

8. The Theatrical Object

Theatrical space is not a void: it is filled by a series of concrete elements of variable relative importance. These are:

- the actors' bodies,
- the elements belonging to the decor,
- the properties.

8.1. How Objects Are Used

Object is a term covering many things. A character can be a speaker, but he can also be a performance object, similar to a piece of furniture. The mute, immobile presence of a human body can signify in the same way as any other object. A group of actors can constitute a decor. There might be almost no difference between an armed guard and a collection of arms when it comes to representing force or violence. It is difficult, therefore, to link our three categories of objects with three autonomous ways of functioning. A prop, an actor, or an element of the decor can demonstrate interchangeable functions. Anything that occupies space can act within that space, and there is movement between the three categories. However, the way objects are used and the relative frequency of these three orders of object characterize a type of theatre. There can be theatre in which the stage is overfull, or theatre in which the stage is an open emptiness. Theatre can use an object strictly as decoration, as an aesthetic object, or it can use an object for the most utilitarian of purposes. There can be theatre in which characters are the only stage objects. Finally, the staging of a play can always overturn the playwright's intended use of objects – fill a Racine tragedy with objects when it seems none are required, or perform one of Hugo's historical dramas, as he himself admitted was possible, with a table and four chairs.

8.2. How to Read Objects

This brings us to the second distinction we can make in connection with the theatrical object: an object can have a scriptural status or a stage existence. There are two levels of lexeme in the theatrical text; some refer us to a representable referent, and others lack that role, but the border between them is blurred. It is clear that the object *heart* cannot directly be represented, and that the 'shores of Crete' in *Phèdre* cannot be represented on stage. But what can we say about the 'borders of Trézène' where the action unfolds? One can show these borders or not. The whole possible interplay of on-stage and off-stage objects offers much scope both to the work of the director and to the imagination of the reader-spectator.

The way we read objects is not simple. How can we determine, at the textual level, what is an object or what can become an object?

a/ The first criterion is grammatical: what in a text is inanimate, is an object. (A character becomes a stage object only when transformed into something inanimate, with the features of the inanimate: non-speech and non-movement.)

b/ A second criterion belongs to content: anything that has the potential to be represented on stage is an object for the theatrical text in question. This is a definition with great latitude. We therefore define the theatrical object, as far as its textual status is concerned, as anything that is an inanimate nominal phrase and which has the potential to be represented upon the stage. Racine's texts are characterized by a remarkable lack of stage objects (see chapter IV, section 3.4.1. 'Spatiality and Totality of the Text'); in the first act of *Andromaque*, aside from parts of the body (*heart, eyes, tears*), we note *towers, ashes, city, countryside* (all of which can be represented not as objects, but as elements of the decor), and certain abstract (metonymic or metaphorical) items such as *fires* or *iron objects*. (We do not need to point out what immediate ideological conclusions can be drawn about a dramaturgy in which no one touches anything, as if the characters had no hands.) In Racine even the decor-object is distant, off-stage and only distant locations are described: the object, indeed the world, is resolutely absent. There is much we can learn from a simple lexical record of all those things that might be considered objects in a given theatrical text; it allows us to list: (a) the kinds of objects that are evoked, (b) the number of these objects, and (c) their on-stage or off-stage nature.

A certain way of occupying space, a certain kind of relation between characters and between them and the world will immediately be obvious. The activity of perceiving and interpreting objects is one of the primary tasks for any reader of the theatrical text.[19]

8.3. Towards a Textual Classification of the Object

We can undertake a typology of the object as it is found in a dramatic text:[20]

a/ When objects appear in the didascalia (or in the dialogue, in cases where they are lacking in the didascalia), the object can be utilitarian: if a duel is to be portrayed, two swords or two pistols are necessary (objects that might then be superseded by entirely different objects); if cooking is done, a stove will be necessary.

b/ The decor-object can be referential; being iconic and indexical, an object refers us to history or to painting (to the picturesque or to the real). All kinds of theatre use this type of object: romantic staging seeks historical accuracy, and an object must conform to the spectator's conventional idea of a given historical decor; the naturalistic object denotes a framework of everyday life.

c/ An object can be symbolic. Its function is then essentially rhetorical: it appears as the metonymy or metaphor of a particular order of reality, be it psychological or sociocultural. Thus in Hugo *the key* is a sexual metaphor and a metonymy of power (the man with the keys is the one with the power). In this case, the symbolic object (whether we are dealing with a cultural object or an object linked to imaginary relationships instituted by the author) is often placed in a signifying system which can be observed with interest throughout an author's entire dramatic output. Thus, in Maeterlinck we see the symbolism of the door, the river, the pond, the ocean, the tower, and the hair; the signifying system of the object in Hugo is a *combinatory* system.[21]

8.4. The Text-Performance Relation and the Object

The object functions in a complex and extremely rich way, and modern theatre tries to exploit all its possibilities.

If we set aside the strictly utilitarian aspect of the object, one which modern staging tends to downplay, we see that the role of the object is essentially twofold and the two aspects are usually combined:

a/ it is a *being-there*, a concrete presence;
b/ it is a *figure*, and it functions in a rhetorical way.

So it is that the actor's body and its various parts constitute a being-there that produces (gestures, acts, stimuli), rather than a signifying sign system. That which is obvious in the case of the actor's body can also apply to material objects: Barthes notes that in Adamov's *Ping-Pong* the slot machine signifies nothing (and it would be a mistake to see it as a symbol). Instead it produces (feelings, human relationships, events).

8.4.1. Towards a Rhetoric of the Theatrical Object

1 / Since the object is both iconic and indexical, its usual rhetorical role in theatre is as the metonymy of a referential reality, and theatre presents the image of that reality. In naturalist theatre or the contemporary *théâtre du quotidien* (kitchen-sink drama), we see objects functioning as the metonymy of the real setting within which the characters live: the reality effect of objects (their iconic nature) is in reality a rhetorical function which refers us to an external reality. Likewise in historical theatre the function of the object is to metonymically refer us to a historical period: a particular item of clothing or a particular weapon functions as the metonymy, or more precisely as the synecdoche (a part for the whole) of the fifteenth century, or of the French Regency. Likewise a given piece of petit-bourgeois furniture can be the metonymy of the entire setting within which petits-bourgeois characters live. The linking of realism and metonymy has long since been described by Jakobson.[22] All metonymic use of the object in theatre is concerned with theatre as story, novel, or image of life. There is no need to add that the staging of a play can emphasize or downplay whatever is included in the stage directions or the dialogue.

The object can also be the metonymy of a character or a sentiment. Romantic theatre frequently exploits this device, from Richelieu's litter in *Marion De Lorme* to the emotion associated with the bouquet of flowers in *Ruy Blas*. In the staging of a play, the director exploits these metonymic echoes even if they are not found within the text. One could also consider as metonymic the indexical role of objects that announce a coming event: a vial of poison, an axe, the red flag of the Commune at the end of Adamov's *Le Printemps '71*.

2 / Many objects have a metaphorical role in addition to their functional role. In particular there is a whole series of objects that figure in dreams, objects that without any doubt are sexual metaphors. A sword can have a metaphorical role even if it is necessary for a duel; a pitcher of water might be necessary to the action, but at the same time it can represent desire. Most objects whose utilitarian or metonymic functions are obvious undergo a metaphorical enhancement, a metaphorization. Thus the accumulation of objects from daily life in a naturalistic theatrical form appears also to be a metaphor for enslavement to the objects, of the weight of objects in daily life, just as in romantic theatre a historical object is at the same time a metaphor of the past as past, of the consignment of the past to the category of ruin. In this last

example we see how metaphorization occurs through a twofold displacement, a double metonymy or double synecdoche: historical object → the past; the past → ruin, death.

Thus we move from metaphor to symbol, especially when the metaphor in question is established on a culturally encoded relation: symbolism in theatre depends primarily upon the object.

8.4.2. The Object as Production

The object is a concrete presence – not so much the iconic figure of a particular aspect of the off-stage referent as the referent itself, not the image of a world, but rather a concrete world. Consider the actor's body and the sheer work it produces. It acts (it moves, dances, demonstrates); much of what makes up theatre is in this shown-acted aspect of the body, whether or not the theatrical text explicitly takes this into account. Likewise there is interplay with the object – the shown, exhibited, constructed or deconstructed object on stage, the object of ostentation, of play or production. The object in theatre is a ludic object. Not that it isn't at the same time the object of resemanticization that for us is one of the key processes of signification in theatre: to interact with an object, a weapon for example, can be productive of meaning.[23]

The object can be shown in its process of production-destruction. The object-product is never portrayed in the French classical period; there the object is functional, rarely rhetorical, never productive. We have to move to quite recent times to find the object in production, not only productive, but also produced. Until modern times (with some rare exceptions in Aristophanes and Shakespeare) objects are presented as being natural; no distinction is made between those that are taken from nature and those that are artefacts of culture (human production). We have to wait until Brecht, for example, before we see the object shifted from its primary use and pressed into other kinds of service, an industrial object shifted away from its work and truly subverted.

a/ The modern interplay with objects, both in the theatrical text and on stage produces human relationships (or more precisely, it makes them visible), such as the famous slot machine in Adamov's *Ping-Pong* mentioned above, a machine that conditions all the relations between the characters. We also saw this in the production of Franz-Xaver Kroetz's play *Travail à domicile* [*The Packaging of Seeds*] by J. Lassalle at the Théâtre de l'Est Parisien in 1976.

b/ This modern interplay with objects also produces meaning through the law of resemanticization. The object ceases to be a given and instead becomes the result of an operation; the fact that it appears as a product involves it in turn at the outset of a production of meaning (the production-product dialectic is operative here). The object becomes a figure for work and for the relationship of the characters with their work. Those on stage cease to receive the object passively, to treat it as part of the setting, the decor, to see it as a tool available to them; instead they act upon it, create it, transform it, destroy it. The entirety of these operations should be carefully analyzed. This can be seen, for example, in the use of *garbage* as an image for a world in which the proletariat retrieves what might still serve a purpose; it can be seen where the use of an object is changed (a *ladder* can become a *bridge*) or when objects from daily life are put to theatrical use.[24] This mobility of the object-sign thus becomes not only an index of the theatrical object's polysemy, but also a complex sign for a creativity of the characters in a play; the theatrical function of the object becomes the icon for the creativity. When we transform household utensils into costumes we are not only saying, 'We are in the theatre,' we are also saying, 'Theatre demonstrates a certain creative relation between people and things, a relation that is intimately linked to their circumstances and to their work.' What might be seen as just a simple theatrical technique is once more shown to be much more significant.[25]

V. Theatre and Time

1. Duration and Theatrical Time

The fundamental question posed by the theatrical text concerns the manner in which it is inscribed within time. We have seen that there are two spaces, an off-stage space and on-stage space; the mediated area between them is a zone in which signs are inverted, a zone which is the audience's area. Likewise the phenomenon of theatre demonstrates two distinct temporalities: the time it takes for a performance to be completed (one or two hours, or more in certain cases or certain cultures), and the time pertaining to the represented action. Clearly, *theatrical time* can be understood as the relationship between these two times, and this relationship depends not so much on the duration of the represented action and the performance time as it does on the mode of representation for a given play. Is it a (mimetic) reproduction of a real action? Is it a ceremony whose duration is significantly greater than the duration of the events it conveys or plays? Once again we find ourselves (as was the case for character and space) dealing with the idea that in theatre there are no autonomous techniques (except in the case of narrowly determined forms of theatrical performance). In other words, the solution that works for a particular theatrical form is not significant in and of itself; rather it brings into question the entire functioning of performance. There can be no one correct form for that temporal relation to take that is convincing or faithful to nature. All forms of temporal relation implicate the entire phenomenon of theatrical signification. This is what we seek to demonstrate here.

To the above we must add that time in the theatre is not easily grasped, either at the level of the text or at the level of performance. It is difficult at the level of the text because, as we shall see, the temporal signifiers are all indirect and vague. It is difficult at the level of performance because important elements such as rhythm, pauses, and articulations are infinitely harder to grasp than elements that can be spatialized. We face the problem common to all scientific investigation in the social sciences: it is easier to grasp the dimensions of space than it is to grasp the dimensions of time.

In any case, what is time in the theatre? Is it the universal time we measure with clocks? Is it the irreversible duration of history? Is it physiological or psychological duration, the period over which tissues age, or lived time, be it Bergsonian or Proustian? Is it the rhythm of human societies and the cycle of rites and ceremonies? The extreme difficulty involved in analysing theatrical time is related to the fact that these perceptions of time can be combined, so that temporality becomes more of a philosophical notion than a semiological one. Theatrical time is simultaneously the image of historical time, individual psychological time, and ceremonial recurrences. Time in Sophocles' *Oedipus Rex* can be analysed in terms of performances on known dates (the Athenian Dionysia), in terms of psychological time of revelation within a given destiny, or in terms of historical time of a particular king, his accession to the throne, and his fall. The difficulty in our analysis is to sort out this confusion, to isolate the various strands of the network, but also to grasp the various signifiers involved.

More precisely, the decisively important factor in the analysis of theatrical temporality is the study of what can be textually grasped, the articulations of the text. It is through textual articulations and the way they function that we can grasp theatrical time (at the level of both text and performance).

1.1. The Unity of Time

Let us return to the distinction between the two temporalities: the time taken for performance and the time pertaining to represented action. This distinction can cast light on the classical concept of performance. There are two opposing theses. According to the first, these durations are two sets that can never completely coincide, but the difference between them tends to become neutralized; a good play is one whose real-life duration is not out of proportion with the duration of the play's action perceived according to its historical duration in real time, a time that is measurable by clock and calendar. This well-known classical doctrine is so arbitrary in the eyes of so many, even its defenders, that it can only be defined by saying that a *day* (twenty-four hours) is seen as approximately equivalent to two hours of performance.

In fact, although because of the possibilities offered by special effects and the off-stage existence of the text, unity of location is more easily complied with; unity of time has always been a constraint, sometimes not too serious, but sometimes unbearable. This is not because it represents too short a duration (two days or a week would not help at all), but rather because it requires us to range clock time and/or historical time against psychological time, the lived time of performance. It requires us to construct a proportional relation between the two concepts of time, and therefore to see them as homogeneous.

At the same time there is a dubious relation established between theatrical time and historical time. We might think that measuring one against the other would amount to giving theatrical time the temporal objectivity of historical time. In fact the opposite happens, for reasons that are not foreign to the way theatrical denegation works: far from historicizing theatre, the unity of time theatricalizes history. Historical duration is separated from the objectivity of the world and its conflicts and is transposed to the domain of performance, although this is not accomplished without some difficulty. For example, in Racine history is perceived not only according to an off-stage perspective – that elsewhere of the Trojan War, of Mithridates' war, of Athalia's conquests – but also according to an outside-of-time perspective, a temporal elsewhere in which Agrippina poisoned Claudius, dispossessed Britannicus, in which Titus conquered Judea with Berenice. History is another temporal place; unity of time, which is an unavoidable brutal slicing up of historical time, deprives human relationships (sociohistorical relationships) of any development, of any unfolding process. Classical theatre becomes, through the action of unity of time, an instantaneous act that excludes the indefinite duration of conflicts as well as the recurrence and return of psychologically determining factors.

1.1.1. History and the Off-stage World

Unity of time, the confronting of real time with psychological time, takes the temporality that governs human relations and cuts it off at both ends. This is true whether we are dealing with the sociohistorical duration of lived, individual time, with the relation of humans with their past, or with the return of the past as something that had been suppressed. In classical theatre unity of time produces the phenomenon in which the full temporal weight of historical time becomes an off-stage reality. It is in the off-stage world, perceivable in the characters' speeches, that we can grasp the relation between the individual and history. This occurs in *Suréna*, with respect to the embassy where the Parthian general and the Armenian Princess, in silent agreement, seal both their absolute love and their political entente; the basic tragic reality is located in a psychological off-stage world that we can grasp as we hear their words. It then becomes necessary that this past be some specific person's past (in other words, as Althusser says, there must be a centralizing specular consciousness), rather than the collective past of the group. History's past, perceived according to an off-stage perspective, is no longer perceived in terms of a conflict unfolding before our eyes, but rather as a symbolic reference. Thus in *Andromaque* the Trojan war is a referential system characterized by its no longer being in question, but rather being there as a purely psychological trace of the historical event. The same can be said of the Judean war in *Bérénice*. The historical conflict is outside of history, that is to say, outside of unfolding history.

Unity of time presents history not as process, but as irreversible, unchangeable destiny. In a tragic text the historical solution is necessarily present from the beginning; it is never independent of the actions of humans. In Corneille's *Sertorius* the hero's freedom is always compromised by the fact – directly linked to the unity of time – that the tyrant Sylla is, at the moment the curtain rises, already out of power, even though the protagonists do not know that. In *Iphigénie* it is interesting to see how a future war (one the spectators already know about, including the outcome) is established as an inevitable event. The uncertainty characterizing the conflict, which is the basis of the dramatic action, cannot have a temporal dimension: Achilles is virtually already dead outside the gates of Troy. Another remarkable example: when Eurydice's final decision implicates Surena's life and saves it (the final scene), Surena is already dead. The tragic opening onto a freely undertaken act is always contained within something already done, already lived that destroys it. The rule of unity of time from classical dramatic art necessarily excludes the phenomenon of becoming.

1.1.2. A Ceremony outside Time

As far as the receiver-spectator is concerned, classical performance presupposes that it is impossible to exploit psychological time, because of the homogeneity of the spectator's lived time and the referential time of the represented story. Spectators can skip the job of going back and forth between their own time and the density of the psychic-historical duration that they are required to imagine. They are not obliged either to fill in temporal gaps in the theatrical text or to perceive the radical heterogeneity existing between their own lived time (outside of the action) and the historical processes presented to them. Unity of time obliges spectators to accept the 'Aristotelian sideration' (momentary blank, in the Brechtian sense of the term). History – which spectators are not obliged to reconstitute – at the same time appears as a stalled spectacle, forever stuck in the past in its immutability, created to be seen, not to be lived: history is a finished spectacle. Claudius is dead forever, poisoned by Agrippina, and that crime forever opens onto the parallel crime caused by the first, the fratricide of Nero. Likewise there is no differenece in character between the two orders of events; individual duration, the psychic past of the protagonists, is seen in the light of eternity. Classical performance is a ceremony that lacks temporal density.

There is thus a solid ideological network that combines the mode of historical reference in tragedy, the unity of time, the specular unity surrounding a given character, and the fatality (permanence) that determines actions and sentiments. It is no accident that Corneille, whose problems with unity of time are well known (see his three *Discours* on the dramatic poem), never succeeds in totally reconstructing this signifying network. The fascination of his theatre stems from that very conflict between the two views of time: one in which the creativity of the hero and of history call upon the spectator to construct the relation between referential time and theatrical time (as in the episode of the battle with the Moors in *Le Cid*), and the other classical view that nothing happens that has not already happened, that performance is like a reproduction of a past that is perpetually already there.

1.2. Temporal Discontinuity

Conversely, any textually inscribed distance between performed time and referential time indicates a passage: of sentiments, of events, of history. Any gap in time leads the spectator (and the reader) to reconstitute a temporal relation that is his or hers not to see, but rather to construct.

The story marches on, the kingdom has become larger or has come apart, the hero who was a child in the first act 'est barbon au dernier' [is an old greybeard by the last], to quote Boileau in his *Art poétique*, lived events are the object of a quest: at the same time those events are imagined to have an autonomous, off-stage, reference. Violating the unity of time requires spectators to set up a dialectic for all that is presented to them. They are required to reflect upon the interval. Each time the stage presents a leap in time, spectators experience the need to invent a process that will fill in the gaps. Likewise they are required to reflect upon the autonomous nature of theatrical time, because the time of performance appears not to be homogeneous to the time of referential history. Meyerhold wrote: 'Episodes allow theatre to do away with the slow rhythm imposed by the neo-classic unity of action and time.'

Thus any form of dramatic writing that involves the stretching of time goes against:

a/ the celebration of theatrical spectacle as a ceremony marked by the seal of temporal unity and as an imitation of a given action that itself is of an atemporal, ahistorical nature;
b/ the classical text understood as an unbroken unity, an uninterrupted discourse with no break in the temporal chain;
c/ the linear rationality of a story in which nothing new happens and in which any movement is no more than the repetition of the same story, or a simple rearrangement of the premises established at the outset of the dramatic narration.

It is precisely on this point that we find the opposition between so-called Baroque drama (Shakespeare, Calderón, etc.) and so-called classical drama. Shakespeare, taking history as process, chose temporal discontinuity, and this led to his rejection by the last diehards of classicism.

It should not be surprising that romantic dramatists caught in the inherent problems of writing history, tried to revive Shakespearean discontinuity, albeit timidly. The romantics indeed wanted to be free to fragment space, but did not want temporal fragmentation, because that entails ideological and technical consequences that they were not ready to accept: the bourgeoisie tried to demonstrate the historical continuity that linked it to the monarchy. The public was not ready to accept a dramatic art that featured temporal discontinuity. This is why romantic dramatists made such efforts to return to history without being totally unfaithful to the unity of time. Thus *Chatterton* strictly observes the unity of time, and melodrama, which does not observe unity of place, at least in the beginning, accepts the twenty-four-hour restriction.

Whenever history is presented in accordance with real time – as in Mérimée's *La Jacquerie* or Hugo's great historical dramas (*Hernani, Le roi s'amuse, Ruy Blas*) – there is an inevitable rupturing of time. We might reflect upon the meaning of Lenz's stretching of time and wonder if perhaps it represents a protest against passional determinism. Even in

Chekhov, unity of time is rejected to the extent that the erosion caused by the passage of time exposes contradictions and disrupts all comfortable compromises. Much of the novelty in Brecht's dramatic art concerns a temporal fragmentation that allows him to measure history's irreversible action in *Mother Courage* or *Saint Joan of the Stockyards.*

1.3. The Dialectic of Time

These differences in the ways performance can present history do not mean that theatrical texts are free of the dialectic between unity and discontinuity, between continuous progress and progress by leaps and bounds, between historical and ahistorical temporality. Even in classical performance, non-time presupposes an abolished time, another time, a reference time that, whether it is valorized or de-valorized, bears within it the catastrophe of which the play's here-and-now is no more than the final enactment. The victory over Troy is a final enactment whose consequences unfold throughout the entire text of *Andromaque. Phèdre* is the story of an aborted process of royal succession that has as corollary a two-fold return to the past: the resurrection of King Theseus, and the restoration of the Pallantides in the person of Aricia. Thus we cannot say that there is no history in Racine, even if history is there only in terms of a destructive past. The unity of time does not totally abolish historical reference, and it is always possible, when staging a play, to adopt an artifice that will emphasize the gap in time that unites and separates a Troy in ashes and a threatened Epirus ('What Troy has saved, Epirus will defend,' *Andromaque*, act 1, scene 2). Conversely, the historical discontinuity, that fractured time in the great Shakespearean historical plays does not prevent the reconstitution of dramatic unity in performance (for example, through the presence of the same actors with the same physiques and the same movements and gestures). This dramatic unity is already established in the text through the unity of discourse and of literary form.

1.4. Space-Time or Temporal Rhetoric

Many especially good examples show how the rhetoric of time functions. Even in classical performance, space and time each appear as a metaphor for the other. In Racine's *Bajazet*, distance in space is equivalent to distance in time. Everything that has to do with time can be portrayed figuratively by spatial elements. When unity of time is not particularly disrupted, there are some rather perverse ways to bring it into question.

In *Lorenzaccio* the central episode, the day of the murder is relatively centred in time, but a detailed study of the march of time in that play would
demonstrate that

- It is impossible to draw up a precise chronology of the play (we even
  note some flashbacks), and impossible to locate oneself within the cas-
  cade of temporal simultaneities and breaks.
- The fact that spatial disruption (each scene takes place in a different
  location) is linked with temporal disruption, indicates a gap in time in
  which the spectator-reader becomes lost. Here space and the dispersion of space truly appear to be the metaphorical signifiers of time and
  its dispersion.

We can easily see the ideological consequences of the above:

a/ The dispersion of the locus of the story means that the story takes
place not only at the royal seat, but in various places. The linking of
the city (seen as a place where there is an accumulation of sociological
loci) with history (seen as complex process, as multiple causality) indicates the rupture of theocentric and monarchical monologism.

b/ This also results from the effects of simultaneity, as we see not only in
Lorenzaccio, but especially in Elizabethan drama, where different parts
of the stage function simultaneously but independently of each other,
indicating the simultaneous presence of the action of different groups
or individuals.

c/ More precisely, this effect of simultaneous actions indicates the presence of several different time frames. In the dramatic action of *King
Lear* there is a concurrence of two time frames: the tragic time, which
is atemporal, involves the king's tragedy (Lear and his companions,
the Fool, Edgar and even Gloucester); the epic time of the action
involves Edmond and Cordelia who raise an army, prepare for battle,
etc. The co-existence of these two time systems indicates a co-existence
of two views of history and even a co-existence of two ideologies.

d/ Recurrences of the same loci can indicate a temporal recurrence; conversely differences between loci allow us to understand time as process. In *Waiting for Godot*, Beckett skillfully brings one and then the
other into play; nothing has changed from one day to the next in the
place of waiting except for the tree which suddenly is covered with
leaves, indicating at the same time something that is happening and
something that remains eternal – irreversibility and circularity.

These examples allow us to see that spatio-temporal rhetoric is the locus for the functioning of time, a determining element in a the meaning of a theatrical work (text and performance).

We also can see the problems that any semiology of the theatre faces in determining temporal elements: the signifier of time is space and the objects it contains. The concrete signifier of time is the totality of a given play's spatial signs.

2. Temporal Signifiers

The fundamental problem concerning time in the theatre is that time must be situated in relation to a here and now which is the here and now of performance and also the spectator's present time: theatre by its very nature denies the presence of both the past and the future. Theatrical writing is a writing in the present. Anything that is to become a sign of time is thus by nature understood in its relation to the present. The signifier of time in the theatre is marked by denial to the same degree as all the other signs of the theatre. We are not at the Sun King's court, even if that is what they are telling and showing us; it is not a spring morning, but rather a winter's night that awaits us when we leave the theatre. The problem with signifiers of time is that they designate a referent that is necessarily off-stage: the difficulty with time in the theatre is that it can be designated as referent but cannot be shown. Time is, by its very nature, outside mimesis: neither historical time nor lived duration can function as a referent constructed on the stage.

For the above reasons, it is more important in theatre than anywhere else to distinguish between text and performance.

a/ For spectators, performance is lived time, time whose duration depends strictly upon the sociocultural conditions in which performance takes place (the short sixty- to ninety-minute modern performances with no intermission, the successive days of performance of mystery plays, the tragedy competitions of antiquity, the long evenings of theatre in the nineteenth century, and the endless unfolding of theatrical festivals). In any case performance represents a rupture in the order of time, a time of festival of whatever kind, whether or not it is part of a ceremony. Performance arrests ordinary time, it is another time, be it a planned link in the chain of days (Athenian Dionysia or 'vendredi habillé' [formal Fridays] at the Paris Opera) or a sociocultural topsy turvy, carnivalesque time.

b/ The theatrical text indicates a reported time, a time that performance will show as a displacement of the here and now: therefore the time in a theatrical text refers us, not to the real time of performance (a time about which the text has little to say), but rather to an imaginary and syncopated time.[1] It is only through the mediation of performance signs that performed time can become duration, a feeling of time on the part of the spectators. This makes an explicit will to speak lived time all the more necessary on the part of the writer (Chekhov, Beckett, Maeterlinck).

c/ On the contrary, in many cases the text does not speak time, but works instead to abolish it – as if theatre were indeed something that does not function within time and performance were supposed to express not only another time, but indeed a non-time. Some dramatists evolve within this syncope of time, and their textual structures are required to show that everything has happened already throughout eternity and that the hero's task is to recover that already-done: elsewhere, with reference to Racine, we have called this the precession of the fated.[2] Time becomes the non-time of myth. Likely it is there, rather than in the use of legends (although the two features are inextricably linked), that we should look for the mythical aspects of Racine's tragedy.

d/ There is one last, constitutive difficulty (linked, as we have seen, to the question of the mimesis of time). Time is something not seen, but only heard spoken; it is something that if it is to be properly accounted for, requires the perpetual invention of visual signs.

2.1. Didascalic Signifiers

The didascalia (external or internal) can, throughout the action, indicate the passage of time and the progress of the action:

- a change of season or a change of time of day (from day to night and the inverse);
- a change in decor, marking a passage that can be denoted as both spatial and temporal since any change in decor, unless otherwise indicated, connotes a displacement in time.

2.2. Rhythms

The number and succession of the events of the fabula, the rhythm of the succession of textual units, the length of those units (above all the average length of sequences, of scenes), give a different feel to temporal duration. The return or the progress of various sequences indicates a progressive or a circular time.[3] But these details are relative: a large number of events presented within a short space of represented time can give the impression of an extremely long time or, on the contrary, of a temporary crowding of events. Other elements are necessary to create the rhythm of time.

2.3. Characters' Discourse

Characters' discourse includes signifiers of time.

a/ Discourse is filled with informing micro-sequences which signal the progress of the action, the march of time, the succession of events: 'To avoid her for six months, and then to see her in a flash' says Ruy Blas in act 3, scene 3 (indicating time that has passed since act 2). Likewise some micro-sequences inform us about *another time*, an off-stage time that is simultaneous or shifted; we see this in Cléone's interrupted recounting of the story of the marriage of Pyrrhus and Andromaque (act 5, scene 2).

b/ An analysis of the temporal functions of the text requires an exhaustive compilation of all the determinants of time (adjectives or adverbs, according to the old nomenclature), and all the temporal syntagmatic units, so as to note recurrences that indicate a particular way in which time functions. In Racine the (often-noted) recurrence of *pour la dernière fois* [for the last time], and also *mille fois, cent fois, encore un coup* [a thousand times, a hundred times, one more time] marks the repetitive nature of the passional situation. *Encore, jamais, toujours* [again, never, always] connote the irremediable and absolute. Likewise there is a lexical opposition between determinants that indicate urgency and those that indicate temporalization (of particular interest in *Bajazet*), where the urgency of the situation paradoxically engenders irresolution and an indefinite stretching out of time.

c/ These observations should not be separated from the analysis of verbal tenses, noting the presence of future or past tenses. The relative frequency of either in the necessarily present-tense system of the dramatic text indicates a precise relation to time. The future tense marks urgency, a push toward the future, or paradoxically it connotes the absence of any future – tragic (or comic) irony showing a future that will never be realized – or the psychology of uncertainty (in Adamov, for example).

2.4. Closure

We can also study the *temporal signifiers of the closure of action*, the terminal events – death, marriage, war, peace – as changes in the meaning of time. The theatrical system of time cannot be understood if we ignore the inventory of signs that connote deterioration or improvement, reintegration (restoration), or the arrival of a new order. We might undertake a whole other study of the lexical fields of final speeches. From a syntactic point of view, in the final speeches of characters, we would have to note changes in the temporal system, the use of the future tense, or alternatively, a return to the present tense. Here is a syntactic example – the frequent use of the imperative as a way to open onto another meaning for time: 'As for us, let us bless our happy adventure' cries Félix at the end of *Polyeucte*, an imperative that is almost required and which connotes the necessary leap to another time, a leap that is indeed an *action*, the final action. An essential example, found in comedy and in Brechtian theatre, is the imperative addressed to the spectator, establishing a new relation with that other time, the spectator's time. This closure of action must be analysed as an autonomous segment in which we see not only the functioning of the end of the time of the action, but also the whole temporal functioning of the text, because an end that involves a restoration of order or an eternal return presupposes another domain of time, another ideological meaning that implies an end opening onto a new order.

2.5. Temporality as a Relation between Signifiers

All of the above leads us to a necessary conclusion: strictly speaking, the textual determinants of time are without meaning in isolation. A temporal signifier has no signified: what does 'it is six o'clock' or 'this morning,' mean? A temporal signifier takes on meaning only in relation to another such signifier; time is a relation.

It is not the number of events that produces a rapid or leisurely rhythm, but rather the relation of that number to the rest of a play's temporal indications. A large number of events in a short space of time can give the spectator-reader the feeling of an acceleration of time. When temporal informants are accompanied by only a little action, the illusion of infinite duration results. All the temporal indicators in *Bajazet* (a play in which no one does anything) give the impression of arrested time.

On the other hand, another type of relation can arise (one that is frequent in Shakespeare) that results from a collision between two temporal planes: for example, human temporality and divine temporality in *A Midsummer Night's Dream*, or, in *King Lear*, the temporality of the old king and that of his daughters who are engaged in the war. In *Le Cid* the crowding of events (emphasized by the care Corneille takes to make it clear that they do not go beyond twenty-four hours) brings to light the collision between the dramatic time of the conflict and the epic time of the hero.

The dramatists of time – Maeterlinck, Chekhov – create a dramatic perception of time by means of a discrepancy between the elements of the decor (shown or simply referred to by characters) and the discourse of the characters. In Maeterlinck, the characters' discourse seems not to move, to be infinitely repetitive, but the elements of the real world move and change, creating unbearable tension and anguish (*L'Intruse, Les Aveugles*, etc.).

In Chekhov, the characters spend their time speaking of time, of their past, of the difference between the present and the past, and of a nostalgia for the future; and yet the decor scarcely changes – only in the tiniest, anguishing shifts. In *The Seagull*, this is seen in the rearrangement of furniture, the changes of season, the rust that they say is taking over the little theatre.

In *Waiting for Godot*, only one day has passed and here we have what was a bare tree, covered with leaves: we are in the domain of theatrical impossibility, in the time that is and yet is not, in the temporality that is unique to Beckett and that creates a repetitive and destructive duration.

Theatre is always this impossible temporal relation, this oxymoron of time without which it could bring to life neither history nor our lived time.

3. Reference

Time is not just duration, nor is it simply the relationship between several temporalities; it is also the moment, that is to say, the reference, the 'referring' of theatrical action at a given moment to a distant past or to the immediate present. This aspect of the problem of time is more relevant to performance than it is to text, but the text does indeed refer to a moment within a duration: the *moment* in *Britannicus* is a precise date during the Roman Empire and the reign of Nero. The theatrical text freezes a moment in the flow of duration, whether it is a well-known moment in history or an obscure instance in the mists of time. It is the task of performance to create signs that can refer to that temporal reference, provided that the reference can be modified and a new system invented.

3.1. Framing

To express time is to displace the *here-and-now*, to install the theatrical phenomenon (text + performance) within a given temporal framework, to establish its limits and ensure its referential anchor. One discovery made through structural analysis is the importance of the beginning, the *incipit*, the first signs around which the others will be organized. The beginning of any theatrical text is filled with temporal indices (didascalia governing the opening and the beginning of dialogue). The exposition presupposes a temporal anchor, if temporality is indeed at play; the didascalia are there in order to mark time or to not mark time, buttressed always by dialogue.

The didascalia mark a moment in history through a series of indices: the names of the characters (historically known or linguistically marked, for example Latin or Greek names); the period or moment in question ('The scene takes place in ... in the year ...'); indications concerning costumes and decor associated with a given time.

a/ This historical past can be abstract: the temporal framework of classical plays is a purely textual index that is not called upon to support didascalia involving local colour. The Rome of *Bérénice* indicates no Pompeian decor, even if the 'torches' and 'lictors' suggest an imaginary off-stage world. Unlike Romantic dramatic art, the historical signifier can therefore be disengaged from any link with a visual, figurable sign that might refer to a given era. On the other hand, this abstract past can indicate the precise moment of the action in relation to an historical event. *Bérénice* begins three days after the death of Vespasian, and Shakespeare's *Julius Caesar* begins on the Ides of March, the day of Caesar's assassination. A play can even be dated in relation to a legendary event: *Phèdre* begins six months after Theseus's departure, and *Horace* begins on the morning of the decisive duel between Rome and Alba. These indications are simple contextual points of reference.

b/ These temporal indications can have the effect of 'presentifying' a historical past; however the signs of the here-and-now should, to the extent possible, be masked by the indexical and iconic signs of the past. This happens in Romantic drama much more than in Shakespeare's plays, which create past imaginary signs.

c/ These signs can indicate the past as past as well as traces of that past in the present. Indices of the past include: micro-accounts of events that refer back to a temporal off-stage world; expository micro-sequences concerning the past of a character or the origin of certain circumstances; the indexical functioning of informing signs (informants of the present, indices of the past); iconic figurations of the past, such as aged settings and ruins (all Hugo's theatre is marked by iconic signs, by decor that portrays the past as ruin, and ruins that invest the present). Finally, in all theatre, the old man is a figure for the living presence of the past, for the eternal cycles of history: a whole interplay is set up between the living and the elements of the past.

3.2. The Here-and-Now

Indexical marks of history may on the other hand be entirely absent. Their absence indicates a zero degree of historicity, an abstract temporal framework (see, for example, the early plays of Adamov). We are led into a present moment, the here-and-now of all instances of performance. This is evident in a series of modern works in which the absence of historical references refers us not only to a rejection of history, but more precisely to a present time; by some sort of rule, the absence of a past historical referent signifies the present; such is the case, deliberate or otherwise, with Genet and Beckett. But, because of an unanticipated paradox, any localization in the present (contemporary reference, fashion, etc.), any reference to the actual or real irreversibly historicizes: the weakness of so-called boulevard theatre or *théâtre d'intervention*, is that they are soon historicized, but without history (that is, they are outmoded, dated).

3.3. Historicizing the Present

On the other hand, a whole complex series of informants describes a temporal situation that is presented not as an abolished past but rather as a present within history. This means that the historicization of the text is such that we can no longer identify what is strictly speaking a signifier of time, because the set of textual signs, from start to finish in the text, constitutes a system of informants and indices that develops right through to the dénouement: each new sign marks the evolution of the contextual situation. Thus, in Brecht's *Saint Joan of the Stockyards*, or in Horvath's plays (*Don Juan Returns from the War; Faith, Hope and Charity*) we can demonstrate, throughout the text, that the paradigm of time is projected upon the syntagma of action. We can see all the signs of the crisis during the 1920s and 1930s with its various unique and historically dated characteristics in the text (didascalia + dialogue) of the three plays mentioned above.

4. Time and Sequences

In the first section of this chapter, we saw how temporality is established particularly within the relationship (continuous-discontinuous) between the spectator's time and the performance time. The second section demonstrated the inadequacy and the relative and non-autonomous nature of the signifiers of time. The third section discussed the meaning of temporal reference. But the essential nature of the signs of temporality seems to us to reside in the manner of articulation of the units that segment the theatrical text.

Some observations:

a/ We once again come up against the fundamental problem of the relation, in the representation between the continuous and the discontinuous, between duration as uninterrupted flow and intervals marked out within that duration.

b/ If we take the text to be a long 'sentence' (a useful comparison) we come up against the problem of the co-existence, in a single text, of different modes of articulation. The comparison with the sentence is perhaps inadequate; a comparison with a verse of a poem's might work better. The verse, according to Juri Lotman in *La structure du texte artistique* (Lotman 1973), is both a succession of phonological units perceived as separate, distinct entities, and a succession of words perceived as inextricably linked to phonematic combinations. The same might be said of the theatrical text, especially because the articulations of the various textual networks are able not to coincide. The problem becomes crucial when we are dealing with short or average-length units.

c/ The mode of writing for theatre and for various types of dramatic art depends closely on theatrical syntagmatic structures, that is to say, on the fact that the sequences (long, average, short) are organized according to tightly knit units (vaudeville, melodrama, tragedy) or more loosely connected units (contemporary theatre, from Maeterlinck to Beckett), or a whole series of variations in between those extremes. There are even cases of (relatively) discontinuous and reversible sequences, as in Brecht, and we cannot rule out the possibility that a given kind of syntagmatic structure will work at a particular level of units but not at another level (smaller units, for example). We see this in the tightly knit network of micro-sequences in Brecht and often in Shakespeare.

d/The effect of performance can confirm or contradict the syntagmatic structuring of a text because performance has its own syntagmatics. The triple opposition – tightly knit versus loosely connected, continuous versus discontinuous, reversible versus irreversible – can be enhanced or violated by the way a play is staged. One might emphasize continuity by leaving fixed elements (decor, objects, and even characters) in place, or by having those same elements recur regularly; one could thus even transform Brechtian discontinuity into continuity. On the other hand, one might emphasize what can be signified by spatio-temporal disruption, thus challenging even classical continuity.

4.1. Three Moments

An initial way to segment the text is sketched by our temporal signifiers. Here three moments are identified in the continuity of a text:

1/a situation that is the point of departure (the here-and-now of the text's beginning),
2/the text-action,
3/a final situation.

This mode of analysis is purely an abstraction carried out with the help of an analysis of content. It presupposes an inventory of the phenomena concerning the beginning and of those involved in the ending, and between the two a series of more or less connected mediations. This abstract operation is important in the determination, not so much of what has happened but of what has been said.

Let us take the complex example of *King Lear*: at the outset, the king relinquishes his crown and divides his kingdom between his daughters. At the end, everybody is dead, except for one who inherits the crown simply by chance. There can be a twofold reading of this final situation: (a) the betrayal of the king who had behaved in a simple feudal manner led to this destruction; (b) Lear overturned the natural order and the natural order is indeed overturned, since his daughters die before him. The mediations here are complex: quarrels and feudal betrayals, the behaviour of ungrateful daughters, and the behaviour of the faithful daughter (although with the same result).

Another, simpler example is found in *Andromaque*. At the outset, Pyrrhus betrays Greece in wanting to marry his captive and, in a way, gives strength and aid to Troy. At the end, Greece has been avenged *vis-à-vis* its own hero through a self-destructive process (death of Hermione, Oreste's madness). The mediations are Pyrrhus's comings and goings between Greece and Troy, and between Andromaque and Hermione.

Dramas involving the integration (or reintegration) of the hero are easily understood, all the more so because that ternary division allows us to account for movement from one space to another (see chapter IV). Here are some examples.

Calderón's *Life is a Dream*: At the outset, the Crown Prince Sigismundo is disgraced and is in prison. At the end, he takes his place on the throne once and for all. The mediations: his comings and goings between spaces allowed him to understand that 'life is a dream.'

Ruy Blas: At the outset, Ruy Blas, who dreams of the Queen, is the lackey of an important lord. At the end Ruy Blas is again a lackey, and he dies. The mediation: through imposture Ruy Blas became a great lord, a reforming minister, and gained the Queen's love. Imagination fails.

The Marriage of Figaro: At the outset, Count Almaviva wants to possess his valet Figaro's fiancée. At the end the Count has bedded his own wife instead. The mediation: a coalition of his opponents overturned his plans. We see how the Count, who sought freely to invade his servants' space, is sent packing back to the space of his own class (in this instance, his own conjugal bed).

This brief tripartite analysis (which reminds us of Brecht's minimalist *fables*) is interesting primarily in the way that it demonstrates the broad outlines of action and its meaning – not only its apparent, denoted, meaning, but especially the direction. It sets aside psychological motivations.

4.2. Long Sequences

We should straight off note that one characteristic of long sequences is that, unlike other sequences, they presuppose the visible, textually indicated interruption of all the networks of the text and of performance. This interruption is provided by the intermission; whether or not it actually takes place, it can be represented by (a) a textual blank (and a textual indication of a new act or scene), (b) a gap in performance, a blackout, a lowering of the curtain, a freezing of the actors' movements, or any other break in the action. Two modes for handling long units – acts and scenes – mark two opposing forms of dramatic art.

4.2.1. Act versus Scene

The act presupposes, at least relatively, that there be unity of time and space and especially that elements present from the beginning will be developed. A change of act does not change those initial givens; they are simply distributed differently, from act to act, like playing cards in successive deals. Whatever the temporal interval between acts, there will be no break in the play's logical progression, and moreover, that interval will not be taken into account dramatically, it will not be posted (to use a metaphor from finance).

On the contrary, dramatic art based on scenes presupposes temporal pauses which by nature are not empty, but full: time has marched on, places and people have changed, and the following scene portrays that change through visible differences from the previous scene. The scene is a portrayal of a new and complex situation seen in (relative) autonomy. Brechtian theatre pushes to a theoretical and practical extreme this idea of the autonomy of each scene, presented as a portrayal of a situation that must be understood in and of itself, as a sort of isolated system with relative closure whose unique structure must be shown. In a way this gives privileged status to the vertical dimension, the combinatory system of signs at a given moment, the functioning of the paradigmatic set.

Here again we are dealing with the well-known opposition between the continuous and the discontinuous: theatre based on scenes interrupts the continuity of the syntagmatic development, seen as a logical succession that goes without saying. The discontinuity of scene makes us think, instead of being carried along by the movement of the *story*. In the theatre we have to show that which does not go without saying, with the pause between scenes, and theatre based on scenes, through its intervals, constrains us to think. Any such gap breaks what Brecht calls identification, a phenomenon we call 'sideration' (a momentary blank) on the part of the spectator; the gap obliges the spectator to put aside not only the action, the succession of the story, but indeed the theatrical universe, and momentarily rejoin his or her own world. Paradoxically, intervals oblige the spectator to come back to a twofold reality – the reality of the spectator beyond the theatre, and a referential reality pertaining to a story that marches on, advancing the action during the interval. In any case, what is seen is the object of denegation; it is the intervals that contain a reference to reality.

4.2.2. Montage/Collage

We can go further: in modern experiments, theatre based on scenes can become montage and/or collage, both of which create meaning by virtue of the fact that they presuppose a rhetoric. We might consider montage (the combination of elements of stories that, while heterogeneous, acquire meaning when we examine their common functioning) to be the result of metaphorization; we know that a metaphor's signified is not simply the sum of the signified's elements brought together (and condensed) by the image, but rather a + x. Collage (the introduction, within dramatic discourse, of a referential element r, a piece of reality that appears foreign to the theatrical referent) can be considered the equivalent, not so much of metaphor as of metonymy; collage constrains the spectator to undertake the same effort to construct meaning out of heterogeneity.

4.2.3. Mixed Forms
Theatre that uses acts and theatre based on scenes are extremes that presuppose a whole series of possible intermediary constructs. Thus the 'days' in the Spanish theatre of the Golden Age are a sort of mixture of movement of place and often time, but with continuity of action. In romantic theatre, for example Hugo, the distinction between act and scene is much reduced: in *Lucrèce Borgia*, the obvious organization into scenes coincides with the effort to exploit *prolepsis*, the anticipation of the scene to come. In *Ruy Blas*, acts 1 and 2 are tableaux (temporal discontinuity and internal paradigmatic organization), but a close temporal unity links acts 3, 4, and 5, which take place over a few hours, in just one location, invoking a form of tragic continuity. In *Lorenzaccio*, Musset combines, in a bizarre way (and we will see just how), a theatre based on scenes and a theatre based on acts. All face the same problem: how are we to understand history, and how is history made?

4.2.4. The Articulation of Sequences
A detailed study of longer units must examine the articulation of sequences, because in all cases the diegetic[4] function of the play will occur, and because there will always be anaphora and recurrence of the elements needed to make the story intelligible. Even a theatre based on scenes creates suspense and is intended to incite spectators to anticipate further developments – if not, they would get up and leave. Take the example of Brecht's *Mother Courage*: certainly each episode has its autonomy. The adventure of each of Mother Courage's children is given as a complete story; however, each story contains elements that are linked with and set into motion the following adventure. Even the death of the mute girl, a death intended to close out the story, is not presented as the

end. The final sequence presents the solitude and impenitent attitude of the woman who lives by war (the camp follower).

In a dramatic art based on acts, the elements involved in suspense are more obvious: at the end of each act, we are offered not a temporary solution but rather a forcefully implied question, whose answer we then await. Act 1 of *Andromaque* should offer a solution: the unambiguous end to non-reception as expressed in Pyrrhus' message to the Greek ambassador Oreste: 'Epirus will save what Troy has saved' (scene 2). In fact the question springs up again. The end of the act sees Pyrrhus's ultimatum to Andromaque: the answer should be expressly given in the following act. The interval is filled by a moment of deliberation on the part of the heroine. The projection of one long unit upon the other expresses tragic urgency. In comparison, each scene in *Mother Courage* is a completed experience that the interval should leave time to digest and understand. We see that time does not have the same meaning for these two different kinds of units.

4.3. The Sequence of Average Length

The problem posed by the sequence of average length is not a simple one. First of all there is the problem of defining such a sequence. In classical theatre, the average-length sequence is textually determined and it takes its place as a (shorter) unit of lesser importance in relation to long units (acts). The classical solution consists in identifying, by scene title and by number, any entrance or exit of a character. Thus the average-length sequence is unambiguously defined according to a certain configuration of the characters. This is not without some confusion: a sudden entry by a confidant, who then leaves just as suddenly, will be labelled a scene, when obviously it is just an articulating segment between two other scenes. We see this with the arrival of Panope, who comes to announce the death of Thésée to Phèdre (act 1, scene 4), or in the short scene (act 1, scene 2) in which Oenone asks Hyppolyte and Théramène to leave before Phèdre's arrival, a scene that is no more than a linking structure, a *passage*. Nonetheless if we undertake the very important study of charting a classical play, sequence by sequence, indicating the presence of characters, we note that these sequences actually correspond to configurations of characters, even to collisions. The table for the average sequences of *Suréna* identifies a wondrous apparatus within which all successive combinations are tried out.

The relation between a long sequence and average sequences in a theatre based on scenes is much more complex. The widely varying length of

Shakespearean scenes means that some of them can be articulated into elements belonging to a lower order while others cannot. As a general rule, when a scene demonstrates a certain complexity, articulations into average sequences are accomplished not as a function of the various entrances and exits of characters (although that could be the case), but rather as a function of exchanges between characters. Thus in *King Lear* the long storm scene between the king and his fool (act 3, scene 3) is articulated into average sequences depending on the type of exchange taking place between the two protagonists. Likewise the scene involving the division of the kingdom (act 1, scene 1) is one long sequence divided into average sequences according to exchanges (a) between Lear and his daughters, (b) between Lear and Cordelia, and (c) between Lear and his daughters' suitors. Most of the characters are on stage all the time. In a general way, a sequence is defined less by its intellectual content than by the movement from one kind of exchange to another, or from one kind of action to another. Sometimes we encounter a problem that we will meet again in connection with micro-sequences: the fact that two ways of segmenting, one carried out as a function of dialogue and the other as a function of didascalia, are simultaneously possible.

Finally, in certain types of dramatic art (Lenz's *Le Précepteur*, Büchner's *Woyzeck*, or, closer to our time, works by Franz-Xaver Kroetz or Michel Deutsch) the scene determines not a long sequence but rather an average-length one. We then have a mosaic, a kaleidoscope of short scenes indicating a kind of dispersed perspective, a scattering of consciousness (and of living conditions). There is a specific example in *Lorenzaccio*, where the average sequences segment the play into scenes (scenes that are articulated according to shifts of location but grouped into acts).

The staging of a play can emphasize or minimize the gaps between average sequences. It can give privileged status to a particular manner of segmenting by the continued presence of actors, for example, or by highlighting pauses between scenes (sometimes scenes are separated by lowering the curtain). Rhythm and movement depend on this mode of articulation, as they do on the continuous/discontinuous relationship with all its consequences for signification.

4.4. Micro-Sequences

However, the concrete effects of time are produced by a segmenting into micro-sequences. These micro-sequences give real rhythm to the text, and they also give it its meaning: tirades, rapid exchanges (classical stichomythia, etc.), and combinations of micro-sequences involving many characters. Scenes can be articulated into many micro-sequences, or can be made up of two or three compact masses. Some scenes flow uninterrupted, while others have clearcut pauses. In some scenes the action is progressive, while in others there are recurring micro-sequences. Finally, some scenes can be articulated at the level of denotation, whereas other scenes demonstrate invisible articulations.

4.4.1. Segmenting into Micro-Sequences

What is a micro-sequence? It can roughly be defined as a fraction of theatrical (textual or performed) time during which *something that can be isolated* happens. But what? An action, a given relation between characters, an idea. If we draw up an inventory of the various ways by which to articulate a pair of micro-sequences, we will gain perspective on the different ways that the segmenting into micro-sequences takes place. Articulation can be accomplished by:

* gestures and movements (didascalia) (in *King Lear*, act 3, scene 7, when Gloucester is blinded by Cornwall's followers, micro-sequences mark the stages in the torture);
* the content of the dialogue, or articulations of that content within a given speech (stages in an argument, in a discussion);
* passional movements which can generally be spotted by a change in syntax (from present to future, or from assertion to interrogation or exclamation);
* in a more general way, the mode of enunciation in dialogue (questions, prayers, orders and responses to them).

This non-exhaustive summary implies an immediately obvious consequence. There will almost necessarily be a conflict between these different modes of segmentation – for example, between gestural elements and dialogue. Furthermore, that conflict is the rule almost everywhere in theatrical text. The life and, we might say, the volume of a text have to do with the fact that it can be articulated in two different ways, that continuity is ensured by gestural elements while dialogue is divided, or that there are temporal shifts between two possible segmentations. Thus in the scene mentioned above, the blinding in *King Lear*, there is non-coincidence between the gestural elements of the followers who blind Gloucester and Gloucester's words. There is a delay in his words, one that tragically marks the victim's inability to understand.

We can go even further: division into micro-sequences presupposes, on the part of the reader-director, a certain idea of meaning. The division (even if it is based on features of the linguistic signifier, even if it is supported by the didascalia) is never established in advance. It has to be effected; it depends on the general meaning which we give or wish to give to the totality of the scene. The division presupposes unspoken elements. The micro-sequence can be understood as a form-meaning that takes shape only at the moment of performance. Certain concatenations can be noted or effected only with reference to earlier sequences in the text.

4.4.2. The Function of Micro-Sequences

In 'Éléments de sémiologie' (Barthes 1964) Barthes establishes an important distinction between kernel-sequences and catalyzing-sequences; the latter are developments and addenda, and are not really indispensable. This distinction is not very rigorous, but it is often helpful for theatrical text where it allows us, as we shall attempt to demonstrate, to distinguish between what is essential and what is accessory.

Barthes' distinction between informing catalysts and indexical catalysts seems less useful, and more debatable, since any catalyst can, at the same time and to different degrees, be both informing and indexical. A catalyst can provide necessary information, while functioning as an index in relation to the rest of the text (it has a place in the diegesis). If we go a little further, we see that all sequences have at least one of the six Jakobsonian functions (see chapter I, section 3.2. 'The Six Functions'). Informants and indices enter into the domain of the referential function. A sequence (particularly a micro-sequence) can have an emotive (or expressive) function, a phatic function (responsible for ensuring contact between protagonists and public), or a poetic function (emphasizing the totality of the message, serving as a link between the networks, or indeed indicating the degree to which paradigmatic structures are projected onto syntagmatic ones). We do not wish to overemphasize the importance of the distinction (sometimes useful but never decisive) between iconic and indexical sequences, since the way theatre functions is both iconic and indexical.[5]

On the other hand, the distinction between *catalyst* and *kernel* is paramount, as long as we do not take the first item of information that catches our attention to be a kernel. We can formulate a hypothesis concerning that *kernel*: it is linked to a *conative* function. It can textually take the form of an imperative (constituting the fundamental sentence, which can be transformed). Thus in *Lucrèce Borgia*, the long banquet scene (act 3, scene 1) is dominated by the (recurring) kernel micro-sequence: 'Drink, let's drink!' (wine/death). In *Andromaque* (act 1, scene 4), two (conative) imperative kernel-sequences oppose each other: 'Marry me!' and 'Leave me alone!' All catalytic micro-sequences are in a way the rhetorical development (verbal or iconic rhetoric) of kernel-sequences. Sometimes this twofold functioning (kernel-catalyst) is much more subtle and masked by unspoken elements of the text. For example, in *Le Cid* the long (essentially expository) story of the battle with the Moors told to the king by Rodrigue (act 4, scene 3) is a rhetorical development (*apologia*) that covers an imperative but unspoken element: 'Do not condemn me for the murder of the Count!'

The conative function is decisive in theatre. Each protagonist tries to make something happen to someone else (to satisfy his or her own desires), with the help of orders, promises, prayers, supplications, threats, blackmail, all of which amount to a conative function.

4.4.3. An Example: *Lorenzaccio*, act 2, scene 2[6]

The doorway to a church. Lorenzo and Valori enter.

Valori. Why is the Duke not here? Ah, Sir! how pleasing all this is for a Christian, all these splendours of the Roman Church! What man could be insensitive to them? Does the artist not find here the heaven his heart seeks? The
5   warrior the priest and the merchant, do they not all find all that they love here? The wondrous harmony of the organs, the spectacular hangings and tapestries, these paintings by the great masters, the warm and soft perfumes emitted by the censer, and the delightful singing of these silvery voices, all of this, in its utter worldliness, might well shock a severe monk, that enemy
10   of pleasure. But nothing is finer, in my view, than a religion that inspires love for it by these means. Why would priests want to serve a jealous God? Religion is not a bird of prey; it is a gentle dove that glides softly above all dreams and all loves.
Lorenzo. Of course; what you say is perfectly true, and perfectly false, as is
15   the case for everything in this world. ·
Tebaldeo Freccia, (*approaching Valori.*) Ah Monseigneur! How nice it is to see a man such as Your Eminence speaking thus about holy tolerance and enthusiasm! Forgive an obscure citizen who is burning with this divine fire, if he thanks you for these few words I have just heard. To find upon the lips of a
20   good man what one has in one's own heart, that is the greatest happiness one can desire.
Valori. Are you not young Freccia?

Tebaldeo. My works have little merit; I am more competent at loving the arts than I am at producing them. My whole youth was spent in churches. It
25   seems to me that only in a church can I admire Raphael and our divine Buonarotti. I remain then for days, contemplating their works, in unequalled ecstasy. The organ music reveals their thinking to me, and allows me to enter their souls. I look at the characters in their paintings, so saintly, on their knees, and I listen, as if the singing of the choirs were com-
30   ing from their open mouths. Puffs of aromatic incense float between them and me, in a light vapour. In it I see the glory of the artist; it is also a sad and sweet vapour that would simply be a sterile perfume, if it were not rising up to God.
Valori. Yours is the heart of an artist; come to my palace, and bring some-
35   thing under your cloak when you come. I want you to do some work for me.
Tebaldeo. Your Eminence does me too great an honour. I am a humble priest in the holy religion of painting.
Lorenzo. Why put off the offer of a job? It looks like you have a frame in your hands.
40   *Tebaldeo.* That is true; but I dare not show it to such great connoisseurs. It is a humble and rough outline of a magnificent dream.
Lorenzo. You are making a painting of your dreams? I shall have one of mine pose for you.
Tebaldeo. Making dreams come true, that is the painter's life. The greatest
45   painters have represented their dreams with all of their powers, changing nothing. Their imagination was a tree full of life; its buds were effortlessly transformed into flowers, and the flowers into fruit. Soon that fruit ripened under a benign sun and, when it was ripe, it soon fell upon the ground, without losing a single one of its virginal grains. Alas! the dreams of medi-
50   ocre artists are plants that are hard to nourish, and that are watered by truly bitter tears so that they barely prosper.

He shows his painting.

Valori. Sincerely, it is a fine painting – not of the first merit, it is true – why would I flatter a man who does not flatter himself? But you do not even
55   have a beard yet, young man.
Lorenzo. Is it a landscape or a portrait? From what angle should I examine it? Sideways, or vertically?
Tebaldeo. Your highness is making fun of me. It is a view of Campo-Santo.
Lorenzo. How far is it from this to immortality?
60   *Valori.* It is not nice for you to tease this youngster. See how his big eyes show

sadness at each of your words.

Tebaldeo. Immortality takes faith. Those to whom God has given wings reach it smiling.

Valori. You speak like a student of Raphael's.

65   *Tebaldeo.* Sir, he was my master. He taught me all I know.

Lorenzo. Come to my place, I will have you paint Mazzafira naked.

Tebaldeo. I do not respect my paint brush, but I respect my art. I cannot paint a courtesan.

Lorenzo. Your God took the time to make her; you can surely take the time

70   to paint her. Do you want to paint a view of Florence for me?

Tebaldeo. Yes, Monseigneur.

Lorenzo. How would you go about it?

Tebaldeo. I would take up a position to the east, on the left bank of the Arno. From there one has the best and largest perspective, and the most

75   pleasant.

Lorenzo. You would paint Florence, its squares, its houses and its streets?

Tebaldeo. Yes, Monseigneur.

Lorenzo. Why then would you not paint a courtesan, if you can paint a evil place?

80   *Tebaldeo.* I have not yet learned to call my mother that.

Lorenzo. Whom do you call mother?

Tebaldeo. Florence, my lord.

Lorenzo. Then you are no more than a bastard, for your mother is a harlot.

Tebaldeo. An open wound can eat away at the healthiest body. But from pre-

85   cious drops of the blood of my mother there comes a fragrant plant that heals all ills. Art, that divine flower, sometime needs manure to nourish it by enriching the soil in which it grows.

Lorenzo. What do you mean?

Tebaldeo. Peaceful and happy nations have at times shone with a pure but

90   weak light. The angel's harp has several strings; the zephyr can waft over the smallest of these, and bring out a soft and delicious harmony. However, only the blowing of the north wind can set the silver string to vibrating. It is the harp's most beautiful and most noble string, yet it vibrates best under a crude touch. Enthusiasm is the brother of suffering.

95   *Lorenzo.* You mean an unhappy people can produce great artists. I would happily be the alchemist working your still. The people's tears drop into it like pearls. By Satan's death! I like you. Families can fall upon the worst times, nations die from misery, and all that inspires your brain. Admirable poet! How do you reconcile all of that with your piety?

100   *Tebaldeo.* I am not making fun of the misfortune of any family. I am saying

that poetry is the sweetest of all sufferings, and that it loves its sisters. I pity unhappy people, but I indeed believe that they produce great artists. Battle fields eventually grow rich harvests, tortured ground can grow celestial wheat.

105   *Lorenzo.* Your doublet is worn. Do you want one of my livery?

Tebaldeo. I belong to no one. When thought seeks freedom, the body should also.

Lorenzo. I'm inclined to tell my valet to beat you up.

Tebaldeo. Why, Monseigneur?

110   *Lorenzo.* Because I feel like it. Have you limped since birth, or was it an accident?

Tebaldeo. I do not limp. What do you mean by that?

Lorenzo. You are either lame or mad.

Tebaldeo. Why, Monseigneur? You are laughing at me.

115   *Lorenzo.* If you were not lame, how could you remain, unless you are mad, in a city in which, because of your ideas on freedom, the Medicis's head valet can beat you up with impunity?

Tebaldeo. I love my mother Florence, that is why I remain here. I know that a citizen can be murdered in broad daylight, in the open street, just on a

120   whim of those who govern, and that is why I carry this stiletto in my belt.

Lorenzo. Would you strike the Duke if he were to strike you, since he often murders needlessly, just for the fun of it?

Tebaldeo. I would kill him, if he were to attack me.

Lorenzo. You tell me this?

125   *Tebaldeo.* Why should that be held against me? I do no one harm. I spend my time in my studio. Sundays I go to the Annunziata or Santa Maria. The Monks think I have a good voice. They dress me in a white robe with red breeches, and I take my place in the choir, and sometimes I am given a small solo part. That's the only time I'm out in public. Evenings, I visit my

130   mistress, and on a beautiful night, we go out onto her balcony. No one knows me and I know no one. Who would be served by my life or death?

Lorenzo. Are you a Republican? Do you admire princes?

Tebaldeo. I am an artist. I love my mother and my mistress.

135   *Lorenzo.* Come to my palace tomorrow. I want to have you paint a picture for my wedding day.

They leave

There is little difficulty in dividing this apparently insignificant scene[7]

into micro-sequences, using the exchanges between characters and the content of their dialogue.

1/ Lorenzo and the Papal Nuncio Valori are chatting under the portal of a church; Valori praises the pomp and splendour of the Catholic church (1–15).

2/ The young painter Tebaldeo Freccia joins the conversation, enthusiastically seconding Valori's statements (16–33).

3/ Valori invites Tebaldeo to come and show him his paintings (34–7).

4/ The three chat: Lorenzo teases Tebaldeo, who is then defended by Valori (38–65).

5/ Lorenzo invites Tebaldeo to work for him, the painter declines, citing his concept of art; Lorenzo argues against that concept (66–104).

6/ The political interrogation of Tebaldeo by Lorenzo (105–34); the final invitation (135–6). *Note*: these last sequences are distinguished from each other solely at the level of content.

a/ We should note that if we refer to gestures and movements, we will come up with a different segmentation. Tebaldeo's movements and gestures, as he insinuates himself into the conversation between Valori and Lorenzo, is perforce prepared by a physical approach, a kind of physical immixing preceding speech (16; the stage direction is *approaching Valori* ... not *approaching Lorenzo*); there is a slight discrepancy here between movements and discourse. Likewise the showing of the painting (52) is separated from Lorenzo's request (38–9) and comes in the middle of a dialogue-sequence involving all three, without interrupting that dialogue (the conversation concerns Tebaldeo's art). These two discrepancies indicate an unspoken background, poses or positionings on the part of Tebaldeo that are not synchronized with his speeches, a disequilibrium that is productive of meaning.

b/ There is no apparent unity to the scene, and in particular there is no apparent relation between the first sequence and the rest of the scene. Why is Valori there (if not to 'speak' about art and religion)? That is a legitimate question because this seems to be a badly constructed scene; it lacks in unity, and there is precious little suspense.

c/ Our impression changes when we identify the kernel-micro-sequence that is in fact dispersed throughout all the segments. Here is what we get if we note all the imperatives and other verbs of command or will:

> *Valori.   Come* to my palace, and *bring* something under your cloak when you come. *I want you* to do some work for me. (34–5)

Lorenzo.   Why put off [*do not put off*] the offer of a job. It looks like you have a frame in your hands [*show your work*]. (38–9)

Lorenzo.   *Come* to my place, *I will have you* paint Mazzafira naked. (66) [present and future orders]

Lorenzo.   Do you want to paint a view of Florence for me? (70) [*do this for me*]

Lorenzo.   Your doublet is worn; do you want one of my livery? (105) [given subsequent unambiguous implications, amounts to: *become my servant.*]

Lorenzo.   *Come* to my palace tomorrow, I want to have you paint a picture for ... (135).

All these imperatives (or equivalents to imperatives) are addressed to Tebaldeo; but they are the response to an unspoken, but connoted imperative:

1/ through Tebaldeo's gestures of intervention (16 – This is quite bold, really! Speaking in this way to a Papal Nuncio! He must really be hungry.);

2/ through the rhetoric of seduction employed in all the speeches Tebaldeo addresses to Valori (immediately followed by the rhetoric of innocence with which he addresses Lorenzo) that establishes a network of meaning with the unsynchronized movements and gestures noted above.

This imperative can be formulated as follows: 'Monseigneur, you who speak so eloquently about religious art, *be* my patron, *buy* my canvasses.'[8] To this Valori, who has clearly understood the supplicative imperative, answers with the imperative '*Come*' (34; understood as 'All right, I shall be your patron.'). After this, Lorenzo intervenes with *Come* (66; understood as 'It is I who shall be the patron'). The recurrence of *Come* in kernel-sequences makes the scene infinitely comical. After Tebaldeo's chatter about '... the characters in their paintings, so saintly on their knees,' 'puffs of aromatic incense,' 'the glory of the artist,' and 'rising up to God,' it is immediately proposed to him that he paint a prostitute. The importance of Valori's presence then becomes apparent.

Let us return to the first sequence, to see if it also contains an *imperative*. Valori's long speech, with its (awful) rhetoric (straight out of Chateaubriand's *Le génie du christianisme*) on the splendours of the Roman Church, directly follows the first sentence: 'Why is the Duke not here?' Where is he? In the church, of course. This Lorenzo, a favourite of the prince, could surely advise his master to go to Mass. The discrete imperative that arises here – '*Be so kind as to advise* Alexandre to go to Mass.' – can be understood as 'Then it will be easy to forget your escapades and have Rome forgive you.' The government might then take on a pious and conforming appearance; the spectator will remember that in act 1, scene 4, Valori complained to the Duke about immorality at the Court and sought Lorenzo's disgrace.

Thus the real meaning of the micro-sequence on religious aesthetics becomes clear; it is a rhetoric of seduction, to which the answer, comically, is Tebaldeo's rhetoric of seduction; Tebaldeo understandably has not understood the unspoken meaning of the speech, only its denoted meaning; thus he takes up the same speech on the relationship between religion and art. Valori's speech takes on its full interest when we note the last sentence on religion 'a gentle dove that glides softly over all dreams and loves' (12–13) – a phrase uttered by a Papal Nuncio who is not unaware that Lorenzo is Alexandre's minion. Valori's solicitation is quite the equal of little Tebaldeo's more open soliciting; thus we see, stunningly, the internal unity of the scene.

Lorenzo's disdainful phrase in answer to Valori's rhetoric – 'Of course; what you say is perfectly true, and perfectly false, as is the case for everything in this world.' (14–15) – is not only a refusal to respond to the question that has been asked and to the real solicitation, but also a formula to *annul* the speech, that is, to present it as if it had no truth-value whatsoever.

We have neglected the other (very rich) functions of this text, so as to concentrate on the *directive* (or conative) function that *organizes* the succession of micro-sequences. Usually, in a text based on dialogue, there is only one principal function that plays that role. We have seen that the recurrence of the kernel-micro-sequence organizes the text around itself, allowing for the production of an acceptable meaning for the whole of the average sequence (scene). The collapse of these rhetorics by Lorenzo transforms the entire scene into a demonstration of an ideology: religious idealism and aesthetic idealism are equals where solicitation and prostitution are concerned. Neither one is the road to action and salvation, but both are redoubtable and mystifying, and the hero turns away from them. It is in this sense that this scene foretells of murder, a solution of despair, the sole, final solution.

4.4.4. Some Consequences

1/ In theatre, more than in any other textual domain, the text takes on meaning only through what is unspoken, and more precisely, through what is implicitly understood, with all the characteristics developed by Ducrot (1980, 131–2): dependence upon relations with context; instability; opposition to literal meaning to which something seems to be added on; discovery through discursive procedures.[9] The implicitly understood, we might add, seems to be that which conditions and sometimes constitutes the central function in the domain of theatre.

2/ At the level of micro-sequences the consequence is that, with rare exceptions, we cannot segment an average sequence into micro-sequences in a linear, unfolding fusion: The example taken from *Lorenzaccio* shows us: (a) the discrepancy in relation to a segmentation based on gestures; (b) the fact that the kernel is dispersed, so to speak, throughout the micro-sequences; (c) the necessity, if we are to account for internal articulations of the text at a minimal level, to resort to even smaller units.

3/ The identification of a recurring kernel in a sequence allows us to orient the staging of a play so as to highlight elements that will be readily perceived by the spectator. Those who become lost in Tebaldeo's aesthetic arguments will clearly see relations such as the request, the supplication, the command, the refusal; they will be aware of a relation of the play's rather obvious socioeconomic and sociopolitical aspects, to the ideologies and their mystification. The search for the kernel allows that which is concrete in the text to speak to us.

4/ It is necessary to study the catalytic micro-sequences, and in particular we should analyse the way Lorenzo interrogates Tebaldeo. Here we are dealing not with the notion of something implicitly understood, but rather something presupposed – presupposed as 'immediately implied' (Ducrot 1980, 133) – a context that is immanent to the message and that contains information outside the message which the speaker considers to be worthy of debate.[10] The purpose of Lorenzo's speech is to bring out the presuppositions in Tebaldeo's speech. For example, Tebaldeo says of his painting: 'It is a humble and rough outline of a magnificent dream.' Lorenzo's reply, 'You are making a painting of your dreams? I shall have one of mine pose for you,' collapses the presupposed content of Tebaldeo's speech. The artist's dream preexists, or is outside of, its realization – a concept Musset rejects.

But here we have departed from sequential analysis in order to touch on what is strictly the domain of discourse, where we find presupposed phenomena: we cannot segment into micro-sequences without at the same time carrying out an analysis of the characters' discourse.

VI. Theatrical Discourse

1. Conditions for Theatrical Discourse

1.1. Definitions

What do we mean by theatrical discourse? We can define it as the totality of linguistic signs produced by a given theatrical work.[1] But that definition is too vague and has more to do with the set of the *utterances* of a theatrical text than with discourse itself as textual production: 'The utterance is a succession of sentences sent between two semantic blanks; discourse is utterance considered from the point of view of the discursive apparatus that governs it' (Guespin 1971, 10).

An initial difficulty arises in connection with theatrical discourse: what are its limits and what, in theatrical activity, can be considered to be discourse? Can theatrical discourse be understood (a) as an organized set of messages whose producer is the dramatist, or (b) as a set of signs and stimuli (verbal and non-verbal) that are produced by performance and whose producer is multiple (dramatist, director, various theatre practitioners actors)? For the sake of simplicity, we will provisionally adopt the view here that theatrical discourse is the set referred to under 'a' above: those linguistic signs that we can attribute to the scriptor (the author) as subject of enunciation.

1.2. Theatrical Enunciation

We are aware that the problems posed by enunciation are not simple, and that theatrical writing does not make them simpler. As for enunciation in its generally accepted sense, we will stick with Benveniste's definition: a 'putting into play of language by an individual act of use' indicating 'the actual act of producing an utterance, not the text of the utterance,'[2] the act that makes the utterance discourse.

The theatrical text, more than any other text, depends closely upon the conditions of its enunciation. We cannot determine the *meaning* of an utterance by considering only its *linguistic component*. We must consider its rhetorical component, its link to the situation of communication in which the utterance is proffered (as Ducrot would have it; see Ducrot 1980); the importance of the rhetorical component is unique to theatre. The 'signification' of a theatrical utterance, if we set aside the situation of communication, is pure nothingness: that situation alone, because it allows for the establishment of the conditions of enunciation, gives the utterance its meaning. Famous theatrical quotations are absolutely meaningless when they are isolated from their enunciative context: 'Go, I do not hate you.' (Chimène speaking to Rodrigue, who has killed her father, from *Le Cid*, act 3, scene 4); 'The poor man!' (Orgon speaking of Tartuffe, from *Tartuffe*, act 1, scene 4); 'For the love of humanity I will give you a gold piece' (Dom Juan speaking to the Poor Man, from *Dom Juan*, act 3, scene 2). These are extreme examples, but they highlight the status of all theatrical texts. The practice of theatre gives speech the concrete conditions for its existence. Dialogue as text is dead, non-signifying speech. To read theatrical discourse is to be involved in something that is secondary to performance; in reading theatrical discourse we reconstitute, in our imagination, the conditions for its enunciation. They alone make possible the production and transmission of meaning.[3] This is an ambiguous task that cannot be fully accomplished because the conditions of enunciation are not tied up with the psychological situation of the character. They are linked to the actual status of theatrical discourse and to the constitutive fact of twofold enunciation. All research on discourse in the theatre is marked not only by the ambiguous nature of the notion of discourse but also by that other ambiguity unique to theatre – whose discourse is discourse in the theatre? It is the discourse of a sender-author and as such can be thought of as a textual (articulated) totality – the discourse of Racine in *Phèdre*. It is also, inseparably, the discourse of a sender-character and in that sense the discourse is not only articulated but also fragmented; it is a discourse whose subject of enunciation is the character, with all the uncertainties that revolve around the notion of character.

Here we see not only ambiguity but also the constitutive, fertile contradiction that is inscribed in theatrical discourse. In the famous scene (which we are happy to quote) where Cinna and Maxime, in the presence of Auguste, argue, one for and the other against absolute power, who is the sender? Where do we situate the speaker Corneille, and can we even speak of such a location? We can get a measure of the incredible naïvety of commentators (a species not yet extinct) who try to find in such speeches the thought, sentiments, even the biography of Corneille (or of Cinna, which is no more relevant).

It is thus impossible to think that the subject is 'at the source of meaning' (to use Michel Pêcheux's phrase): theatrical discourse is the best example of the non-individual character of enunciation.

1.3. Twofold Enunciation

How then can we explain this twofold enunciation we find in theatre? We know that within the theatrical text we are dealing with two distinct textual levels (two sub-categories of the textual totality): one, whose immediate subject of enunciation is the author, includes the complete set of didascalia (stage directions, place names, names of characters); the other, whose mediate subject of enunciation is character, invests the entire dialogue in the play (including monologues). It is in connection with the latter sub-category of linguistic signs that we might speak of 'a linguistics of speech that studies the way speaking subjects use signs.'[4] These textual layers that make up dialogue are marked by what Benveniste calls subjectivity.

The totality of the discourse conveyed by a theatrical text is made up of two sub-categories:

a/ a reporting discourse whose sender is the author (scriptor);
b/ a reported discourse whose speaker is the character.

There is therefore a process of communication between character-'figures' which takes place within another process of communication, one that links the scriptor to the audience. We can now understand why any reading that does not include theatrical dialogue within another process of communication cannot fail to miss the effect of meaning proper to theatre. To read the scene involving Phèdre's admission to Hippolyte without taking into account Racine's relation to the spectator is necessarily reductive. Dialogue is an encompassed phenomenon within an encompassing phenomenon.

In all performance we see a twofold situation of communication: (a) the theatrical situation, or more precisely the *stage* situation, in which the senders are the scriptor and the practitioners (director, actors, etc.); (b) the performed situation that is constructed between characters.

Thus we must identify the fundamental ambiguity that so marks theatrical discourse. Its conditions of enunciation (its context) are of two orders – those that are encompassing and the rest: (a) concrete *stage* conditions of enunciation, and (b) *imaginary* conditions of enunciation, constructed through performance.

The first are determined by the code of performance (anterior to any theatrical text): they are conditions of performance, the audience's relation to the stage, shape of the stage, etc.; they are taken up and modified by the director's (written or unwritten) 'text';[5] they are also found in the didascalia, which indicate (1) the existence of this unique process of communication, theatrical communication, and (2) to some extent, the stage code that governs that communication.

The second (the imaginary conditions of enunciation) are primarily indicated by the didascalia (although important elements can, as we have seen, be found within dialogue). It is as if the speech situation were manifested by the textual layer that we call didascalia, whose proper role is to formulate the conditions for the exercise of speech. We can see the consequences of such a basic fact:

1/ The twofold role of the didascalia (determining both stage and imaginary conditions of enunciation) explains the ambiguity mentioned above, as well as the confusion between these two types of conditions.
2/ The didascalia,[6] in governing performance, have, as their specific message, the imaginary conditions of enunciation.

In other words, the specific message that theatrical performance expresses is not so much the discourse of the characters as it is the conditions for the exercise of that discourse. From that flows a pre-eminently important fact that is often overlooked in textual analysis, although intuitively but clearly perceived by spectators: theatre expresses not so much speech, but as how one can or cannot speak. All textual layers (didascalia + didascalic elements within dialogue) that define a situation of communication between characters, by determining the conditions of enunciation for their speeches, have the function not only of modifying the meaning of these dialogue-messages, but also of constituting autonomous messages, expressing the relation between speeches and the possibility or impossibility of relations between humans. In Brecht's *Galileo Galilei* the famous scene in which the Pope, in full papal regalia, progressively demonstrates decreasing good will towards his friend Galileo (scene 12), is less an expression of a speech than it is of the new conditions of enunciation for the speech of that same character. Many modern works, those by Beckett for example, are concerned not so much with discourse as with the conditions for the exercise or non-exercise of speech. Hence it is almost impossible to carry out a simple textual analysis on them. In *Endgame* the old men's speeches come out of a garbage can, and the message is less in the speeches than it is in the speech-garbage can relation. What can you say when your message comes out of a garbage can? The condition of enunciation for discourse constitutes the message and is thus part of the totality of the discourse conveyed by the object-theatre, addressing the spectator. The didascalic textual layer has the characteristic of being both a message and an indication of the contextual conditions of another message.

1.4. Discourse and the Process of Communication

We are thus faced with a process of communication that has four elements (2 times 2):

1/ the reporting discourse (I) has the scriptor IA as speaker-sender (at the level of performance the various practitioners of theatre are added as senders IA') and the audience IB as receiver;
2/ The reported discourse (II) has the character[7] IIA as sender-interlocutor and another character IIB as receiver.

Thus we have not only a 'syntax serving two masters' (sender I and sender II)[8] but indeed a much more complicated structure in which the four voices function almost simultaneously throughout the entire duration of the theatrical text; the voices of the senders mingle together just as the voice and the listening activity of the receiver-speaker and the receiver-public are mingled.

We will try successively to examine the function of reporting discourse as it is realized by the four voices, and then the function of reported discourse in its principal relationship with the character speaker, and in dialogue between interlocutors.

2. The Discourse of the Scriptor

By discourse of the scriptor we mean the reporting discourse that is linked not only to the scriptor's desire to write theatre, but also to the set of stage conditions for enunciation: to the scriptor *IA* (author) is added the scriptor *IA'* (practitioner, director, etc.).

When we speak of the communication situation and the conditions of enunciation dependent upon them, we do not mean conditions of production at the level of the scriptors *IA* and *IA'*. The study of the relations of the production of texts (and of performances) to their sociohistorical conditions goes beyond our present work. That task, an absolutely necessary one, is not possible for us now and is outside the scope of our present study.

We shall settle for an examination of the general characteristics of theatrical discourse, dealing first with the most important of those characteristics. Theatrical discourse is not declarative or informative; it is conative (with a predominance of what Jakobson calls the conative function) and its mode is the imperative.

2.1. Theatrical Enunciation and the Imperative

This is a paradoxical statement. If we read a theatrical text printed on the pages of a book, it is not immediately obvious to us that its status is radically different from that of a novel or a poem. But when we remember that the theatrical text is doubly present upon the stage – as a set of phonic signs emitted by the actors and as a set of linguistic signs that govern non-linguistic signs (the complex semic totality of performance) – it becomes clear that the status of the written text (text, canvas, script, musical score, etc.) is that it governs the signs of performance (although necessarily, in performance there are autonomous signs produced with no direct relation to the text). On that point, what is obvious for the didascalia is no less obvious for the dialogue, which is equally important in governing performance signs, directly or indirectly. It does so directly because dialogue is spoken on the stage, and indirectly because dialogue, as much through its structures as through its indices, conditions auditory-visual signs.

If in a given item from the didascalia we meet the syntagma *a chair*, it is impossible to transform it into 'there is a chair.' The only transformation that accounts for the functioning of the didascalic text is '*place* a chair ...' (on stage, in the area where the action is taking place). But the line, 'Take a seat, Cinna.' also has the characteristic of organizing the presence on stage of a seat. Further, the same sentence, within the text written by Corneille, is an instruction to the actor to say it. We would add – and it is less obvious – that the text as a whole, through its very structures, governs the functioning of the signs of performance.

The theatrical text is modalized:

a/ as an imperative addressed to the stage practitioners (do or say this or that, put a chair there, a table, a curtain, say this phrase);

b/ as an imperative addressed to the public (see, hear [and/or imagine] what I have *ordered* the practitioners of the stage to show [impose upon, propose to] you).

The status of the theatrical text is the same as the status of a music score, a libretto, or a choreography. They all lead to the construction of a sign system through the intermediary of mediators:

a/ the actor, a creator-distributor of phonic linguistic signs;

b/ the director (set designer, props director, actors, etc.).

The discourse conveyed by theatrical text is of a unique nature: it has an *illocutionary force.*[9] It appears as a speech act that presupposes and creates its own conditions of enunciation; in this aspect it is analogous to an infantry manual or a missal. Theatrical speech, classically, develops as follows: X (author) says that Y (character) says that (utterance); a much more accurate formulation would be: X (author) orders Y (actor) to say that (utterance), and X (author) orders Z (director) to see to it that (didascalic utterance) [for example, that a chair be placed on stage].

The fundamental characteristic of theatrical discourse is that it can only be understood as a series of orders given with a view to stage production, with a view to performance; it is addressed to receiver-mediators who are charged with the responsibility of re-transmitting it to a receiver-public.

2.2. We Are in the Theatre

A consequence: theatrical discourse rests on a fundamental presupposition – we are in the theatre. In other words, the content of its discourse has no meaning outside a determinate space (the area in which the performance takes place, the stage, etc.) or outside a determinate time (the time of performance). The dramatic author declares from the start:

a/ My speech is sufficient to give the stage practitioners the order to create the conditions of enunciation for my discourse; it constitutes in and of itself that order, and therein lies its illocutionary force.

b/ My discourse has no meaning outside the framework of the performance; each sentence of my text presupposes the affirmation that it is said or shown on stage (that we are in the theatre). We are indeed dealing with a presupposition, in the sense in which Ducrot uses the term,[10] because whatever the sentence (whatever its affirmed element) might be, we can make it undergo negative or interrogative transformations without changing the presupposition. For Dom Juan's line to the Poor Man: 'Go, I give it to you out of love for humanity,' we can write, 'I do not give it to you ...,' or 'Do I give it to you?' without affecting in any way the presupposition *we are in the theatre.*

This has several consequences. Let us take an example: in Racine's *Iphigénie,* Arcas says, 'But everything is sleeping, the army, the winds and Neptune'; this sentence can possibly have some significance, but it cannot have meaning. Strictly speaking, it is neither true nor false – you cannot speak of it that way. But if we add the presupposition we are in the theatre, we get: (on stage) 'Everything is sleeping, the army, the winds and Neptune.' This sentence presents more difficulties and will have referential value only if the staging of the play, by constructing a mimetic referent, gives it that value. The only question we can answer with a yes or no clearly brings the presupposition into focus: 'Did the actor portraying Arcas just say, on stage, "But everything is sleeping, the army, the winds and Neptune"?' The answer can be 'Yes, he did,' 'No, he forgot to say that,' or even 'The director told him not to say that.'

This simple example shows quite clearly where denial is situated in the theatre. Of course, theatrical speech has imperative value, but by that very fact it cannot have informative or *constative* value (to use Austin's term[11]). The message it conveys is not referential, or more precisely, it does not relate to the stage referent. It speaks only of what is on stage (what is and what should be). When Arcas says, 'But everything is sleeping ...':

a/ Racine gives the order to the actor to say, 'But everything is sleeping';

b/ the actor informs the spectator 'what is on stage.' But 'what is' finally can be no more than the actor's speech. The totality of theatrical discourse is both limited by and informed by the basic presupposition. What appears obvious in connection with Arcas's line is no less so (although it is much less evident) when a speaker-character says to another speaker-character, 'I love you,' or 'I hate you.' Such messages convey no constative information, they give us no information about anybody.

Denial in the theatre, something that initially has only psychic meaning, acquires a linguistic reality through the basic presupposition. Theatrical discourse appears to be disconnected from referential reality, and its sole connection seems to be with the stage referent; it is 'disengaged' from the effective forces of real life. This simple observation casts some doubt on all speculations that assimilate theatre in the sacred, making performance a locus of contact with the sacred. We would more readily say the opposite: by the fact of denial, theatre is a locus where sacred words are no longer sacred, where those words can no longer baptise, pray to the gods, or sanctify a marriage; theatre is a locus where the juridical has no value, where one can neither swear an oath, sign a contract, nor conclude an agreement.[12]

Thus the presupposed premise strongly entrenches all of the scriptor's discourse within the framework of theatrical communication, with its autonomy and its disconnectedness from reality.

2.3. The Discourse of the Scriptor as a Totality

If the discourse of the scriptor takes on meaning only in terms of theatricality, there is nothing to stop us from also considering it, at least provisionally, as a 'total poem,' to be approached through textual analysis alone – indeed through 'infinite' poetic analysis, as was done, for example, with Baudelaire's *Les Chats* (Jakobson, Lévi-Strauss). Of course we can consider *Phèdre* or *Bajazet* as poetic totalities and analyze them as poems by Racine. That is what so much of traditional textual explication or modern criticism does, with greater or lesser success. There is nothing to stop us from subjecting, if not the whole of the dramatic text (a project that smacks of paranoia), at least a sample to that analytical practice, not to give the chosen fragment a meaning (I believe the reader understands this), but rather to make stylistic discoveries. Of course there is a 'style' that is Racine's, or Maeterlinck's; Leo Spitzer, for example, studies litotes in Racine.[13] There are perfectly legitimate analyses dealing with the lexicon of Corneille or Molière, or with syntax, and even more importantly, with prosody. We will not accord special attention to ways of reading that are well known for their wide diversity, but which do not deal with the theatrical text as a unique object of study.[14]

2.4. Scriptor's Speech, Character's Speech

Among the many false problems that punctuate critical thought on the paradoxical subject of the theatre, without doubt the worst is the one that raises the question of the subject of theatrical discourse. When Hermione speaks, who is speaking? Is it Racine or the fictive object we know as Hermione? In the face of such a brutal and absurd inquiry, criticism beats a hasty retreat. We do not dare put the question in that way, but we are quite brave enough to ask whether Lorenzo is Musset. (Sometimes we say outright: Lorenzo or Perdican is Musset; it is well known that romanticism is individualistic and subjective ...) We dare, with some reservation, to ask ourselves who the 'reasoner' is in a Molière play, and if his discourse is really Molière's discourse.

Our theory of the four voices in theatrical discourse has the merit of allowing us to avoid this frantic, vain search for the thought, the personality, or even the biography of the author. From the moment we discover these four voices, theatrical discourse can be no more than a relation between these voices. In particular, within dialogue the voice of speaker *I* (the scriptor) and the voice of speaker *II* (the character) are both present, even if they are not easily identifiable as such; the voice of the author invests-disinvests the voice of the character in a sort of rhythm, a pulsating action that shapes the theatrical text. Thus the long speech of Don Carlos in *Hernani* (act 4, scene 2) invests both Don Carlos' voice as he reflects upon the empire he awaits, and Hugo's voice as he reflects upon power in the nineteenth century. It would be pointless to look there for conditions during the nineteenth-century empire or for an echo of Hugo's ideas. We can say the same of the three speeches in Corneille's *Cinna* concerning supreme power (act 2, scene 1). Again we have particularly meaningful political discourse; but this observation can be relevant to the whole of textual dialogue. The biographical *I* is hidden in theatrical discourse: thus the autobiographical speech of an *I-Hugo* includes only the most obscure of topographical or onomastic allusions.[15] If Charles Mauron or Lucien Goldmann,[16] through various approaches, can identify the presence of the Jansenist *deus absconditus* in a Racinian text, it is not strictly speaking at the level of discourse, but rather in reference to the work's structures.

Because theatrical discourse is the discourse of a subject-scriptor, it is the discourse of a subject that is immediately stripped of his or her *I*, the discourse of a subject that denies his or her subjecthood, that declares himself or herself to be speaking through the voice of another, or several others, to be speaking without being a subject: theatrical discourse is a discourse without a subject. The function of the scriptor is to organize the conditions for the sending of speech while at the same time denying responsibility for that speech. Discourse without subject, but in which two voices are invested, voices in dialogue – this is the first, primitive form in which we see *dialogism*[17] within theatrical discourse. It is easy to postulate the existence of such a dialogism, but more difficult to find its sometimes almost unidentifiable traces. Two procedures are perhaps feasible, as long as we do not isolate them from each other: to decipher theatrical discourse as the conscious/unconscious discourse of a scriptor, or to understand it as the discourse of a fictive subject (with an equally fictive conscious/unconscious relation). Both these procedures are illegitimate and fruitless if they claim to be connected with, and to explain, any given psyche (the creator's, the character's), because what is accomplished by theatrical discourse is precisely the escape from the problem of individual subjectivity. Theatrical discourse is by nature an inquiry into the status of speech: who is speaking to whom, and under what conditions can one speak?

2.5. The Sender-Scriptor and the Receiver-Public

To return to the four voices, we note that there is a process of communication between a sender and a receiver, and that in this process the voice of the audience is far from insignificant.[18] It is not only heard concretely, but also always presupposed by the sender. In theatre one can only say (write) what can be heard: in a positive way or in a negative way (through self-censorship), the scriptor responds to an audience's voice. For example in the theatre of the nineteenth century, the presence of the courtesan character is a response to social demand. Every theatrical text is a response to a *demand* on the part of the audience, and it is from that perspective that theatrical discourse is most easily articulated with history and ideology. It is very interesting to identify (all kinds of approaches are possible) elements that are common to all theatrical discourse of a given era, or more precisely, common to a genre that is linked to a particular type of theatre and stage. Thus for example, stylistic studies of melodrama,[19] popular drama in the nineteenth century, or Elizabethan drama, have less to do with a kind of discourse common to the scriptors in question than with the discourse shared by the receiver. The vocabulary of melodrama informs us less about the writing habits of its authors then it does about the audience's way of listening. Even if the author takes a stand that opposes spectators' expectations (as does Hugo, and more recently, Jean Genet), that refusal cannot escape inclusion within the theatrical discourse itself. Whether the scriptor situates himself or herself within the dominant ideology of his time, or claims to oppose it with a counter-discourse, the phantom of the dominant discourse will be present, in some form, within the text. Already classic analyses of discourse[20] have shown that theatre must be approached in a unique way: an important form of dialogism present in a theatrical discourse sets in opposition within a single text two ideological discourses that in general are themselves quite identifiable.

We see the problem that arises not only in connection with classical theatre, but with any type of theatre that is not contemporary: how can we develop a new relation between a textual discourse created with a specific audience in mind, and an audience that has changed, that shares neither the culture nor the preoccupations of the original intended audience? The simplest reflex is to deny the problem and see the relation between the discourse of the scriptor and the voice of the spectator as based on a universal human nature, on passions that have always been and always will be. Another trap is the attempt to reconstitute the author's discourse along with its historical conditions of enunciation, while at the same time denying the presence of a contemporary audience and the voice specific to it.

In this connection we now discover yet another voice, one that modulates the scriptor's voice – the voice of the sender that we call the director (and the other practitioners of theatre). To the scriptor's text T we add the director's text t': to the IA–IB relation we add, or substitute an $I'A$–B relation. In productions staged by Planchon or Vitez, K.M. Grüber or J. Lassalle,[21] the discourse expressed by Bérénice, presupposes a new receiver: the contemporary audience. A dialogue is established between the director's voice and the author's voice, a dialogue that of course cannot be deciphered at the level of the theatrical text and which takes on its meaning only within the framework of the signs sent out by performance. That is the domain in which we must bring together a semiology of theatrical discourse and a semiotics of performance. Here we take measure of the degree to which this concept of the scriptor's discourse runs the risk of being itself arbitrary, unless we can demonstrate the relationship between the four voices implicated in the process of theatrical communication.

3. The Character's Discourse

Here we are dealing with the area in which reading habits and traditions governing commentaries of theatrical texts make a new kind of analysis more difficult. It will be useful to bear in mind what was said in chapter

III about the relationships between the character's discourse and the functioning human being that putatively is the vehicle for that discourse. Suffice it to recall that (a) the notion of character is relatively recent and historically dated and is in no way a universal in theatre, (b) that the character's discourse is far from being the wherewithal with which to constitute a psychology of the individual-character. It is through the semiotic-character totality and its syntactic function that we can identify the conditions of enunciation of that discourse and therefore understand it.

3.1. The Character's Discourse as Message: The Six Functions

Whatever criticism we might make of the functions Jakobson identifies for discourse, it nonetheless remains true that an analysis of the character's discourse according to those functions remains useful and fruitful.

a/ The *referential* function: At the level of content we can make an inventory of what the character tells us about other characters and about himself or herself: it is thus clear that what the character can tell us about his own psychology is a very thin layer among all other layers of referential information (although it is the domain in which commentators' achievements are the most facile, where their conclusions appear all the more brilliant for the fact that they run no risk of being refuted by other analyses). The character's discourse informs us in the area of politics, religion, philosophy; it is the tool by which the other characters (in the exposition, for example) and the audience can acquire knowledge. Perhaps even more – and this is a fundamental part of its referential function – it demonstrates how a given instance of speech is spoken in relation with a situation: this is where we find the *realism* of the character's discourse. However, it is also true that the referential function of the character's discourse cannot be analysed without reference to other discourses.

b/ The *conative* function: The character's speech is, or can be, action, because it incites the other characters to action (and/or to other discourse). Thus the result of Cinna's speech on monarchical power is to prevent Auguste from abdicating (*Cinna*, act 2, scene 1). The study of the conative function should be carried out not only in the area of verbal mood (an obvious application) but also in connection with the entire *rhetorical* function of discourse, argumentation, and all that makes a character into an orator: command, persuasion, etc., and all the modalities of discourse seen as an act governed by the conative function.

c / The *emotive* or *expressive* function: In theory this function is linked to the sender; it is the means by which the receiver perceives sender's emotions. In theatre this function is directed toward the receiver-spectator and must imitate emotions which deep down he knows no one is feeling, so as to induce them in the receiver-spectator. Again, syntax and even semantics alone are not sufficient to clarify the emotive function of the character's discourse; neither lexical features (the vocabulary of passion) nor syntactic characteristics (exclamations, breaks in syntax, jerkiness) are enough to indicate the emotive function. The famous 'You will be there, my daughter' – Agamemnon's invitation to his daughter to attend his own sacrifice – induces emotion only because of the relation of that speech to its context (*Iphigénie*, act 2, scene 2). Here a strictly linguistic analysis shows its limitations with respect to theatre: in theatre semantics must be complemented and completed by pragmatics.

d / The *poetic* function: In theory this function only indirectly affects the discourse of the character-subject of enunciation. If we can analyze the poetic function of a theatrical text, we can do so only if the analysis is applied to the entire discourse or to its elements (sequence by sequence). The analysis cannot be carried out upon one textual layer (spoken by the actor-character) taken in isolation. In certain very rare cases, we can grasp not only the 'style' of a given character, but indeed an individual poetics. Thus in Shakespeare's *King Lear* we can analyse a poetics proper to the Fool's discourse or even to Lear's discourse (starting from the moment in the wild when he declares himself to be a 'fool'). In these cases, it would be difficult but not impossible to look for poetic elements that are proper to the character's discourse – in other words, to seek out the internal organization of this discourse; of course, this should be done with all the reservations inherent to the study of the poetics of a necessarily dispersed and scattered text. There is another major reservation: what we are dealing with is less a poetics of discourse than it is a poetics of the text (a text that is necessarily not closed). This would lead us, somewhat arbitrarily, away from what is strictly the domain of theatre (see Ubersfeld 1981).

e / The *phatic* function: If theoretically this notion is clear, in practical terms it poses genuine problems when we try to determine it textually. The phatic function invests any message proffered by an actor-character. Thus, whatever the character expresses, she or he is also saying, *I'm speaking to you, do you hear me?* This is an eternally twofold phatic function: it addresses the receiver on stage at the same time as it addresses the spectator. It is extremely interesting and important to identify textual determinations that indicate a phatic relation with another (a speaker *or* a spectator). The textual aspect of contemporary theatre often leans in the direction of exhibiting the phatic function to the detriment of the other functions. Pushed to the extreme, some of Beckett's or Adamov's dialogues can appear to be pure communication alone, with no other content than the fact of communication itself and the conditions under which it takes place. Perhaps the most striking example is *Waiting for Godot*, where the greater part of the messages seem to have no meaning other than to affirm, maintain, or simply seek contact. In that case it is very difficult to determine the phatic function at only the linguistic level, very often that function is signalled by a gesture or through an object denoted in discourse – for example, the shoes in *Waiting for Godot* or the slot machine in Adamov's *Ping-Pong*. Through a kind of paradox the clearest sign of phatic function of the character's discourse is the nullification of any referential or conative content. When discourse appears to be about nothing, we know that the essential function of that discourse is phatic; it is speaking communication. What is extremely obvious and basic to modern theatre is also found in all other theatrical discourse, even that of classical characters. For every instance of a character's discourse, we must study not only the discourse in and of itself with its various functions, but also (a) the conditions of enunciation responsible for the power or weakness of that discourse (backed up by bayonets, or the vain supplication of the conquered), and (b) any relationship with accompanying gestures which might cancel out or limit the effects of the discourse in question.

In concluding our discussion of the prime importance of the phatic function of a character's discourse, we are brought back to problems that are of the domain of pragmatics. Nothing can be demonstrated about the character's discourse that will not have a relation with the two 'discourses' that accompany it – that of the *context* and that of the *gestural* (see Ubersfeld 1981). The textual component, as we could demonstrate for each of the functions, cannot be understood without the other two components.

3.2. The Character's Language

The words which they call out to each other I report
What the mother says to her son

What the employer says to the employee
What the wife replies to her husband
All the begging words, all the commanding
The grovelling, the misleading
The lying, the unknowing
The whining, the wounding ...
I report them all.
>   B. Brecht, *The Playwright's Song*, translated by John Willett (Brecht 1976)

It is entirely by design that we use the vague word *language*, a word that accounts for all aspects of what is said by the character.

3.2.1. The Character's Idiolect

In certain specific cases the character uses a separate language; in the textual layer where the character is the *subject*, there are linguistic particularities brought to light by the theatre. In all of these unique cases language serves to give the character the status of 'foreigner' or 'stranger.' Thus popular characters are portrayed as not knowing how to use their masters' language: for example, peasant characters in plays by Marivaux or Molière (even when they are portrayed more nobly elsewhere in a given play, as is the case for Martine in *Les Femmes savantes*). Their artificial language has no referential value and serves only to distance them. This is also accomplished in a different way with provincial accents and turns of phrase reminiscent of their *patois* (cf. in Molière, in *Monsieur de Pourceaugnac*, or in *Les Fourberies de Scapin*). In later times, the *simpleton* of melodrama is also portrayed as someone who wishes to speak the language of his masters, especially since he already serves their values and ideologies, but speaks it with comical distortions. In all of these cases the character's idiolect serves to elicit a superior laugh from the spectator at a character who does not know how to use the community's linguistic tool. In theatre, linguistic difference is rarely considered to be specific. It is rather seen as designating those who are outside of the group, in a position of inferiority.[22]

3.2.2. The Social Code

This aspect, emphasized by Brecht, is a defining aspect of certain forms of theatre. However, we might well consider that all characters in theatre speak the language of the social layer to which they belong. This 'obvious fact' needs to be treated with some care: are we talking about the social layer to which a character is supposed to belong or the layer to which the scriptor belongs? (We are deliberately avoiding the word 'class' because it presupposes that one is conscious of belonging to a particular class.) Are we not dealing instead with the imaginary language which the scriptor assigns to the social layer to which the character belongs? The language of Racine's kings is imaginary; it is neither Racine's language nor that of Louis XIV. The language of the capitalist Puntila (*Mr. Puntila and his Man Matti*) is no more Rockefeller's or Ford's language than it is Brecht's. This means that the language of the characters of a play is not conceived to reflect with referential precision the language of the social being it purports to represent. However, it is clear that Alceste's language is coded differently from the language of the petty noblemen (who belong to the same social layer as Alceste, but not to the same group). What is socially encoded in the character's discourse is the borrowing from a particular kind of discourse that already exists in the society around the character, a discourse the character uses as an encoded system. Thus when Célimène says to Alceste, 'No, you don't love me in the way *we're supposed* to love' (*Le Misanthrope*, act 4, scene 3), this posits a discourse that presupposes the existence of not so much love but a discourse on love[23] in the social group to which they belong. The 'social' aspect of the character's language is not a reflection of reality but rather the 'citation' of a kind of social discourse. Here we are dealing with the important problem of the plurality of discourses within the discourse of a given character (Bakhtinian *dialogism*); one of the most interesting aspects of this problem is the borrowing, by a given social class, of the discourse of another class (usually from the dominant class). This problem is especially current in theatre and we encounter it often. For example, in forms of theatre immediately contemporaneous with *théâtre du quotidien* (kitchen-sink drama) the characters created by Franz-Xaver Kroetz, Michel Deutsch, and Jean-Pierre Wenzel cannot speak their own discourse, but are obliged to borrow the dominant discourse (*discourses*) in order to expose their own particular problems.

3.2.3. Subjective Discourse
Such an analysis reduces the subjective aspect of the character's discourse: the presence, within his or her discourse, of both the interlocutor and social discourse, reduces the importance of subjective enunciation. In the famous example, 'I have not kissed him yet today,' (*Andromaque*, act 1, scene 4), scholarly tradition sees a spontaneous maternal exclamation; perhaps, but the statement is to a much greater extent a (double-edged) weapon against Pyrrhus. It is a swing at him that could be paraphrased as follows: In reply to Pyrrhus who has just asked, 'Were you look-

ing for me Madam?' Andromaque answers, 'It's not you I'm looking for, nor you that I love, but the child Astyanax; he is what is left of Troy' ('Since once a day you let me be alone / with all of Hector and Troy I own').[24] A character's discourse conveys not so much subjectivity as intersubjectivity.

The character's discourse declares itself as speaking its own subjectivity, as being 'man within language.' Theatre is where what Benveniste calls 'the individual act of appropriating language' is best carried out. This act:

introduces the one who speaks as he is found in his speech ... The presence of the speaker in his utterance means that each instance of discourse constitutes an internal centre of reference. This situation will be manifested by the interplay of specific forms whose function is to place the speaker in a constant and necessary relation with his utterance ... In the first instance we have the emergence of personal indices (the *I-you* relation) which can be produced only within and through utterance: the term *I*, denotes the individual who is proffering the utterance, the term *you*, the individual who is present as receiver. The many indices of ostension (*this, here*, etc.) share this same nature and are implicated in the same structure of utterance. They are terms that imply a gesture that designates an object at the same time as the term is pronounced (Benveniste 1974, II:82).

Theatrical discourse is indeed centred on utterance, on *I-you* discourse (as opposed to a *he* discourse, an objective discourse), a *here-and-now* discourse in which what Benveniste calls *embrayeurs* (shifters) function. However, and this is the fundamental paradox of theatre, and of its possibilities – what characterizes shifters is that they *have no referent*: who is *I*? where is *here*? when is *now*? Specifications that are outside the discourse are needed if it is to have its referent: theatrical performance, as we have shown, constructs that referent. This allows it to have an infinite number of *here-and-now*s, and therefore also many *I*s. The theatrical *I* is never exclusively linked to an historical and biographically determinate *me*; if 'Cleopatra' speaks, it is not really Cleopatra, but an actress.

It is on these two points (the *I-you* relation, and the described system above involving the present) that we should focus the analysis of the character's discourse as subjective discourse. The *I-you* relation implies a constantly renewed relation between a character and his or her subjectivity, and a relation between that subjectivity and other subjectivities. At any moment in the action the *I-you* relation indicates movement in the area of intersubjective relations. Every reading gives rise to the question: what does a character, in a given sequence, do with his or her *I*?

We shall examine two opposite examples. The first is Phèdre's self-reflexive speech in the long scene of confession to Hippolyte (act 2, scene 5). Here Phèdre expresses her own *I* alone (usually in the position of subject), sometimes in the form of metonymy:

> I see the King, see him, speak to him, thrill.
> My mind is wandering. My lord, my madness
> speaks the thing it should not.
> ...
> Yes, Prince, for him indeed I yearn, I languish Theseus.
> I love him, ...
> I love. But never think that even while
> I love you I can absolve myself, or hide my face
> from my own guiltiness.

We could quote the whole of Phèdre's discourse, not only in this scene but almost throughout the text. This is a good example of self-reflexive discourse whose subjectivism, functioning at the level of action as well as the level of interpersonal discourse, calls up the illusory commentary involving a psychology of person.

The second, contrary example is Ruy Blas's anonymous speech addressing a ringing apostrophe to the ministers (*Ruy Blas*, act 3, scene 2), in which, although he is the prime minister, he cannot say *I* because he has no identity, because he bears a usurped name.

An analysis of the tense system will also reveal the relation of the character to time and action. In Adamov's early plays the hero (the central character of all of his dream stories) cannot speak of himself or his own action in the present. His self-reflexive speech always uses the future tense (sometimes the conditional), reporting any given act at an action time that is in perpetual forward flight. Here again, the character's subjective discourse has less to do with the psychology of a person who cannot speak in the present and who perpetually puts off his indecisive acts until the next day (*Le sens de la marche, Les retrouvailles*) than it does with a certain kind of interpersonal relations which regulate the action and are regulated by it.

Here we touch on the problem of the *modalization* of enunciation, a problem that corresponds to an interpersonal, social relation and that therefore requires a relation between the protagonists in a given instance of communication.

A sentence can have only one obligatory modality of enunciation – declarative interrogative, imperative, exclamative – that specifies both the type of communication between speaker and listener(s),[25] and also the speaker's commitment to his own discourse (expressed by 'perhaps,' 'probably,' 'of course'). Syntax has a major role in the modalization of enunciation, and in that respect the status of theatrical discourse is no different from that of dialogue in the novel. (For example, see the speech made up entirely of negatives, in which Madame de Clèves turns down Nemours, on the last page of Madame de La Fayette's novel.) But in theatre there is a reversion of modalization upon the content of discourse. Modalizing the enunciation of discourse is not so much a matter of giving it a particular 'colour' as giving it another meaning; the modalization in fact becomes the content of the message. What is said is not the object of a given instance of questioning and uncertainty; rather that questioning and uncertainty bring into play a certain type of relations of language with the interlocutor. 'You do not answer me?' Hermione asks Pyrrhus, who is no longer listening (*Andromaque*, act 4, scene 5); the message of this sentence is not really its question and awaited answer, but is in fact the phatic appeal to Pyrrhus. Even more than classical theatre, modern theatre both depends upon and operates upon modalization. In modern theatre speech is marked by uncertainty, it is expressly cut off from any realist referent, it displays its subjectivity. Modalization in modern theatre statistically plays a much more important role than it does in classical theatre. For example in the famous first sentence of Beckett's *Endgame* we can observe modalization setting in: Finished, it's finished, nearly finished, it must be nearly finished.

3.3. Heterogeneity of the Character's Discourse

A character on stage is expressed, in theory, by a single actor (and when this is violated it is perceived in fact as a violation). On the other hand, in many forms of theatre – and we are not just thinking of Brecht – there is an effort to align the character's discourse with a given everyday referent: this is the way a marquis speaks, or a valet, a butcher, a CEO, a farmhand in Picardy. Thus there is an often powerful 'reality effect' in the discourse of a character, which gives that speech at least an apparent consistency that overrides any discrepancies. Some forms of theatre depend on the consistency of a given character's speech, as in various comic types or the naturalism of certain characters in Goldoni or Chekhov (although this is certainly not true of all of their characters). In other cases it is the uniformity of 'style' in a Corneille or a Racine that produces an effect of consistency in a given character's speech.

This consistency is more apparent than real, at least in less conventional theatre. In a character's theatrical utterance we see heterogeneous discourse: alongside subjective discourse we will find quoted discourses: speeches that convey general opinion, 'the wisdom of nations,' aphorisms, proverbs, maxims, utterances in the third person, set apart as objective elements. The most subjective theatrical discourse is the vehicle for a mass of other discourses borrowed from cultural areas and belonging to society in general or, more often, to the social level at which the character is developed. It is not an overstatement to say that much of Brechtian distancing consists in ridding the utterances of the characters of the illusion of monocentrism, so that utterances of diverse provenance can be juxtaposed in the discourse of those characters. More precisely this effort consists in juxtaposing subjective discourse with discourse set at a distance, objective discourse. There is a very good, almost legendary, example in *The Good Person of Szechuan* where the main character is split into two characters with opposing discourses. What is often referred to as a character's inner conflict is, in theatre, a collision of discourses. At each step we come up against the fundamental fact that, even in monologue, a character's discourse functions only through dialogue, implicit or explicit. Any reasonably detailed analysis of discourse will inevitably show that a character's discourse is not a continuous flow but rather the juxtaposition of different textual layers among which there is a relation, generally a conflicting one. We can go further: it is these various discursive layers that make dialogue possible. The relation between a character's discourse and dialogue is truly dialectical. It is not possible to analyse a character's discourse as an isolated monad, but conversely, the textual heterogeneity of that discourse makes it possible to place it in relation to other discourses.

4. Dialogue, Dialogism, Dialectics

Theatrical speech, even in a monologue, is essentially 'dialogued.' Theatrical dialogue is less a series of textual layers with two or more subjects of enunciation than it is the verbal emergence of a speech situation that has two confronting elements.

4.1. Dialogue and Situation of Dialogue

It is of course important to do what all classical[26] dramatic art does, namely to note the diverse forms of dialogue and their combination within the whole of a dramatic text: dialogue that takes the form of long, elaborately constructed speeches in which characters confront each other rhetorically and passionately; stichomythia (in which characters exchange whole lines or hemistichs), as in the most intense moments of a tragedy; interrupted speeches or babblings exchanged in classical comedy; multiple scenes which weave the speakers' exchanges together; fake dialogue almost completely dominated by one speaker whose speech is simply punctuated by the replies of another speaker whose only role is to feed the momentum, as we see in scenes from classical tragedy or romantic drama where someone confides in an other; parallel dialogues without exchanges (with or without asides) as are found sometimes in Shakespeare, and often in the so-called theatre of the absurd. It will be useful to describe all these forms of dialogue, at least in formal terms.

We can say that the manner of exchange constitutes a sign that makes it possible to construct meaning, and is in and of itself a vehicle for meaning. However, it is clear that we would not 'understand,' as we indeed sometimes do, the meaning of a scene played in a foreign language if other elements were not also deployed. The basis of dialogue is the *relation of power* between characters: this formula must be understood in its widest sense. The relation of love can also be a relation of domination; to desire is to be a supplicant, and therefore in a position of 'inferiority' *vis-à-vis* whoever holds the object of desire. This situation produces a whole complex of relations between the various forces at play, forces which determine the very conditions under which speech takes place. Thus, as is so clearly demonstrated by Ducrot (1974 and 1980), any 'asking' scene presupposes that the character who asks is in a position to perform the asking role, that the 'juridicial' relations between the one asking and the one asked are such that a parallel relation in language is possible, and that the one asked is obliged to answer, or is willing to answer. The famous scene with Auguste and his counsellors (*Cinna*, act 2, scene 1) is meaningful only through its relation to the implicit order from Auguste, an order that no one can ignore by virtue of his role as master, a master who can oblige those around him to tell him whether or not he should abdicate.

A theatrical dialogue thus has a double layer of contents, it delivers two types of messages; a single sign system (linguistic signs) carries a twofold content:

a/ the content itself, the utterances of the discourse;
b/ information concerning the conditions for the production of those utterances.

To neglect that second layer of information because it is less obvious amounts to distorting the meaning of the utterances themselves, as we will attempt to demonstrate with some examples. Theatrical dialogue is based upon a presupposition that governs it: the presupposition that one of the interlocutors, for example, is in a position to decide the nature of the instance of dialogue and to impose that decision. We can go further: the primary message of theatrical dialogue is precisely the verbal relation at play and the presuppositions that govern it. That verbal relation itself is dependent on relations (usually of dominance) between characters, because those relations appear as an imitation of relations that operate in the real world. They are the primary matter of mimesis. There is no need to add that the way we perceive them is entirely dependent upon social relations, to use the term in its broadest sense.

4.2. Dialogue and Ideology

On this point of the ideology-discourse relation, we come back to Robin's lucid analysis, commenting on a text by Haroche, Henry and Pêcheux (Robin 1971, 102). She points out that:

- Ideologies[27] are not neutral elements, but rather social forms, class ideologies.
- Discourses cannot be reduced to ideologies any more than ideologies can be superimposed upon discourses. It is observed that discursive systems are a component of ideological systems,[28] in other words, that ideological systems govern discursive systems.
- Discursive systems can be perceived only as a function of the conditions of their production, the institutions that spawn them and the constitutive rules of discourse: as Foucault says, we do not say just anything, at just any moment in time, just anywhere.
- Words can be analysed only as a function of the combinations, the constructions in which they are used (ibid., 104).

This analysis is all the more applicable to theatrical dialogue for the fact that it takes on its full meaning only in relation to what Robin calls the *discursive positions* of speakers. These discursive positions can be identified through the explicit content of discourse, but they can be identified even more easily at the level Robin calls the *unasserted*, a 'pre-construct' of discourse, analogous in the way it works to the *presuppositions* defined by Ducrot – in other words the common basis, the assertion that is not cast in doubt and upon which dialogue is constructed, with all its divergences.

For example, it is clear that a Shakespearean dialogue in which a king is one of the speakers, presupposes maxims that define the feudal relation between the king and his vassals (the discursive position), with all of the sociohistorical changes to those relations that were introduced during Shakespeare's time: the contradiction that arises opposes those presupposed maxims and the different, new discursive positions that the vassals' revolt produces. In the exchanges between Lear and his rebellious daughters (along with the constructed discourse and its familial, moral, affective, even political arguments) there is a change in the relation of power between the old king and the newly ruling women.

We can see the mediations by which ideology becomes established within a theatrical text, less at the level of explicit content (and even of its connotations) than at the level of the presuppositions that govern relations between characters. Thus, the ideological consequences of the crisis in feudalism at the end of the sixteenth century in England are perceived less at the level of the content of dialogues than at the level of the language situations that arise between the characters: the entire texts of *Richard II* and *Macbeth* can be better understood if we read their dialogues in that way. This is unique to theatre: what can be perceived through critical appraisal alone in non-theatrical texts (discursive or novelistic), in theatre can be put into a given form and exhibited through staging. It is as if the director's task were precisely to show 'visually' the situations for language and, by extension, the discursive positions.

4.3. Questioning Dialogue

Our questions about dialogue initially are questions about the production of dialogue. The power of dialogue's impact on the spectator stems most often from the gap between the discourse that is enacted and the conditions for its production, or indeed the abnormal nature of the conditions of its production.

The initial effort to understand the text of a dialogue must involve questions about:

a/ the relations of *dependency* between the characters involved within a given sociohistorical structure (master-valet, king-subject, man-woman, lover-loved, asker-asked, etc.)

b/ the degree to which these relations affect speech relations between speakers, with all resulting consequences for the *illocutionary force* of the utterances involved: The meaning of an imperative utterance depends on whether it is possible for the speaker to be obeyed. We must therefore ask several questions of the text: who is speaking? who has the right to speak? who is first to speak? etc.

c/ the presuppositions upon which the very existence of dialogue rests – not to be confused with the presuppositions that govern the utterances of dialogue.

4.4. Contradictions

The answers to these questions lead us to some obvious conclusions that hardly need noting, but often, they allow us to see how dialogue functions through certain contradictions.

4.4.1. Contradictions between Speech and Discursive Position

A servant does not speak in the presence of his master, a court jester does not insult his king: *King Lear* and many other Shakespeare texts show how this contradiction can in fact generate meaning. We have just seen that dialogue in a Hugo drama will assign speech to someone who is not in a position to speak, who is in an 'impossible' position: a courtesan speaks to a chaste king, a lackey to government ministers or to the queen. Meaning is shifted: it is focused, not on the signification of the utterances but, through the absurdity of the situation, on the conditions for the production of the effectual speech and the possibility of its being heard. If we come back to the notion of verisimilitude in drama, we note that it has less to do with psychology than with the conditions under which dialogue can take place. Although Baroque drama often expressly exploits this contradiction, classical drama seeks to lessen it. But contradiction is there nonetheless and it gives the classical stage its power and its meaning: there is a well-known example from *Andromaque* (act 1, scene 4) in which we see the confrontation between the heroine and Pyrrhus: this scene indicates a possible reversal of the master-slave, conqueror-conquered, relation. The entire dialogue is built upon the conflict inherent in the twofold presupposition: Andromaque in a position of weakness, Andromaque in a position of power. We can even ask ourselves if the meaning of the scene is not to show this reversal within the speech situation, a reversal that is effected by the conqueror (but as a result of what power coming from both within and without him? – a question asked but unresolved, a psychological breach that cannot be filled by the words love or passion).

4.4.2. Contradiction between Conditions of Enunciation and Content of Discourse

This is the way much of Marivaux's theatre works – the conditions for the production of discourse are turned upside down producing the unexpected effects of his dialogue. *Le jeu de l'amour et du hasard*, a play in which the masters and the valets trade their discursive positions, is an excellent example; another characteristic example is *La double inconstance* in which the hypocritical speeches of the masters disguise their actual speech situations.

In Beckett this contradiction takes on a different face: the conditions of the production of discourse are hidden, and our ignorance about them produces the dialogue's suspense; this is the case with the uncertainty concerning the relations of power underlying the Hamm-Clov speech relations in *Endgame*.

We have a fine example in *Lorenzaccio* (act 2, scene 2); the scene analysed demonstrates the interplay of articulations.[29] The invitations from Lorenzo and Valori ('Come to my place ... I will have you paint ...') answer an unspoken element in the young Tebaldeo's discourse, an understood element by which he has offered his services ('hire me, buy from me')[30] and whose indexical traces are easily noted in discourse and gesture. Thus we can appreciate Tebaldeo's true discourse situation: he is a supplicant, repeating Valori's remarks (which in fact he has misunderstood) like a sycophantic parrot, and putting up with the indiscrete interrogation of his patron-to-be. We can see that mimesis is functioning in the miming of a discourse situation of not only an artist of the Renaissance but also of the artist or the literary hack of the early nineteenth century: the defence of moral independence and of the autonomy of art (art for art's sake), although produced under conditions of servitude; the defence of a fair price and the free choice of selling a painting-object or a book-object, when in fact the artist is a slave whose entire works the master forcefully buys in advance by establishing a purchasing monopoly. This extraordinary scene shows how reference is sought not so much in the sociohistorical referents of the utterances as in the actual situation in which the dialogue is produced.

4.5. Utterances in Dialogue

4.5.1. Productive Speech

We can conclude that dialogue is the development or the shaping of two discursive positions in confrontation with one another. This is shocking for those who are accustomed to seeing theatrical dialogue as a portrayal of conflicts in which the autonomy and freedom of passional or rhetorical speech is the rule. This autonomy (which the mirror of theatre demonstrates to be illusory)[31] does not exclude the development of a speech-action dialectics in which speech appears to be a factor for change in the action and a backlash that modifies its own conditions of production.[32] But even in French classical theatre, a special area, examples of dialogue in which speech is truly productive are infinitely rarer than we might think. The Greeks' persuasive speech is best deployed in almost juridicial conditions in which the prevailing code makes it possible to use a logical discourse: for instance, relative equality of discourse situations. We might say that Corneille's dramatic art constitutes a major effort to bring together and construct the conditions for exchange that make productive speech possible; his speakers can convince and be convinced. In Racine, however, a non-productive dialogue is brought into play, in which, despite appearances, no one convinces anybody. This is another way of looking at the *phatic function* of dialogue and confirming the fact that the way utterances are strung together and exchanged is more important than their content.

4.5.2. Dialogue and Dialogism

Utterances themselves are caught up in a system of contradictions that sometimes are dialectically resolved, but sometimes exist side by side. We have seen that a character's discourse includes juxtaposed utterances that are linked to different discursive systems. This initial form of dialogism is of enormous interest because it presupposes that a character is not always coincident to himself or herself and this brings into question the unity of that character. The contradictions of history emerge through the character's discourse, well beyond any individual psychology. We can read even the great deliberative monologues of the classical age in this way – the stanzas of *Le Cid*, and also, if we look at them more closely, Racine's passional monologues – because the monologue includes utterances and maxims which do not share all of the same presuppositions.

We can demonstrate that dialogism within a character's discourse is not simply a fracturing into two *voices*, as Bakhtine would have it. It is rather a collage (or montage) of radically different utterances.[33] Moreover, dialogism is involved not just in particular forms of modern theatre, but rather in all theatre: it is constitutive of theatrical dialogue, through an unexpected device, of a common or shared presupposition. If there is dialogue (and dialogism), it is because all consonances and dissonances, all conflicts and agreements occur in relation to that common core. When Bakhtine rejects the concept of dialogism in theatre he is right to the extent that he recognizes that common core. He is wrong because it is that very common core, the shared presupposition, that makes it possible for theatre to mount the confrontation, juxtaposition, montage and collage of different voices. If we are going to debate an issue, there must at least be agreement on one basic point, whatever it might be, about which there is no question, a point that although unformulated, is the very basis of the exchanged speech. Take the famous example 'the King of France is bald': we can debate, and agree or disagree on the issue of the King of France's baldness, but we have to at least agree on the fact (the presupposition) that France has a king. Everything will come to a halt if someone cries out, 'But there is no King of France!' We should note in parentheses that in certain forms of theatre, Ionesco's for example, the dialogue continues regardless; we can demonstrate that Ionescan dialogue characteristically functions with no shared presupposition. But also, it is neither dialogic nor dialectical – it is absurd.

We see precisely that in Musset's *Lorenzaccio* the hero faces utterances that belong to several different discursive formations or systems, and these in turn belong to different ideological systems: Philippe Strozzi's 'liberal' discourse, with its cultural connotations of heroic latinity, and the 'ultra' and 'Jeune France' discourse so obvious in Tebaldeo's utterances.[34] At each point the dialogue can take place only because Lorenzo demonstrates that he shares those (contradictory) presuppositions upon which the interlocutor's speeches are based. This explains the central and focusing position of the hero. He functions as a 'specular conscience,' to use Althusser's term,[35] a position that is also destructive, through the successive neutralization or suppression of the discourses he faces.

We could cite other examples, including Nero, who is temporarily beaten by Burrhus (in *Britannicus*, act 4, scene 3), because he is obliged to adopt formally the *presuppositions* of Burrhus's discourse. Further, we should not think that presuppositions are only political or ideological: a presupposition that underlies a given dialogue might be either *I love x* or *x loves me* (with the reservation that the latter case may or may not be articulated with ideology).[36] As for the *comic*, one of its sources is the presence in a single dialogue of different presuppositions that are not perceived by the parties involved; another is the perfectly hypocritical adoption of a presupposition that the speaker does not in fact espouse. We see this in Valère's dialogue with Harpagon when he is obliged to adopt the presupposition that *money is everything* (*L'avare*, act 1, scene 5). The final ceremony in *Le malade imaginaire* makes concrete the presupposition underlying all of Argan's speeches: the presence of the doctor will magically make him better by simple contact.

4.6. Some Procedures for Analysing Dialogue

We can use the above to decide on future directions to take in our research on theatrical dialogue.

a/ We need to establish the discursive positions of various speakers and, more concretely, their speech situations, which can sometimes go unperceived, masked by an apparent obviousness of meaning (meaning of the utterances): often it is an unspoken element in the discourse that conditions the speech situation. We need to look for indices – such as gestural factors, modalizations – that will allow us to recognize the 'true' situation, the real relations between characters. We must draw up the inventory of the twofold domain of the *implied* (Tebaldeo truly wants to sell his painting, Valori wants something from Lorenzaccio, Andromaque does not have freedom of movement), and of the *presupposition* (art is by nature a supplicant, art is free, a captive must submit to her conqueror) that determines the discursive position of speakers.

b/ We need to look for the presuppositions that condition dialogue itself. Thus in Tebaldeo's scene, Lorenzo and Tebaldeo share the following presuppositions: Florence = decayed, corrupted mother; art = natural growth that is nourished by an earth made rich by rotting material. These presuppositions allow dialogue to function where there is difference, by conflict (or by addition) not at the level of the presupposition (that which is is beyond any denial, or questioning, in that it has the status of a postulate), but the level of the *affirmation* (that which is immediately implicated, which one can *deny*, about which one can ask questions). It is important to remember that it would be useless, in any given dialogue, to look for a presupposition that could be reduced to an ideological-political formula. Thus in Maeterlinck's *L'intruse*, an extreme example, the presupposition is *fantastic*: the whole multiple, complex, elusive dialogue, with several characters, presupposes that death is a person who enters people's homes. There is a corollary task here: we must note the multiple presuppositions within the discursive levels attributed to a given character. The fact that there are many such presuppositions makes it possible for the character to enter into dialogue with many others.

c/ We need to study created utterances (with their historical references) that will allow us to see how the affirmation of discourse functions, the explicit utterances. Thus in that same scene with Tebaldeo, the affirmation involves an artist's freedom, with all that it implies in his life (a recurring discourse in Musset – see *Le fils du Titien*), or the link between art and historical catastrophe. These created utterances can be studied (a) according to their own functioning and the way they are joined together in dialogue, (b) in their relation to any given discursive formation or system, and (c) in their relation to the presuppositions involved.

4.7. Some Concluding Remarks

a/ It is possible to establish not only a semantics of theatrical discourse, but indeed perhaps even a semiology, because the preconstruct (or presupposition) is anterior to the signified of utterances. But such a semiology cannot be understood if it is separated from a pragmatics which would determine conditions for the exercise of discursive speech.

b/ Theatrical discourse appears to be a practice of which a considerable component is social discourse in the form of preconstructions or presuppositions, a social discourse that no one in particular is responsible for and of which no one is the subject. The idea of responsibility, of the right of ownership of one person over his or her language, is thus not applicable here. This non-individual characteristic is made more obvious in theatre by the fact that one and the same discourse can come from different lips.

This kind of analysis is important because it demonstrates the inclusion of social discourse in the form of quotation, formula, maxim, proverb, internal objection, within that very discourse (or discourses). Thus we can show that the dominant discourse does not act solely through speech, but also upon speech, informing relations between characters. Here we touch upon recent theatrical forms that in France and Germany are called *théâtre du quotidien* (kitchen-sink drama); where dialogue is concerned, the writing shows remnants – ragged yet persistently surviving and destructive – of the dominant discourse from the mouths of those who would not at all be expected to have anything to do with the dominant discourse. Hence the surprising critical virtues of that theatre. It is at this level of theatrical discourse, particularly where dialogue is concerned, that the ideology-writing relation in theatre is the most obvious.

Conversely, theatre as a practice allows us to demonstrate how ideology is not only performance but also production, because it conditions relations between people (discourse and actions).

c/ This kind of analysis is not without consequence. First, it shows us that at the level of discourse we cannot completely escape mimesis, even if we use that word in the non-naturalistic sense of a miming of conditions for the production of speech. Next, the importance of theatre is emphasized by the fact that it shows us the role of speech in relation to situation and action. It is from this perspective that the spectator's 'Brechtian' thinking can be carried out – to demonstrate the importance of a given discourse, what it amounts to, what it means (in the most concrete sense).

d/ The fundamental role of the staging of a play in relation to a discourse that in theory pre-exists it is to demonstrate what is preconstructed, to make us see what belongs to the domain of the unspoken (or of the connotative or indexical spoken). Staging shows who is speaking and how it is possible or impossible to speak. Sometimes, and this has been the rule throughout history, change in discursive formations or systems results in the loss of meaning and immediacy of a particular element: the task of directing is to construct and exhibit a parallel or similar presupposition, similar in the way triangles are similar. We see this when Bernard Sobel reconstitutes a preconstructed anti-Semitism that is both different from and similar to Marlowe's in *The Jew of Malta*; he does this in order to demonstrate it, to exhibit it as an 'ideological' presupposition. Directing a play from the classical age requires not only a display of the presuppositions involved, but also the replacement of those that have fallen into disuse, that no longer function.

To conclude, we might say that theatrical discourse is just part of an overall practice, characterized by the fact that it is also a social practice involving not only the spectator, but also directors, actors, and technicians as practitioners in an economic circuit (see Ubersfeld 1981).

A Prelude to Performance

We have tried to demonstrate that theatrical activity – although certain aspects may remain unclear, and although an intellectually and psychologically complex effort is required – can be analysed, like any other activity, with the help of procedures that are still of a rather rudimentary nature.

What can be accomplished by our semiological analysis? It reminds us to pay attention to signs, to the text's materiality with all its possible significations. These semiological procedures should be seen as prudent investigations that prevent us from leaping at the first meaning that suggests itself, from forgetting our true purpose and setting off in pursuit of shadows.

These semiological procedures give us the ability to draw up an inventory of the many possibilities offered by the theatrical text. They allow us to make an inventory of all that goes into making a text so rich, and they allow readers as well as professionals (actor, director, etc.) to make choices. Textual determinations present themselves as they really are – independent, yet linked. They are also linked with the receiver, with his or her own choices for possible readings and ways of listening.

Far from leading to a relativist despair, to the 'anything goes' of an impressionist reading or of an anarchical invention, these procedures can simultaneously open up a whole field of possible readings and assign privileged status to a reading that accounts for the greatest number of such possibilities. Our analyses are intended to be precise, of course, instead of imposing constraints, they can stimulate the pleasure and intellectual curiosity of the artist who creates an object that will circulate in the real world.

The Real and the Body

The fascination that theatre exerts – in perpetual crisis but indestructible – in the first instance relates to the fact that it is an object in the world, a concrete object that is composed of not images but rather real objects and beings – above all, the bodies and voices of actors.

Theatrical practice is 'materialist': it states that there is no thought without the body. Theatre is body, and the body is primary, demanding the right to live. But in all its activity it is subject to concrete conditions, and these conditions are social. One can be an idealist (in the philosophical sense of idealism versus materialism) when reading, but idealism is less easy when one is actually involved in theatrical activity.

The theatre is body: it states that emotions are necessary and vital and that it – the theatre – works with and in the service of emotions: our whole purpose is to find out what it does with them.

The Cleaning Rags and the Serviettes

If theatre produces emotions it is because it is a mirror of the world – but a strange mirror that brings things close up, exaggerates, syncopates. In theatre the impossible reigns, theatre works with the impossible, and is made for expressing the impossible. It is where mutually exclusive categories can come together in the same place; things that contradict reality find a place in theatre, but instead of covering them over, theatre openly displays them. Theatre is an acrobat that can leap over the bar that the binary nature of the sign represents. Theatre constantly violates structural constraints.

The circularity characteristic of rite and myth is compromised by the workings of theatre. The main figure exploited in theatre is the *oxymoron*. Theatrical time is an oxymoron. Myth is repetitive, but theatre succeeds in having the myth express what it has not expressed before: we see this in the way Aeschylus rewrites *Prometheus*, and in the three *Electras* of the Greek theatre.

Theatrical space is an oxymoron; it is the domain for miming the real – both sign and referent. The character is an oxymoron, a living actor who is also a textual figure.

Theatre: the hero wipes down his glorious nudity with a rag, while a delicate serviette cleans the floor.

Theatre: a princess is a goosegirl, her donkey-skin dress the colour of the moon. Theatre is a locus for disorder: Oreste, the matricidal criminal, is innocent-guilty, absolved by the gods. Theatre displays insoluble contradiction – obstacle before which logic and morality must give way; theatre offers phantasmic, dream-world solutions ...

What can be done with this disorder? There are three solutions. One is to return everything to a state of order. After all, following saturnalia things return to normal, transgressions are punished and the legitimate king regains his throne. Another is that disorder can simply continue, exacerbated and irretrievable, to its ultimate destruction with the ever-expanding entropy of the world. Another is that a new order can be established; Athena absolves Oreste, and tomorrow becomes today.

Theatrical oxymoron is the figure for contradictions that make things move forward. But theatrical activity can also present things only to cover them almost immediately with an impenetrable veil. Popular theatre shows just enough to hook the spectators and make them feel comfortable. Theatre proclaims the unacceptable and the monstrous; it is a hole that the spectators must plug as best they can, otherwise their little craft will leak. There are many kinds of theatre that quickly plug those holes, seal the breaches, and file down the tiger's teeth. Other kinds of theatre require us to think, to seek solutions: 'Ladies and gentlemen, in you we trust: There must be happy endings, must, must, must!'[1]

Exorcism, Exercise[2]

When reflecting on theatre, we keep coming up against the same contradiction. The theatre is a figure for real experience, with all of its explosive contradictions – contradictions which the stage makes us see in terms of oxymoron. That experience, in the reduced area of the stage, can be perceived by the spectator as either exorcism or practice. Theatrical experience is a scale model. As such, it lets us skip its counterpart in real life, it exorcizes that real-life counterpart, it makes us live according to impulses that daily life disallows: murder, incest, violent death, adultery, and blasphemy, all that is normally forbidden is there on the stage. Here, death and pain are death and pain at a distance. Banalities: we are in that special domain of *catharsis*. Where there is in fact an insoluble conflict, catharsis offers a dream-world solution, and we go out feeling content: things will turn out alright without us.

But the scale model is also a tool for learning and understanding: to transform, as theatre does, the insignificant into the significant – to semanticize signs – is to give oneself or others the power to understand conditions for the exercise of speech in the world, to understand the relation of speech to concrete situations; discourse and gestures designate the unspoken that underlies discourse. Theatre, being a scale model of power relations, appears as an exercise in which one achieves mastery over a test object that is smaller and more easily managed than its real-life counterpart.

Exorcism, exercise: do not think that these two views of theatre are mutually exclusive. In theatre there is a perpetual oscillation between them, a state in which emotions trigger thoughts that in turn rekindle emotion. The spectator is then, perhaps, excused from actually undergoing what he or she undergoes in real life. What Artaud calls the Plague is a violent release, for the spectator, of a given specific, overwhelming, but productive emotion: the spectator is made to experience something to which she or he is absolutely obliged to give meaning.

Pre-existing Meaning

It follows from all this that meaning in theatre does not exist before performance, before what is concretely said and shown; moreover it cannot exist without the spectator. This gives rise to the insoluble difficulties posed by any hermeneutics of the theatre: how are we to decipher a meaning that has yet to be produced? The theatrical text belongs to the order of the undecidable. It is the practice of theatre that constitutes that meaning, that constructs it. To read the theatre is simply to set out the conditions for the production of that meaning. This is the task of the dramaturge, the semiologist, the director, and the reader; it is your task, our task. And it is not irrational to note that this meaning, the meaning that always precedes our reading, in large measure escapes rigorous formulation. We are not denying the presence of the lived phenomenon in theatre, and we recognize that the meaning constructed for all is also each one's memory. What is so unique to theatre is the fact that, because it is no longer (as the poet said) 'one person's voice' – since the scriptor has voluntary withdrawn – it so implicates the spectator that it ends up being the voice of us all.

Notes

Foreword

1 For a list of her major works, see the bibliography.

2 The translation is ours.

3 See, for example major reviews by P. Pavis, in *Sub-stance* 18/19 (1977): 225–6; A. Daspre, in *La pensée* (juin, 1978): 151–3; J.-C. Fizaine, in *Romantisme* 19 (1978): 121; M. Issacharoff, in *Poetics Today* 2:3 (1981): 255–63; S. Jansen, in *Revue Romane* 17 (1982): 111–21; M. Corvin, in *Revue d'histoire littéraire* 2 (1983): 310–14.

4 The Paris School of Semiotics is the name given to the group of researchers from Europe and North America who participated in A.J. Greimas's ongoing seminar from 1964 to the present. Although Greimas passed away in 1992, the *Groupe de recherches sémio-linguistiques de l'Ecole des hautes études en sciences sociales* in Paris, continued to function and to meet on a bi-monthly basis. What distinguishes this school from other semiotic movements attempting to elaborate a theory of general systems of signification is their definition of the sign. If, for a number of semiotic theories, the sign is first and foremost an observable phenomenon, as J.-C. Coquet notes, 'from the perspective of the *Paris School* it is first and foremost a construct' (Coquet 1982, 5). It is obvious that the initial choice of this postulate has weighty theoretical and practical consequences.

5 See J. Veltrusky (1977); and also P. Bogatyrev in L. Matejka and R. Titunik (1976). For an overview of the *Prague School* contribution to the study of theatre, see M.L. Quinn (1995).

6 See Carlson (1993, 498); Issacharoff (1981, 255); Toro (1996, 43).

7 This very critical issue of fidelity to the text was the subject of ongoing discussion between Anne Ubersfeld and Pierre Larthomas, who, in *Le langage drama-*

tique, deplores the way directors sometimes interpret certain classical plays, making the text a simple pretext (Larthomas 1995, 35).

8 A.J. Greimas and J. Courtés criticize the triangular model aimed at accounting for the structure of the sign in which the symbol or signifier is linked to the referent not directly but through the intermediary of the reference or signified: 'In this interpretation, the reference, instead of being viewed as a relation, is reified and is transformed into a concept – a hybrid entity, neither linguistic nor referential – the expansion of which includes a class of referents' (Greimas and Courtés 1982, 259–60). Ubersfeld avoids this reification by opting for a strategy that addresses not the referent given *a priori* but the referentialization of the theatrical sign, that is to say the study of the procedures through which is constituted the referential illusion, or the meaning effect 'reality' or 'truth,' proposed by Roland Barthes.

9 The actant, be it subject, object, predicate, etc., only exists in a junctive relation with the other actants. As such it accounts for the organization of narrative discourse at the level of narrative syntax.

10 The narrative schema is considered as recording the 'life meaning' through its three essential domains: the qualification of the subject (mandate sequence), which introduces it into life; its realization by means of which it acts (action sequence); and finally, the sanction (evaluation sequence) – at one and the same time retribution and recognition – which alone confirms the meanings of its actions and installs it as a subject.

Introduction

1 See Ubersfeld (1981).
2 See Hjelmslev's distinctions between the form and matter of expression, and between the form and matter of content (Hjelmslev 1961). See also Metz (1974).
3 See Szépe and Voigt (1981).

I: Text: Performance

1 Hjelmslev's distinction (Hjelmslev 1961).
2 Those who we prefer to call 'practitioners' or 'artists.'
3 In his remarkable analysis 'La Parole soufflée' in *Writing and Difference* (1978) Derrida shows how Artaud's attempt, as far as the theatrical text is concerned, is pushing things to the limit. We note that the materiality of the theatre resides also in language (*phonè*).

4 A study of relations between people based upon physical distance. See Hall (1959, 1966).

5 In the program for the production of Brecht's *A Respectable Wedding*, by Vincent and Jourdheuil (1973–1974), the name of each character was accompanied by a 'novelized' biography.

6 The French text uses the word *didascalies* to refer to stage or production directions. In our translation we have used the English equivalent, *didascalia*, which is borrowed directly from the Greek.

7 Stage and performance directions have never been absolutely non-existent, of course, but authors did not deem it necessary to record them. The first edition of Shakespeare does not include directions, and the directions printed in later editions are derived from the text.

8 If the *objective* writing of the *Nouveau roman*, for example, is proposed as counter-example, we would answer that novelistic writing cannot erase the subjective mark of the writing subject by covering it with another subjective marking. See chapter VI, 'Theatrical Discourse,' for a less summary approach to the problem of 'objectivity' in theatre.

9 Our translation retains the French forms of names cited by the author from plays written in French.

10 Perhaps only the actor's body can be seen as a system of signs that is articulated into parts and whose signifier/signified relation is relatively arbitrary.

11 The existence of stimuli is not exclusive to theater or even to mounted spectacles. Many signs that we perceive in any act of communication function both as signs and as stimuli. The sign (or more precisely, signal) danger is understood as a sign but can also make us run for our lives. For example, in erotic literature the colour system is a set of both intelligible signs and of stimuli.

12 The comparison Saussure makes is that of a sheet of paper; it cannot be divided in terms of its thickness, but it has front and back surfaces that are independent of each other (the arbitrary nature of the sign) but indissociable. Hjelmslev extended this distinction by opposing the level of expression and the level of content, a distinction that is further broken down into form/substance of expression, and form/substance of content.

13 We can say that indices also have to do with connotations, that is with secondary meanings; see chapter I, section 2.6. 'Denotation, Connotation.'

14 In theatre icons are signs that serve to represent things, signs that have a paradigmatic value; they can be substituted for things. Icons are the very source for theatrical mimesis; an actor is the icon of a character.

15 For Hjelmslev, connotations are the content of a level of expression made up of the set of denotative signs, in this position he is joined by Roland Barthes (Barthes 1964).

16 See Umberto Eco (1972, 69 ff.) on the semioticization of the referent.

17 'The metalinguistic function is the function in language by which the speaker takes the code he is using ... as object of his discourse' (Dubois 1973). Defining the words we use is an activity that belongs to the metalinguistic function.

18 'In this way the theatre leaves its spectators productively disposed even after the spectacle is over. Let us hope that their theatre may allow them to enjoy as entertainment that terrible and never-ending labour which should ensure their maintenance ... for the simplest way of living is in art' ('A Short Organum for the Theatre,' in Brecht 1964, 205). See Ubersfeld (1981).

19 See the remarkable work by Denis Bablet (Bablet 1971).

20 See 'A Short Organum for the Theatre' (in Brecht 1964).

21 See chapter IV, section 8 'The Theatrical Object.'

22 'That is great art: everything in it is shocking,' from 'On Epic Theater' (Brecht 1972, 113).

23 These relations should be studied: we should note that the emotion provoked by the spectacle of pain is not pain, but rather something else ('pity' accompanied by a kind of pleasure?). It should not be forgotten that it is not one particular emotion that gives rise to theatrical pleasure, but rather the whole of the ceremony: to find pleasure in only one part (a scene, an interpretation) is a 'perversion'; a successful performance is an act in its totality.

24 An autobiographical account heard by this author and attested to by other witnesses.

II: The Actantial Model in Theatre

1 See the whole of this discussion in Eco (1972).

2 Thus, for example, *La dramaturgie classique en France* (Schérer 1950) produces the most surprising effects when its concepts are applied to African or Far Eastern theatre.

3 Surface-level determinations consist of: characters, speeches, scenes and dialogues, everything that has to do with dramatic art; deep structures: consist of the syntax of the dramatic action, its invisible elements and the relations between them. Thus beneath the many adventures of the Knights of the Round Table is the *Quest for the Holy Grail.*

4 *Tabular*: posits a piling up of simultaneous (spatio-temporal) signs, even at the moment of reading.

5 For these functions, see Bremond (1966).

6 Greimas (1987). Remember that Greimas's work is not specifically in the area of theatre, but rather all narrative forms.

7 For the concept of the archi-actant, see Greimas (1983, 211).

8 We should note the ideological significance of the arbiter function: it presupposes that, below the forces we see in conflicting relations, there is a deciding or conciliating force, a power that is above the conflict.

9 A reader (Florence Dupont) has pointed out to me that, beyond the City, the whole order of civilization that prohibits incest – an order seen in Apollo's oracle – plays the role of sender. Proof, once more, of the complexity of the potential occupants of the *sender* position, and of the need to take cultural differences into account as precisely as possible.

10 This was admirably demonstrated in Robert Bresson's 1974 film *Lancelot du Lac.*

11 Here interdisciplinarity must enter into our considerations. Theatrical semiology, anthropology, and history are of great mutual help.

12 This would produce a fundamental triangle:

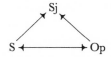

The conflictual element would be the sender-opponent couple. For example, in Racine's *Esther,* the action portrays conflict between God, protector of the Jews, and the minister Aman; this conflict occurs at a level above the instruments Esther and Assuérus (God being manifested by Mardochée).

13 Subject and receiver are one and the same when the subject acts *for himself or herself,* as is the case in amorous quests.

14 *Vs* (the abbreviation for *versus*) means 'opposed to.'

15 Another analysis, that of Oswald Ducrot, might clarify this connection with its reference to the idea of *the complex predicate* (see Ducrot 1980, 121).

16 *Cf.* the quasi incestuous character of this love, echoed by Tebaldeo, who calls Florence 'my mother,' which is connoted by the two maternal figures, Marie Soderini and Catherine.

17 It is probably not difficult to read Macbeth's desire as the (frustrated) desire for his wife; the rest would then be *mediate* desire: being great, a king, virile, etc., in order to be loved by her.

18 So it is with Michel Hermon's direction of Ford's play, *'Tis Pity She's a Whore,* at the Théâtre de la Cité in 1974. Annabella and her desire are given privileged status; this is a textually perceivable structure, but one that is left in the shadows because of the constraints of the code.

19 Here André Green's psychoanalytical reading of *Othello* (Green 1979) can clarify actantial analysis and be clarified by it in turn. Thus we might read a sort of circulation of (homosexual) desire and hatred.

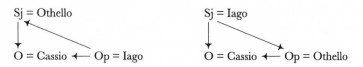

These structures might also be doubled by the presence of Desdemona as the desired and devalued feminine object.

20 See our study of the structures of melodrama (Ubersfeld 1976).

21 See chapter IV, section 6.1. 'The Content of Dramatic Space.'

22 It would not be difficult to analyse Alceste on the one hand, and Célimène on the other, as anguished subjects, torn between their desire and their will to become integrated within the group.

23 It is clear that Philinte does not occupy an autonomous position in relation to the rest of the group. Since he is not Alceste's ally, but rather his opponent, we can see how the actantial model brings to light a conflict that is masked by the apparent psychological determinations (friendship) of speech. It goes without saying that a precise analysis of that same speech would show the conflictual and oppositional nature of Philinte's speech (see chapter III, section 3.2. 'Character and Paradigms'). In this same vein, notice the exchanges between the opponents: they construct an opposing paradigm toward which Arsinoë moves; Arsinoë is an apparent helper to Alceste but is in fact an opponent to the twofold subject Alceste-Célimène, as is immediately denoted by Alceste's speech.

24 'L'ambiguïté du récit: la double lecture de Dom Juan de Molière,' in Rastier (1973).

25 *Dialogic*: Since Bakhtine (1970a; 1970b) we have used the term dialogism to describe the simultaneous presence of two voices within one literary text, bringing to light a contradiction at play.

26 This is the activity of the writer, the practitioner (director or actor), and the spectator.

27 Furthermore, right from the first scene Théramène points out to Hippolyte that it was paternal prohibition that established Aricie as an object of desire for the son.

28 Phèdre wants to buy Hippolyte with the help of royal power: 'Find him Oenone, find this ambitious boy, show him the glitter of the Aethenian crown' (act 3, scene 1).

29 See chapter V, section 4 'Time and Sequences.'

30 Vladimir Propp shows that sometimes a single sphere of action is distributed among several characters, or a single character can be involved in several spheres of action (Propp 1968, 80–1).

31 Seme: the minimal unit of meaning.

32 Nominal System + Verbal System

33 This basic observation allows us to go beyond the psychological quarrels involved in the love or in Titus's ultimate satiation. Understanding of this view was demonstrated magnificently in the production of *Bérénice* mounted by K.M. Grüber at the Comédie Française in 1984.

34 A bishop, a cardinal, or a simple village priest can say mass and administer the sacraments.

III: The Character

1 We use *metatext* for the commentary-text intended to prolong and elucidate a given literary text.

2 We use the term *relative* in order to account for this fact: the general rule of the character's permanence (provided textually, for example, by his or her name) can be the object of inversions and distortions. A character can be disguised and his name changed. Does this mean that a dialectic of permanence/change is set up around the character, a dialectic designed to bring into question one or another of the character's distinctive features? That is the question posed by the character.

3 We should note that truly individual determinations are difficult in theatre, where an actor-individual must take them on or imitate them whether or not she or he is physically similar. It is clear that current tendencies toward de-individualization liberate the actor from that enslavement. Actors are no longer obliged to imitate a particular person and copy her or his individual features; actors no longer have to be the 'rubberfaced' mimes that theatre of the individual requires.

4 There is no need to point out that the difficulties encountered in the psychological analysis of the character-individual are not solved by psychoanalysis: a being on paper does not have a subconscious and will therefore have no psyche. What can be deduced analytically, albeit with its own attendant problems, is a certain knowledge as to the author's psyche (cf. Charles Mauron's work on Racine or Baudelaire). It is not clear, however, whether or not that knowledge enlightens us at all in regards to the author's theatre.

5 For determination of *actantial models*, see chapter II, section 3.1. 'Actants.'

IV: Theatre and Space

1 However schematic that construction might be, indeed even if it is nothing but black curtains.

2 See Beaumarchais's famous text in which Figaro presents the hall where his case is heard both as theatre and as a representation of social hierarchy.

3 For example, in Ariane Mnouchkine's *1789* (Théâtre du Soleil, 1970), there was a double interaction of the actors in the audience space and the spectators in the actors' space: the actors came down into the seats to tell the spectators about the storming of the Bastille, so that the spectators were standing surrounded by huge puppets.

4 Thus, for example, the very simple syntagma 'the bird sings' can be the object of any number of paradigmatic substitutions for the word *bird* (not only various kinds of songbirds, but anything that can sing). The totality of these possible substitutions constitutes a paradigm. G. Genette demonstrates the importance of the syntagma/paradigm relation for linguistic spatiality:

'By rigorously identifying language's *speech* and by assigning to it the primary role in linguistic functioning, which we will define in terms of a system of purely differential relations in which each element defines itself by the place it occupies in the tableau of the whole and by the vertical and horizontal relations it maintains with its related and proximate elements, then it is undeniable that Saussure and his successors have identified a mode of existence for language that we will have to call spatial' (Genette 1969, 45).

5 For example, the use of blanks and white space gives a spatial value to the poetic page, especially with the experiments of Mallarmé and Apollinaire (1963).

6 This passage is quoted by Umberto Eco (1972, 174).

7 Ibid., 175.

8 When Eco, in criticizing the notion of iconicity, ironically notes that 'the true, complete, iconic sign of Queen Elizabeth is not Annigoni's portrait but rather the Queen herself (or her double produced in science-fiction)' (Eco 1972, 174–5), he is offering a kind of definition of *the iconicity of the spatial sign in theatre*.

9 We should note that the equivocal nature of the meaning of *referent* in linguistics is unavoidable (and even exacerbated) when we are dealing with the theatrical spatial sign. In his seminar, Jean Peytard stated: 'In the domain of space, there is necessarily a projection of things upon words: the referent devours the signified.'

10 This is not to say that there is no 'semanticism of the real world,' but rather that it is theatre's task to bring it forth.

11 We must also study these elements not only in their static combinations, but also in their *transformations* (in relation to the fabula in question), in order to demonstrate how the stage space becomes creator, conveyor, and transformer

of its own meanings. Conversely, an important part of theatrical semiotics consists in observing, within a given staging of a play, how the activity of *arrangement within space* is carried out. There remains the task of studying the *spatialization code* and drawing up the *history* of stage space and 'stageography' (scénographie) in relation to the text. (See 'L'espace théâtral et son scénographe' in Ubersfeld 1981.)

12 *Cf.* also Hugo: 'My self can be broken down into Olympio: the lyre, Herman: love, Maglia: laughter, Hierro: combat' (Hugo 1870).

13 We find no contradiction between the Freudian analysis of *Oedipus Rex* and an anthropological analysis of myth (contrary to the position of Jean-Pierre Vernant and Pierre Vidal-Naquet in *Mythe et tragédie dans la Grèce ancienne*); in fact, the concept of space allows us to understand how different (and sometimes perforce contradictory) meanings can co-exist because they are deployed in the *same field.*

14 We should not forget that here, as is the case everywhere in theatre, there are no absolutes: this parasitic effect can, in certain cases, appear to be a deliberate meaning: any sign can be implicated in 'resemanticization.'

15 See Mannoni (1969).

16 Thus the panels and placards should be seen not as an effect of authentic history, but rather, and more importantly, as markers of the locus of theatricality, the point at which denial is reversed.

17 'Une esclave là-haut./Mais une reine ici. Comte, à chacun son lot ... /Tout ce que le soleil éclaire est sous ta loi;/Tout ce qui remplit l'ombre, ô burgrave, est à moi!' [Up there I am a slave; down here a queen. Each mortal has his destiny! ... / All that the sun reveals up there, is yours; all that foul gloom conceals down here, is mine!] (Hugo, *Les Burgraves*, part 3, scene 2).

18 See our analysis of Hugo's dramatic spaces in *Le roi et le bouffon* (Ubersfeld 1974, 407–57).

19 Teachers could find much material here for simple, highly informative exercises.

20 See our analysis in *Le roi et le bouffon* (Ubersfeld 1974, 582 ff.).

21 Ubersfeld (1974, 425 ff. and 528 ff.).

22 'So-called realistic literature that is closely connected to the principle of metonymy' (Jakobson 1964, 244).

23 In cinema we see Charlie Chaplin playing Hitler, tossing a balloon-globe that eventually bursts in his face (*The Great Dictator,* 1940).

24 These two examples are taken from the production of Brecht's *The Caucasian Chalk Circle* by the Turkish director Mehmet Ulusoy (1974) – a sieve, quite conveniently, becomes a helmet.

25 For more on objects and performance, see Ubersfeld 1981, chapter III.

V: Theatre and Time

1 A time punctuated by abstract chronological points of reference.
2 See Ubersfeld 1991.
3 In Brecht's *Mr. Puntila and his Man Matti*, the temporal signifiers indicate a rapid succession, the pulses between the master's drunken time and his lucid time.
4 *Diegetic*: that which pertains to the story and its succession of events.
5 All iconic signs undergo the process we call *resemanticization*, which is analogous to what Umberto Eco calls *the semiotization of the referent* (Eco 1972, 69).
6 Translated from Alfred de Musset, *Lorenzaccio*, ed. Robert Abirached (Paris: Gallimard, 1978) 163–72.
7 It is debatable to claim that this scene helps to prepare the ending on the ground that when Duke Alexandre poses for Tebaldeo, he has to take off his coat of mail, enabling Lorenzo to steal it. The coat of mail is not necessary to the action and need never have been introduced in the first place.
8 Lorenzo recognizes this meaning: 'Why put off *the offer of a job?* (38).
9 We have been attempting to carry out this procedure.
10 See Ducrot (1980, chapter 4, 'La présupposition dans la description sémantique').

VI: Theatrical Discourse

1 We should remember that the theatrical text *when performed* functions in a two-fold way:
 a/ as a set of phonic signs emitted in the course of the performance, with a double sender (the author and the actor) and a double receiver (the audience and the *other* actor).
 b/ as a set of linguistic signs (message) that govern a semiotic complex: space, objects, movements of the actors, etc. (signs made from diverse expressive matter). Dialogue and didascalia both govern the performance signs (see chapter VI, section 1.3. 'Twofold Enunciation').
2 Benveniste (1970, 12–13). For further discussion on this problem of enunciation, see the excellent summary by Dominique Maingueneau (Maingueneau 1976, chapter III).
3 This is the perspective taken by Stanislavski in his work (sometimes pushed to unhelpful extremes): he seeks to imagine the living being who speaks when given theatrical words and the psychic and material conditions of enunciation of those words.

4 Ducrot (1980, 70). However, one might think that the notion of discourse constitutes precisely a way to get beyond the *language/speech* distinction.

5 On this point concerning the director's text *T'*, see chapter I, section 1.2.3. 'Performance and Textual Activity.'

6 By didascalia, we mean here not only the actual didascalia but also all other elements, including dialogue, that have a function in governing performance. We call these other elements internal didascalia (see examples in Shakespeare or Racine).

7 See chapter III, section 2.3. 'The Character as Subject of Discourse.'

8 Volochinov (quoted by Marcellesi), in connection not with theatre but simply with reported discourse: 'A dynamic linguistics having three dimensions, the author, the author of the reported discourse, the linguistic construction, a combination of the *tone* of the character (empathy) and the *tone* of the author (distancing) within one and the same linguistic construction' (Marcellesi 1974, 195).

9 On the question of acts and illocutionary force, see Ducrot (1980) and Searle (1969). Illocutionary force is what determines how an utterance should be received by the receiver (assertion, promise, order).

10 See Ducrot and Todorov (1979, 272):

'... the opposition of what is *affirmed* and what is *presupposed* ... The utterance, "Jack continues to act foolishly" affirms both (a) that Jack has acted foolishly in the past and (b) that he is acting foolishly in the present. Now affirmations (a) and (b) seem to have to be separated within the global description of the utterance, for they have different properties. Thus (a) is still affirmed when (b) is denied ("It is false that Jack continues to act foolishly') or when it is the object of an interrogation ("Is Jack continuing to act foolishly?"). The same does not hold true for (b). Moreover, (a) is not affirmed in the same way as (b): (a) is presented as self-evident or as already known and impossible to put in doubt; (b) on the contrary is presented as new and ultimately debatable. Thus we call *(a)* a presupposition and *(b)* an affirmation. Although there is general agreement on the properties of affirmations and presuppositions, it is very difficult to find a general definition of the phenomenon. The effort may be made along three lines:

– From the logical point of view: the presupposition will be defined by the fact that, if it is false, the utterance can be called neither true nor false (the falseness of the presupposition establishes a 'hole' in the truth table of the proposition).

– From the viewpoint of use conditions: the presuppositions must be true (or regarded as true by the hearer) in order for the use of the utterance to be "normal"; otherwise it is unacceptable. But this "deontology" of discourse to which we are then referring remains to be more precisely defined.

– From the viewpoint of intersubjective relations in the (pragmatic) discourse: the choice of an utterance introduces a certain modification in the relationships among the interlocutors – according to the presupposition included in the utterance. Presupposing would then be a speech act with illocutionary value, by the same token as promising, ordering, interrogating.'

11 Austin (1970).

12 Florence Dupont (in a paper given at the Bourg-Saint-Maurice seminar in 1976) points out that the Romans were so sure of this that they did not allow citizens to become actors, on the grounds that the juridical force of a citizen's word might be perceived as overriding the status of theatrical speech, meaning that even on stage the citizen-actor's speech would retain its juridical force (for the freeing of a slave, for example).

13 See 'L'effet de sourdine dans le style classique: Racine' (the muting effect in classical style: Racine) (in Spitzer 1980).

14 On this type of analysis, see Roman Jakobson, *Questions de poétique* (1973) and the fine handbook by Delas and Filiolet, *Linguistique et poétique* (1973).

15 See Ubersfeld (1974, 477–9).

16 See Goldmann (1964).

17 On this subject, and on the presence of several voices within a text, see Bakhtine (1970a).

18 See chapter I, section 3.3. 'The Receiver-Audience.'

19 See the special issue of *Revue des sciences humaines* on melodrama (no. 162, 1976).

20 See Robin (1973).

21 Productions respectively at Villeurbane (1971), Paris (1971), Ivry (1979), and the Comédie Française (1984 and 1993).

22 We know about the problems encountered by Balzac and others when they tried to have theatre legitimately use *slang*. We might also cite the grouping of various populations in the Ottoman Empire, where popular theatre elicited superior laughter at the linguistic particularities of non-native peoples.

23 The same *formula* 'loving the way you're supposed to' is found on the lips of Pierrot the peasant (*Dom Juan*, act 2, scene 1), but there it is discursively developed in a different way. The humour comes from the fact that it is borrowed from another class.

24 Here, the choice of a reading that gives privileged status to individual feelings or interpersonal relations will have an impact on performance.

25 See Maingueneau (1976, 110, 119).

26 See, for example, Schérer (1950) and Larthomas (1995).

27 We define ideology, following Louis Althusser, as 'the way in which men live out their relations with their conditions of existence.' Althusser defines practical ideologies as 'complex formations of montages, notions, representations, images on the one hand, and on the other, montages of behaviour, attitudes, gestures. The whole of this functions as a set of practical norms governing the attitude and concrete stance of men concerning real objects and their social and individual existence, as well as their history' (quoted in Robin 1973, 101–2).

28 'We speak of ideological formation in order to characterize an element that can be implicated as a force confronting other forces within the ideological conjunction characteristic of a given social formation, at a given moment in time. Each ideological formation thus constitutes a complex set of attitudes and representations that are neither "individual" nor "universal," but which are related more or less directly to class attitudes in conflict with each other' (Robin 1973, 104).

29 See chapter V, section 4.4.3. 'An Example: *Lorenzaccio*, act 2, scene 2.'

30 In the protagonists' dialogue there are also clear enough indices of homosexual seduction or propositioning – the individual and the political are closely linked.

31 Once we see the emergence in a character's 'text' of several contradictory or at least divergent discourses concerned with different discursive structures, it becomes difficult to see speech as the product of a free consciousness, of an autonomous and creative 'subject.'

32 An examination of this dialectics in each sequence of average length (scene) would be a uniquely fruitful undertaking and would be useful for pedagogical purposes.

33 We have a *montage* when disparate elements take on meaning through their combination, through a construction of which they are the components. We have a *collage* when meaning is created through their very difference or heterogeneity, as opposed to their combination.

34 See 'Révolution et topique de la cité: *Lorenzaccio*,' in Ubersfeld (1991).

35 See 'Vers un théâtre matérialiste' in Althusser (1977).

36 It would be interesting to show how the Oedipal structure of the family (and of the psyche) can function as a presupposition. It would be sufficient to identify how the analytical and the ideological are articulated.

A Prelude to Performance

1 Bertolt Brecht, epilogue to *The Good Person of Szechwan*.

2 Ubersfeld uses the French word 'exercice,' which would normally be translated as 'practice' (following the meaning of practice for 'exercer' as in 'exercer une profession' or any other activity). In the following section we have
translated 'exercice' as 'exercise' or 'practice' as appropriate to the context.

Bibliography

Adamov, Arthur. 1959. *Ping-Pong: A Play in Two Parts*. Translated by Richard Howard. New York: Grove Press.

Althusser, Louis. 1977. *For Marx*. Translated by Ben Brewster. London: NLB.

Apollinaire, Guillaume. 1963. *Calligrammes, poèmes de la paix et de la guerre*. Paris: Gallimard.

Artaud, Antonin. 1958. *The Theater and Its Double*. Translated by Mary Caroline Richards. New York: Grove Press.

Austin, John Langshaw. 1970. *Quand dire, c'est faire*. Paris: Seuil.

Bablet, Denis. 1971. *The Revolution of Stage Design in the 20th Century*. Paris: L'Amiel.

Bakhtine, Mikhail. 1970a. *Poétique de Dostoïevski*. Paris: Éditions du Seuil.

– 1970b. *L'oeuvre de François Rabelais et la culture populaire au moyen age et sous la rennaissance*. Translated by Andrée Robel. Paris: Gallimard.

Barthes, Roland. 1964. *Éléments de semiologie*. Paris: Seuil.

– 1966 (ed.) *Communications 8: L'analogue structurale du récit*. Paris: Seuil.

– 1969. *Le degré zero de l'écriture: Suivi de elements de semiologie*. Paris: Conthier

– 1970. 'Par ou commencer?' *Poetique* 1: 3–9.

– 1972. *Critical Essays*. Translated by Richard Howard. Evanston: Northwestern University Press.

– 1982. *A Barthes Reader*. New York: Hill and Wang.

Benveniste, Émile. 1970. 'L'appareil formel de l'énonciation.' *Langages* 17: 12–18.

– 1974. *Problèmes de linguistique générale, II*. Paris: Gallimard.

Blanchot, Maurice. 1955. *L'espace littéraire*. Paris: Gallimard.

Bogatyrev, Petr. 1977. 'Semiotics in the Folk Theatre.' In Matejka and Titunik, eds., 1977, 33–50.

Boileau-Despreaux, Nicolas. *L'art poétique*. Presented by H. Benac. Paris: Hachette 1962.

Brecht, Bertolt. 1964. *A Short Organum on Theatre*. In *Brecht on Theatre: The Development of an Aesthetic*. ed. and trans. by John Willet. New York: Hill and Wang

– 1972. *Ecrits sur le théâtre.* Paris: L'Arche

– 1976. *Bertolt Brecht: Part Two,* trans. John Willet. London: Methuen

Bremond, Claude 1966. 'La logique des possibles narratifs.' In Barthes, ed. 1966.

Carlson, Marvin. 1993. *Theories of the Theatre.* Ithaca and London: Cornell University Press.

Chabrol, Claude, ed. 1973. *Sémiotique narrative et textuelle.* Paris: Larousse.

Coquet, Jean-Claude. 1982. *Sémiotique. L'école de Paris.* Paris: Hachette Université.

Delas, Daniel, and Jacques Filliolet. 1973. *Linguistique et poétique.* Paris: Larousse.

De Marinis, Marco. 1993. *The Semiotics of Performance.* Bloomington: Indiana University Press.

Derrida, Jacques. 1978. *Writing and Difference.* Translated by Alan Bass. Chicago: University of Chicago Press.

Dubois, Jacques. 1973. *Dictionnaire de linguistique.* Paris, Larousse.

Ducrot, Oswald. 1974. *La preuve et le dire: langage et logique.* Paris: Mame.

– 1980. *Dire et ne pas dire: principes de sémantique linguistique.* Paris: Hermann.

Ducrot, Oswald, and Tzvetan Todorov. 1979. *Encyclopedic Dictionary of the Sciences of Languages.* Translated by Catherine Porter. Baltimore: Johns Hopkins University Press.

Eco, Umberto. 1972. *La structure absente: introduction à la recherche sémiotique.* Translated by Ucciol Esposito. Paris: Mercure de France.

Elam, Keir. 1980. *The Semiotics of Theatre and Drama.* London: Methuen.

Genette, Gérard. 1969. *Figures II.* Paris: Seuil.

Goldmann, Lucien. 1964. *The Hidden God: A Study of Tragic Vision in the Pensées of Pascal and the Tragedies of Racine.* London: Routledge and K. Paul.

Green, André. 1979. *The Tragic Effect: The Oedipus Complex in Tragedy.* Translated by Alan Sheridan. Cambridge: Cambridge University Press.

Greimas, Algirdas Julien. 1973. 'Les actants, les acteurs et les figures.' In Chabrol 1973.

– 1983. *Structural Semantics: An Attempt at a Method.* Translated by Paul Perron and Frank Collins. Translated by Danielle McDowell, Ronald Schleifer, and Alan Velie. Lincoln: University of Nebraska Press.

– 1987. *On Meaning: Selected Writings in Semiotic Theory.* Translated by Paul Perron and Frank Collins. Minneapolis: University of Minnesota Press.

Greimas, Algirdas Julien, and Joseph Courtés. 1982. *Semiotics and Language. An Analytical Dictionary.* Translated by Larry Crist et al. Bloomington: Indiana University Press.

Greimas, Algirdas Julien, and Jacques Fontanille. 1993. *The Semiotics of Passions.* Translated by Paul Perron and Frank Collins. Minneapolis: University of Minnesota Press.

Grotowski, Jerzy. 1969. *Towards a Poor Theatre.* London: Methuen.

Guespin, Louis. 1971. 'Problématique des travaux sur le discours politique.' *Langages* 21: 3–24.

Hall, Edward T. 1959. *The Silent Language.* Garden City, New York: Doubleday.
– 1966. *The Hidden Dimension.* Garden City, New York: Doubleday.
Helbo, André. 1975. *Sémiologie de la représentation: Théâtre, télévision, bande dessinée.* Bruxelles: Éditions Complexe.
– 1987. *Theory of Performing Art.* Amsterdam and Philadelphia: John Benjamins.
Hjelmslev, Louis. 1961. *Prolegomena to a Theory of Language.* Madison: University of Wisconsin Press.
Hugo, Victor. 1841. *Littérature et philosophie mêlées.* Paris: Klincksieck 1976.
– *Carnets intimes, 1870–1871.* Paris: Gallimard 1953.
Jakobson, Roman. 1963. *Essais de linguistique générale.* Paris: Éditions de Minuit.
– 1973. *Questions de poétique.* Paris: Editions de Seuil.
Larthomas, Pierre. 1995. *Le langage dramatique.* Paris: PUF.
Lévi-Strauss, Claude. 1976. *Structural Anthropology,* vol. 2. Translated by Monique Layton. New York: Basic Books.
Lotman, Juri. 1973. *La structure du texte artistique.* Translated by Anne Fournier et al. Paris: Gallimard.
Maingueneau, Dominique. 1976. *Initiation aux méthodes de l'analyse du discours: problèmes et perspectives.* Paris: Hachette.
Mannoni, Octave. 1969. *Clefs pour l'imaginaire ou, L'autre scène.* Paris: Éditions du Seuil.
Marcellesi, Jean-Baptiste, and Bernard Gardin. 1974. *Introduction à la sociolinguistique: la linguistique sociale.* Paris: Larousse.
Martinet, André. 1969. *Linguistique, guide alphabéthique.* Paris: Denoël-Gonthier.
Matejka, Ladislav, and Irwin R. Titunik. 1977. *Semiotics of Art.* Cambridge, MA: MIT Press.
Melrose, Susan. 1994. *A Semiotics of the Dramatic Text.* Houndsmills, Basington: Macmillan.
Metz, Christian. 1974. *Language and Cinema.* Translated by Donna Jean Umiker-Sebeok. The Hague: Mouton.
Meyerhold, Vsevolod Emilievich. 1973. *Écrits sur le théâtre.* Translated by Béatrice. Lausanne: Éditions La Cité.
Morris, Charles. 1946. *Signs, Language and Behavior.* New York: Prentice Hall.
Mounin, Georges. 1970. *Introduction à la sémiologie.* Paris: Éditions du Minuit.
Mukařovský, Jan. 1934. 'Art as Semiotic Fact.' In Matejka and Titunik 1977, 3–9.
Nespoulous, Jean-Luc, Paul Perron, and André Roch Lecours, eds. 1986. *The Biological Foundations of Gestures: Motor and Semiotic Aspects.* New Jersey: Lawrence Earlbaum.
Pavis, Patrice. 1977. 'Ubersfeld Anne, *Lire le théâtre.*' *Sub-stance.* 18/19: 225–6.
– 1982. *The Languages of the Stage.* New York: Performing Arts Journal Publications.
Peirce, Charles S. 1931–5. *Collected Papers.* Cambridge: Harvard University Press.
Prieto, Luis J. 1966. *Messages et signaux.* Paris: Presses universitaires de France.

Propp, Vladimir. 1968. *Morphology of the Folk Tale*. Austin: University of Texas Press.

Quinn, Michael. 1995. *The Semiotic Stage: Prague School Theatre Theory*. New York and Washington: Peter Lang.

Rastier, François. 1973. *Essais de sémiotique discursive*. Tours: Maison Mame.

Robin, Régine. 1971. 'La sémantique et la coupure saussurienne; langue, langage, discours.' *Langages* 24:1.

– 1973. *Histoire et linguistique*. Paris: A. Colin.

Rosa, Guy. 1991. 'Ubersfeld Anne.' In *Dictionnaire encyclopédique du théâtre*, edited by M. Corvin. Paris: Bordas, 849.

Schérer, Jacques. 1950. *La dramaturgie classique en France*. Paris: Nizet.

Searle, John R. 1969. *Speech Acts: An Essay in the Philosophy of Language*. London: Cambridge University Press.

Souriau, Etienne. 1950. *Les deux cents milles situations dramatiques*. Paris: Flammarion.

Spitzer, Leo. 1980. *Études de style*. Translated by Eliane Kaufholz, Alain Coulon, Michel Foucault. Paris: Gallimard.

Szépe, György, and Vilmos Voigt. 1981. 'Alternative sémiologique.' *Kodicas-Code: An International Journal of Semiotics* 20: 83–95.

Toro, Fernando de. 1996. *Theatre Semiotics*. Toronto: University of Toronto Press.

Ubersfeld, Anne. 1970. *Armand Salacrou*. Paris: Seghers

– 1974. *Le roi et le bouffon: Étude sur le théâtre de Hugo de 1830 à 1839*. Paris: J. Corti.

– 1976. 'Les bons et le méchant.' *Revue des sciences humaines* 162(2): 193–203.

– 1977. *Lire le théatre*. Paris: Éditions Sociales.

– 1981. *L'école du spectateur: Lire le théâtre 2*. Paris: Éditions sociales.

– 1985a. *Le roman d'Hernani*. Paris: Comédie-Française-Mercure de France.

– 1985b. *Claudel, autobiographie et histoire: Le partage de midi*. Paris: Messidor.

– 1990. *Vinaver dramaturge*. Paris: Librarie théâtrale

– 1991. *Le théâtre et la cité: De Corneille à Kantor*. Bruxelles: Éditions Complexes.

– 1992. *Théophile Gautier*. Paris: Stock.

– 1993. *Le drame romantique*. Paris: Belin.

– 1994. *Antoine Vitez: Metteur en scène et poète*. Paris: Les Quatre Vents.

– 1996. *Le dialogue du théâtre*. Paris: Belin.

Ubersfeld, Anne, and Georges Banu. 1978. *L'objet théâtral*. Paris: CNDP

Van Dijk, Teun A. 1973. 'Grammaires textuelles et structures narratives.' In Chabrol 1973, 177–207.

Veltrusky, Jiří. 1977. *Drama as Literature*. Lisse: Ridder Press.

Vernant, Jean-Pierre, and Pierre Vidal-Naquet. 1981. *Tragedy and Myth in Ancient Greece*. Translated by Janet Lloyd. Sussex: Harvester Books.

Index of Terms

presupposed, 157, 203n10
psyche, 86

receiver, 38–44
receiver-audience, 20, 22–3, 168
reference, 138–40
referent, 12, 18–20
resemanticization, 15, 125
role, 67–70

sequence, 141–57
sequence of average length, 146–7
sign, 12–13

signified, 12
signifier, 12
space (dramatic), 115–16
symbol, 13, 124
synecdoche, 81, 124
syntagmatic, 14–15, 142

theatralization, 27–8; of character,
    92–3
theatricality, 7

understood (unspoken), 157
unity of time, 127–8

Index of Authors and Titles